SLENDER WAS THE THREAD

Slender was the Thread

KASHMIR CONFRONTATION, 1947–48

Orient BlackSwan

SLENDER WAS THE THREAD: KASHMIR CONFRONTATION, 1947–48

ORIENT BLACKSWAN PRIVATE LIMITED

Registered Office
3-6-752 Himayatnagar, Hyderabad 500 029 (Telangana), INDIA
e-mail: centraloffice@orientblackswan.com

Other Offices
Bengaluru, Chennai, Guwahati, Hyderabad,
Kolkata, Mumbai, New Delhi, Noida, Patna

First published 1969
Reprinted as a Sangam paperback 1973
Reprinted in hard cover by Orient Longman 1986, 1988, 1994
This paperback edition published by Orient Blackswan Pvt. Ltd 2020
Reprinted 2022, 2023, 2024, 2025

ISBN 978-93-5287-849-9

040357

Typeset in
Times New Roman Mt Std 10/13
by Manmohan Kumar, Delhi

Printed in India at
B.B. Press, Tronica City, Ghaziabad, UP 201 103

Published by
Orient Blackswan Private Limited
3-6-752 Himayatnagar, Hyderabad 500 029 (Telangana), INDIA
e-mail: info@orientblackswan.com

To
The officers and men of
161 Infantry Brigade
who demonstrated that courage and patriotism
never go out of fashion

Contents

Foreword

I have read a number of accounts of the defence of the Kashmir Valley when the tribal raiders from the North-West Frontier, actively aided and abetted by Pakistan's armed forces and Government, descended in October 1947 on an orgy of killing, looting, pillage, plunder and rape. Their object was to devastate the Valley and to seize Srinagar.

How a fistful of the Indian armed forces, taken initially by surprise, confronted the invaders and ejected them from the Valley has been told before. It has never been told so vividly and in such faithful detail as in this book by Lieutenant General L. P. Sen, then acting Brigadier in command of 161 Infantry Brigade which faced some fierce fighting in the Valley. In the Kashmir operations of 1947–48, Indian soldiers fought for the first time under Indian commanders at every echelon.

It was 161 Brigade which, under its stubborn, resourceful commander stemmed the wave of invaders at Uri in that fateful winter.

'Bogey' Sen's account is racy and readable but it is also remarkable for its perceptiveness and depth. A good journalist is one who can see the news behind the news. Equally a good soldiers can at times intelligently anticipate the real move and motive behind a feint. It is paradoxically less easy to do so against unsophisticated tribesmen, brimming over with more bravado than brains. The author effectively demolishes some widespread legends and fancies on the military prowess of tribal warriors such as the much vaunted Mahsuds, Waziris, Afridis and Mohmands. According to the author, they "will only attack troops who are careless and present him with an easy ambush from which he can escape unscathed, and he will attack isolated bodies of men when the numerical odds are greatly in his favour, closing in when the garrison has expended its ammunition, and overpowering it by sheer weight of numbers."

General Sen writes easily and often with grace, which cannot be said of most military commanders. He projects, for instance, revealing cameos of political personages like Sardar Vallabhbhai Patel of whom he relates a characteristic anecdote, and of military commanders like the often irascible but capable General Kulwant Singh. His narrative of the burning of Baramula is absorbing. The story of the Kashmir fighting is rounded of in a reflective last chapter which throws into harsh relief the permutations and combinations behind the British attitude to Kashmir. General Sen states bluntly what has never been so forthrightly stated before—that as a result of Britain's political hangover on Kashmir, neither Britain, Pakistan nor Kashmir has been the beneficiary. The only beneficiary has been China. A shrewd point which needed making.

I put down the manuscript of this book far more enlightened than when I began reading it. I am sure other readers will benefit equally.

New Delhi
15 August 1969

FRANK MORAES

Preface

In late October 1947, at what was virtually a moment's notice, a battalion of the Indian Army was flown into the Kashmir Valley. It was followed on succeeding days by further units, and eventually established itself in Kashmir as 161 Infantry Brigade. By the third week of December 1947, the only land route into the Valley over the Banihal Pass was snowbound, and 161 Infantry Brigade spent the next few months completely isolated from the rest of the Indian Army. During this period it faced many crucial situations but the unbounded courage of the officers and men saw it through crisis after crisis. These efforts have unfortunately been known only to those who were involved in the actions and, through personal narration, to a few others. This book is an effort to place on record, and enable a wider section of the public to know, what exactly happened in Kashmir during those grim days.

A rapid survey of the attitude adopted by the rulers of certain Princely States at the time of the partition of the sub-continent into India and Pakistan has been included in the first chapter on the advice and insistence of the late V. P. Menon. Although a very sick man, he gave me a great deal of his time when I paid visit to his Bangalore home in 1965. He was quite certain that it was necessary to portray the problems which faced the newly-born Dominion of India and acquaint the reader with the circumstances in which Indian troops entered the State of Jammu & Kashmir. When I said to him that his authoritative treatment of this subject in his book *The Story of the Integration of Indian States* was available, he clinched the issue by remarking: "You can't attach my book as an Appendix, can you?" I am most grateful to him for giving me the factual data. His death, soon after our last meeting, has denied me the opportunity of keeping a promise to present him with a copy of this book if and when it was published.

Although the subject of the book is, in the main, warfare, an attempt has been made to portray the events in language that can be readily understood by those with little or no knowledge of military matters or terminology. This necessitated passing the script to a cross section of friends with the request that they point out what parts were obscure. Their comments and suggestions have been most useful. To all of them I owe a debt of very sincere gratitude. Also to the large number of officers who served in 161 Infantry Brigade for recalling anecdotes. My acknowledgments are also due to the Directorate of Public Relations, Ministry of Defence for permission to reproduce photographs.

This contribution is not designed to solve the problem of Kashmir. Its main object is to portray a critical stage of the past, a stage in which a relatively small body of extremely gallant men gave unflinchingly of their best, and made my role as their Brigade Commander so simple.

New Delhi
9 August 1969

Chapter 1

A Vulnerable Prize

SIR HARI SINGH, who became the ruler of Jammu and Kashmir in 1925, was sensitive to any form of outside intervention in his State. Provided, however, that the visitor did not engage in political activity, he could enter the State without difficulty and was indeed made welcome. A major portion of the State revenue came from the large influx of tourists during the summer months. No entry permit was necessary. One had only to fill up a form at the Custom Post, giving particulars of where one intended to reside, the probable date of departure, and a declaration that no prohibited items, a list of which was handed to the visitor, were being brought in. Customs Posts were located on the motorable routes into the State, at Domel and Kohala for those entering the Kashmir Valley, and at Suchetgarh in the case of entry via Jammu Province.

Two major roads converged at Domel from the area of the subcontinent now forming West Pakistan. One beginning at Wah from the main Grand Trunk Road from Peshawar to Lahore, and the other at Rawalpindi. The tarmac road from Wah, wide enough for two lanes of traffic and with a gradual rise, was the better and more popular of the two. It runs through Abbottabad, Manshera and Garhi Habibullah to Domel. The other route, from Rawalpindi, involves climbing the hill road to Murree and then dropping down to Kohala before proceeding to Domel by a road that runs almost parallel to the Jhelum River. This route is subject to landslides in the hilly sections and has many hairpin bends. From Domel, the junction point of the two routes, the road runs alongside the Jhelum via Chinari, Chakothi and Uri, then though the river gorge at Mahura, and on to Baramula where the Kashmir Valley starts. From Baramula to Srinagar is a gently climbing tarmac road, lined for most of its length by tall chinar trees, with paddy fields and orchards stretching for miles on both sides.

The route to the Kashmir Valley from the south began from the Grand Trunk Road at Wazirabad, and ran through Sialkot and Suchetgarh to Jammu. Soon after leaving Jammu, it enters mountainous terrain and winds its way through Udhampur, Kud, Ramban and through the tunnels constructed under the 9,290-ft. Banihal Pass in 1955, and then descends into the Valley to proceed via Anantnag to Srinagar. It is now an all-weather route, but until the tunnels were constructed, the road ran over the Pass and was snowbound from mid-December to April. Movement across the Pass by any type of vehicle or animal, or even man, was impossible during the winter months. Even at other times, the Banihal route was the worst of the three leading into the Valley. Motoring on this narrow and steep road, with blind corners and hairpin bends, required excessive low-gear running of vehicles entailing abnormal wear and tear, and imposed a severe strain on the drivers. Many sections of the road were also subject to frequent landslides. During the pre-Partition days, visitors to the Valley from the Punjab or further east avoided this route if possible, preferring the longer but less hazardous route via Rawalpindi and

Murree, or, if time was of no consequence, did the extra mileage to Wah and took the easiest road.

The partition of the sub-continent presented Pakistan with all the three major roads leading to Jammu and Kashmir. A road route of a sort did enter the State from what is now India. It ran from Madhopur to Kathua and on to Samba and Jammu, but it was intersected by numerous bridgeless tributaries of the River Ravi and other minor streams, which had to be crossed by ferry or by using the fords over the shallower streams. Not surfaced with tarmac, it powdered very quickly, while a shower of rain would make any attempt at speeding extremely dangerous as even light traffic caused severe rutting.

There had been no railway system of any description in the Valley. The rail route in undivided India terminated at Jammu town, from Sialkot. It would have been difficult but not impossible to extend the broad gauge railway line beyond Havelian and on to Domel, from where a light railway could have followed the alignment of the road into the Valley. It can only be assumed that the Maharajah, unlike most of his brother-Princes who welcomed the opening up of their territories for commerce, did not view such a facility as being either necessary or desirable.

Two airstrips did exist, one at Srinagar and the other at Jammu, but they were for the exclusive use of the Maharajah's private light aircraft. As this was rarely utilised, the airstrips had no concrete runways. Although a number of airline companies were operating in the sub-continent, and Srinagar and Jammu could have benefited from their services, the towns were not on any scheduled air route. Neither of the airstrips was equipped with navigational aids, crash-fire tenders or arrangements for refuelling. For anything other than a light aircraft to attempt landing on them was risky.

Virtually the entire traffic within and out of the State was, therefore, dependent on motor or animal transport. As all the petrol, oil and lubricants had to be imported from outside, the State was peculiarly vulnerable even if it had possessed large and well-equipped armed forces, which it did not.

The Jammu and Kashmir State Forces amounted in their strength to about an Infantry Division, and consisted mainly of infantry battalions with hardly any artillery and other supporting arms. It had been inconceivable that the State would be subjected to any form of attack from without. Major General H. L. Scott, the Chief of Staff of the State Forces, had therefore deployed the units in accordance with the requirements of internal security.

This was the position on 15 August 1947, the day on which the sub-continent stood partitioned into the Dominions of India and Pakistan. While most of the Princely States had cast their lot with one or the other Dominion, the Maharajah of Jammu and Kashmir was among the few who remained undecided. His indecision was to prove costly and fateful to the people of his own State as well as to India and Pakistan.

On 24 March 1947, Lord (now Earl) Louis Mountbatten had been installed as Viceroy of India, replacing Field Marshal Lord Wavell. Empowered by the British Government to put into effect its resolve to transfer power, Lord Mountbatten commenced negotiations with the two major political parties, the Congress and the Muslim League. He tried without success to persuade Muhammad Ali Jinnah, leader of the Muslim League, to a federal scheme which would retain the unity of India. The story of this unavailing effort was narrated by the last British Viceroy in the following words, in the course of the Nehru Memorial Lecture he delivered in Cambridge on 14 November 1968:

> I first tried very hard to revive the Cabinet Mission plan with him (Mr. Jinnah) in order to retain the unity of India, but he wouldn't hear of it. He insisted on the partition of India into a Muslim State, to be called Pakistan, and the very large non-Muslim residue, which he used to refer to as Hindustan. He wished to include not only the provinces, like Sindh, which had a very large Muslim majority, but also Bengal and the Punjab which had very large non-Muslim minorities. I told him that if he insisted on partitioning India he would have to agree to partition these two provinces and only to include the Muslim majority areas in Pakistan. He objected violently to 'a moth-eaten Pakistan.' He pointed out that it was unreasonable to divide these great provinces, as

> their inhabitants were primarily Bengalis or Punjabis, which was more important than whether they were Muslims or Hindus. I then applied the same logic to the whole of India, claiming that a man was an Indian first and foremost before he was a Muslim or a Hindu. Therefore the whole of India should not be partitioned. This annoyed him....
>
> I tried to tempt Jinnah by offering him Bengal and the Punjab unpartioned provided he would agree that though the provinces with Muslim majorities would have self-government they must be within an overall federal government at the centre. However, he said he would sooner have a moth-eaten Pakistan that owed no allegiance to a central government than a larger and more important area which came under it.
>
> I then ascertained from the Congress and Sikh leaders that, heart-broken though they were at the very thought of partitioning India, if the Muslim League would not accept a transfer of power on any other basis, they would have no option but to accept if they were not to remain indefinitely under British rule.

On 3 June 1947, the Viceroy announced what is commonly referred to as the Mountbatten Plan for the partition of the sub-continent. The date for the transfer of power to the two Dominions of India and Pakistan was advanced from the earlier target of June 1948 to 15 August 1947. Aware of the rising tempers, Mountbatten evidently thought that the quicker the Plan was executed, the less would be the agony. It requires no skill to be critical of the deficiencies that follow the implementation of any plan, but in this particular case it is debatable whether Mountbatten's sharp acceleration of the original date was a wise decision. It allowed only 73 days to partition a sub-continent which is the size of Europe less Russia and consisted of 11 provinces directly administered by the British and 565 Princely States. The problems that had to be ironed out were numerous and complex.

The leaders of the Congress party were consistent in their stand that the partition of the sub-continent on a religious or 'two-nation' basis was neither feasible nor acceptable to them. Such an approach would have reduced the status of the 40 million Muslims who would be left in the Dominion of India to that of aliens or second-class citizens, whereas the Congress party stood for modern secular democracy. The division of the provinces as it eventually took place was in the nature of a political division. Though certain areas with predominantly Muslim population were allotted to Pakistan, in the case of Bengal and the Punjab, the Legislatures of the two provinces were consulted. It was agreed that the western half of the Punjab and the eastern half of Bengal should go to Pakistan, and the other halves to India. A referendum was held in the North-West Frontier Provinces, even though its population was more than 90 per cent Muslim. The area voted for Pakistan, the referendum being boycotted by Khan Abdul Ghaffar Khan and his followers who, like the Congress party, stood for secular democracy and would have preferred to exercise a third option—not given to them in the referendum—of independence, Pakistan being ideologically unacceptable to them and the area not being contiguous to India.

In the event, the two wings of Pakistan were formed by the North-West Frontier Province, Baluchistan, Sind and West Punjab in the West, and by the eastern half of Bengal in the East.

On the transfer of power by Britain, paramountcy was retroceded from the King Emperor to the 565 rulers who had never exercised any authority in respect of External Affairs, Defence and Communications during British rule. The States ranged from the largest, Hyderabad, with an area of 82,000 square miles, a population of 16 million and a revenue of Rs 260 million, to Vejanoness, with an area of under one-third of a square mile, a population of about 200 and a revenue of Rs 500 per annum. Of the 565 States, 140 were fairly large and their rulers were described as "fully empowered"; a further 70 were in an intermediate bracket, the rulers exercising wide but not absolute powers; and the remainder, which were Estates rather than States, had rulers with limited powers of jurisdiction. In 1945, an Attachment Scheme had been formulated under which a large number of these Estates were placed under the control of the adjoining larger States. With paramountcy lapsing, the Attachment Scheme also expired. Each of the 565 rulers was expected to accede to either of the two new Dominions according to his choice, and not on the basis of the religious beliefs of the people of the State.

The vast majority of the Princely States were linked irretrievably by geography with the territory which was to form the Dominion of India. By 15 August 1947, the Instrument of Accession to India had been signed by the rulers of all the States geographically contiguous to it, with the exception of Jammu and Kashmir in the north, Junagadh and some smaller adjoining States in the Kathiawar peninsula on the west coast, and Hyderabad in central India.

Junagadh, bounded on three sides by States that had acceded to India and on the fourth by the Arabian Sea, was the largest State in Kathiawar. It did not have a contiguous border with West Pakistan, the maritime route between its main port, Veraval, and Karachi in West Pakistan being 325 nautical miles. With an area of 3,400 square miles and a population of about 7 million, of whom 80 per cent were non-Muslims, the territory of Junagadh was, like that of many of the other Kathiawar States, splintered. It had enclaves in the bordering States of Gondal, Baroda and Bhavnagar, all of which had acceded to India, while other States which had also acceded to India had enclaves in Junagadh. All these factors pointed in but one direction: the Kathiawar States had to accede, as a whole, to one or the other of the two new Dominions. They were much too mixed up territorially to do otherwise.

Sir Mahabatkhan Rasulkhanji, the Nawab of Junagadh, had always maintained that Junagadh's future lay in the formation of a self-contained group of Kathiawar States. When in April 1947, weeks before the announcement of the Mountbatten Plan, articles appeared in the local Press suggesting that Junagadh was considering joining Pakistan, the Dewan of the State, Khan Bahadur Abdul Kadir Mohammed Hussain, firmly repudiated any such intention. But on 15 August, with Abdul Kadir, a sick man, and Sir Shah Nawaz Bhutto, a Muslim League politician from Karachi (and father of Zulfikar Ali Bhutto who later became prominent in Pakistan's public life), installed in his place as the Dewan, the Government of Junagadh announced its accession to Pakistan. The Government of India had received no prior intimation of this decision, and only received confirmation of it on 18 August in a reply to a telegram sent to the Dewan. It was not till after nearly a month, on 13 September, that Pakistan informed India that it had accepted the accession of Junagadh and had signed a Standstill Agreement with the State.

Junagadh's decision infuriated the other Kathiawar States, and protests poured into Delhi. Lord Mountbatten, now the Governor General of the Dominion of India, despatched his Chief of Staff, Lord Ismay, to Karachi for consultations with the Government of Pakistan. On his return to Delhi, Lord Ismay stated that, in his opinion, the Government of Pakistan was trying to provoke India into taking a step which would discredit her in the eyes of the world and obtain sympathy for Pakistan as an aggrieved Party. Junagadh, he stressed, was an economic and an administrative unit firmly embedded in Kathiawar, and as such could only be a liability to Pakistan in every sphere.

The Khan of Manavadar, the Ruler of a small State with an area of about 100 square miles, contiguous to Junagadh on three sides and bordered on the fourth by Gondal State which had acceded to India, who had not till then made a decision, also announced that he had entered into a Standstill Agreement with Pakistan and had asked that Dominion to accept his accession. However, the Sheikh of Mangrol, a very small State adjoining Junagadh, who had also not announced his choice, now signed a Standstill Agreement and Instrument of Accession with India. The Nawab of Junagadh refused to recognise Mangrol's accession to India, asserting that Mangrol as an "attached State" was his vassal and had no right to conduct negotiations without his authority. This position the Sheikh of Mangrol refused to accept, maintaining that with puramountcy lapsing on 15 August, he was independent of Junagadh. Apprehensive that other "vassals" might follow Mangrol's example, the Nawab of Junagadh despatched his State Force troops into Babariawad, an area comprising Estates whose rulers challenged the Nawab's overlordship and promptly acceded to India. The Government of India thereupon requested the Nawab of Junagadh to remove his State Force troops from Babariawad.

In order to protect the areas that had acceded to India, an Infantry Brigade of the Indian Army was despatched to Kathiawar.

The Brigade Commander was instructed not to violate Junagadh territory in any way and not even to enter Mangrol and Babariawad, which had acceded to India but whose accession was being contested by Junagadh and Pakistan, but to deploy his troops only in the other territories that had acceded. On 25 September, the Dewan of Junagadh sent a message to the Government of India in which he stated that the State Force troops in Babariawad would not be removed, and that both Mangrol and Babariawad were integral parts of Junagadh. A telegram was despatched by the Government of India to Liaquat Ali Khan, the Prime Minister of Pakistan, demanding that Junagadh State Force troops be withdrawn from Babariawad. Two days later, on 1 October, the subject was discussed between the Prime Ministers of India and Pakistan at a meeting of the Joint Defence Council which was being held in Delhi. While discussion was in progress, information was received that Junagadh State Force troops had entered Mangrol State.

This provocative act could have been met with retaliation, but the Government of India decided not to move Indian Army troops into either Babariawad or Mangrol but to continue peaceful efforts to secure the withdrawal of the Junagadh State Force troops. As neither Pakistan nor Junagadh issued instructions for the withdrawal of the State Force troops, the Commander of the Indian Infantry Brigade deployed in Kathiawar was instructed on 4 October to prepare plans for the occupation of Mangrol and Babariawad in case it should prove necessary. Further exchange of communications between India and Pakistan, and India and Junagadh, bore no fruit. Eventually, on 1 November, the Government of India despatched civil administrators, each accompanied by a small token force, to take over the administration of Mangrol and Babariawad.

The unsettled conditions in the area had caused a cessation of all trade with Junagadh. The food position became precarious, and the Nawab, realising that an untenable opposition had been reached, decided to abandon the State. He flew to Karachi with most of his family members, but not before ensuring for himself a life of ease by emptying the State Treasury of its cash and securities. With the departure of the Nawab, local political forces came into operation and began occupying various parts of the State. This compelled the Dewan, Sir Shah Nawaz Bhutto, to approach Samaldas Gandhi, the leader of a political party which had assumed the title of Arzi Hukumat (Provisional Government), to take over the reins of the government and to restore law and order. However, influential citizens of the State, including prominent Muslims, persuaded Sir Shah Nawaz to hand over the administration to the Government of India instead of the Arzi Hukumat. On 7 November, Sir Shah Nawaz made a request to this effect to the Government of India.

Prior to taking over the administration of Junagadh, the Indian Government cabled the Prime Minister of Pakistan to inform him that it was acceding to the request of the Dewan in order to avoid disorder and possible chaos in the State. The message stressed that the Government of India desired that a quick solution be arrived at, which should meet the wishes of the people of the State. It suggested that representatives of India and Pakistan meet to discuss the matter at the earliest possible moment.

The take-over of the State on 9 November was peaceful, without a single untoward incident. Two days later, the Prime Minister of Pakistan replied to the Indian cable. He stated that the Dewan of Junagadh had no authority to enter into any negotiations or settlement with India, and that the taking over of the administration and the sending of troops into Junagadh by India was a breach of international law. He demanded the immediate withdrawal of Indian troops.

The Government of India stated in reply that if it had not taken over the administration of the State, the Arzi Hukumat would have done so, and that might have resulted in bloodshed. It had acted on the request of Sir Shah Nawaz Bhutto and his colleagues of the Junagadh State Council, who had stated that the administration had collapsed. Further, Sir Shah Nawaz had taken the decision with the unanimous approval of not only the State Council but also the leaders of public opinion in the State.

In the absence of any constructive proposal from Pakistan, the Government of India decided to hold a referendum to ascertain the wishes of the people regarding accession as soon as normalcy had been restored. The referendum was held on 20 February 1948. In Junagadh, more than 190,000 votes were cast out of an electorate of 200,000. Those voting for Pakistan totalled 91, and the rest voted for India. In Mangrol, Manavadar and certain adjoining Estates, Pakistan's share of the 31,434 votes cast was 39. Thus ended a chapter full of incident, but one which could have been avoided if Pakistan had not encouraged the Nawab of Junagadh in his folly.

Hyderabad, as noted earlier, was the largest of the Princely States in undivided India. The Nizam who ruled this overwhelmingly non-Muslim State made known his aspiration for independence outside both the future Dominions as early as in April 1946, when the President of his Executive Council told Lord Wavell, the then Viceroy of India, that Hyderabad would prefer, on paramountcy lapsing, to become an independent State. After the Mountbatten Plan was announced on 3 June 1947, the Nizam of Hyderabad remained silent, biding his time, and announced on 15 August that he was entitled to and would assume the status of an independent sovereign. He was immediately informed by Lord Mountbatten that his intention was not a possibility and the State could not become a Dominion.

On 17 August, the Nawab of Chhatari, President of the Nizam's Executive Council, wrote to Mountbatten expressing a wish to enter into negotiations. This was agreed to, but on 25 August, the date on which the Hyderabad delegation was due to arrive in Delhi, the legal expert Sir Walter Monckton, K. C. who had been engaged by the Nizam as his Constitutional Adviser, informed Lord Mountbatten that he had resigned his position. He said that a violent attack had been made on him in the Hyderabad Press, engineered and organised by the Ittehad-ul-Musilmeen, a communal organisation in the State. The leader of this organisation, which was militaristic in nature, was a sciolist named Kasim Razvi who had organised and armed a large body of men, whom he named the Razakars into a Brigade. The Nawab of Chhatari also tendered his resignation but it was refused by the Nizam. As a result of the Nizam's issuing a statement condemning the attack on the delegation, Sir Walter Monckton withdrew his resignation.

Negotiations with the Hyderabad delegation commenced, but they met with little success. Each draft agreement, and there were a large number of them framed, was brought back to Delhi with the insertion of some unacceptable clause. It became obvious that the Nizam had no intention of surrendering his sovereignty, as there was a constant demand for the right to enter into direct political relations with foreign powers. Meanwhile, disquieting information was received in Delhi that Hyderabad was negotiating with a Czechoslovak firm for the supply of arms and ammunition valued at £3 million.

On 22 October, a final revised draft was hammered out in Delhi, and, having been agreed to by both sides, was handed to the State delegation which left for Hyderabad the same day with the promise that it would return to Delhi on 26 October with the Nizam's acceptance. This draft was debated by the Nizam's Executive Council for three days, and eventually accepted by a majority. The Nizam was approached on the evening of 25 October and the document placed before him, but although he approved, he postponed the signing until the next day. On 26 October, the delegation again approached the Nizam, but once again he postponed the signing to the next day.

On 27 October, Kasim Razvi and his Razakars staged a demonstration. They surrounded the houses of the members of the delegation—Sir Walter Monckton, the Nawab of Chhatari and Sir Sultan Ahmed—made inflammatory speeches through loudspeakers, and made it impossible for the delegation to leave for Delhi.

On the morning of 28 October, the Nizam produced a surprise for his delegation. He introduced Kasim Razvi into the meeting. Razvi did not mince his words: he said that a fresh delegation should be formed to negotiate with the Government of India, that India, tied up with trouble elsewhere (the invasion of Kashmir by raiders from Pakistan had commenced), would be too hard put to refuse Hyderabad's demands if the State insisted strongly enough. Despite the warning by his Executive Councillors that the course suggested by Kasim Razvi would be most harmful, perhaps even disastrous to the interests of the State, the Nizam showed a strong inclination towards

Razvi's suggestion. Thereupon the members of the delegation resigned and a new delegation was formed. It was composed of Nawab Moin Nawaz Jung, Hyderabad's Minister for Police and Information, one of the dissidents in the Executive Council when the 22 October draft agreement had been discussed, Abdur Rahim, a prominent member of the Ittehad-ul-Musilmeen; and P. V. Reddy, a nonentity with no opinion of his own.

Lord Mountbatten was most annoyed at this sudden change in the membership of the delegation, and when Nawab Moin Nawaz Jung attempted to resume negotiations on the basis of the very first State draft, it was evident that the Hyderabad delegation intended throwing to the four winds the hard work that had been put into several weeks of conferences, consultations and drafting. This was clearly unacceptable. The leader of the delegation was informed that the last draft had received the acceptance of the State Executive Council and the agreement of the Nizam, and there was no question of re-opening the issue from the start. Lord Mountbatten told Nawab Moin Nawaz Jung that the Nizam must make up his mind whether he intended to rule his State himself, or be ruled by the Ittehad-ul-Musilmeen.

The conferences that followed bore no fruit. The Nawab of Chhatari, finding matters intolerable, resigned as President of the Executive Council. The Nizam, on Razvi's advice, appointed Mir Laik Ali, a prominent businessman of Hyderabad and Pakistan's representative to the United Nations, to succeed the Nawab. With other nominees of Razvi also included in the Executive Council, the Government of Hyderabad was now fully under Kasim Razvi's control.

The Razakars launched on brigandage, joining hands with the Communists. Kasim Razvi encouraged Razakar and Communist bands to make incursions into the neighbouring Indian provinces of Bombay, Madras and the Central Provinces. On 12 April 1948, in a statement to the Associated Press of India, he declared that he would plant the family flag of the House of Hyderabad on the Red Fort in Delhi.

On 22 May, the mail train from Madras to Bombay was attacked during its halt at Gangapur station in Hyderabad State. Two passengers were killed, eleven seriously wounded and thirteen kidnapped. A large number of other travellers were manhandled and subjected to indignities as the Hyderabad State Railway Police looked on.

On 18 June 1948, negotiations between India and Hyderabad State finally broke down. It was probably timed by Kasim Razvi to take place round about this date, as Lord Mountbatten's tenure of appointment as Governor General of India was to conclude on 21 June. He had striven valiantly to persuade the Nizam to a sensible course. Lord Mountbatten's failure was attributable in a not unimportant measure to the anti-Indian attitude of a section of the British Press and certain British politicians who argued that Hyderabad could and should be independent. These statements stoked the fires of ambition that smouldered in the Nizam and Kasim Razvi.

Although the Nizam had banned the Communist Party in his State in 1943, he lifted the ban at the instance of Kasim Razvi. The latter was now able to supply the Communists openly with arms and ammunition and to co-ordinate their activities with those of the Razakars. Raids on the borders of the neighbouring provinces of India and on the railway trains passing through the State were stepped up. Law and order broke down within the State and across its borders. Indian police and troops had to be despatched to protect the population of the adjoining provinces. In August 1948, the Nizam was sent a sternly worded request by the Government of India to take strong measures to bring the situation under control and to disband the Razakars. Whether he had the power to do so is doubtful, and the request fell in any case on deaf ears.

As the situation worsened steadily, Indian troops were ordered on 13 September 1948 to march into Hyderabad. The Hyderabad State Forces laid down their arms within four days, after offering token resistance. The casualties suffered, about 800 in all, occurred mainly among the Razakars and the Communists. A ban was placed immediately on the Razakar organisation. Kasim Razvi was arrested on 19 September. The Communists were then engaged, but they proved a much harder nut to crack. Operating mainly by night, they put the arms handed to them by the Razakars to effective use, and it took nearly three years to bring them under control.

Soon after the installation of a Military Governor, the Nizam issued a proclamation, which brought Hyderabad State into line with the other geographically linked Princely States that had acceded to India.

Till October 1947, the Maharajah of Jammu and Kashmir, like his counterpart in Hyderabad, entertained visions of becoming a sovereign ruler outside the Dominions of India and Pakistan. He had been informed by Lord Mountbatten, when he was still the Viceroy of undivided India, that it was not a feasible proposition and that he must accede to the Dominion of his choice. The Maharajah's hesitation had little to do with the fact that the majority of the State's population was Muslim. The major political party in the State, the National Conference led by Sheikh Abdullah, although predominantly Muslim in its membership, was strongly inclined towards India. The Maharajah sat on the fence for reasons of his own personal ambition.

Since no decision was conveyed by the Maharajah till 15 August 1947, Lord Mountbatten despatched Lord Ismay to Srinagar to persuade Sir Hari Singh to take one course or the other. The mission was infructuous, but, as an interim step, the Maharajah signed Standstill Agreements with both India and Pakistan. India abided by the Agreement. Pakistan did not.

In the case of Junagadh and Hyderabad, which were separated by vast distance from Pakistan, the Government in Karachi (the then capital of the new Dominion) could only offer political support to the rulers who held out against accession to India despite their States being surrounded by Indian territory. Pakistan based its support to the Muslim rulers of these two predominantly non-Muslim States on the ground that, under the Mountbatten Plan, it was entirely for the rulers to opt for accession to either Dominion.

Jammu and Kashmir, on the other hand, was contiguous to Pakistan as well as to India. The beautiful Kashmir Valley, famed as the Switzerland of the East, was a tempting prize, and a vulnerable one that was apparently within easy grasp. It suited Pakistan in this case to deny the ruler his option and to harp on the religious composition of the State's population. Ironically, however, it was the popular

Muslim leaders of Kashmir—Sheikh Mohammed Abdullah, Bakshi Ghulam Mohammed, Mirza Afzal Beg, Ghulam Mohammed Sadiq and Syed Mir Qasim, to mention the foremost—who rejected the two-nation theory and called for accession to India since it was a modern democracy more suited for achieving their people's progress in the conditions of the twentieth century than the semi-theocratic Pakistan.

Lacking support from anyone but a small section of the people of Jammu and Kashmir, Pakistan resorted first to economic coercion and then to naked force.

In an attempt to bring pressure to bear on the Maharajah, Pakistan cut off all supplies of food, petrol, salt and other essential commodities on the import of which the State depended. As the main communication lines ran from what was now Pakistan territory into Jammu and Kashmir, the sanctions left a strong mark. In order to exert even stronger pressure, a series of raids against the border posts of the State Forces were organised in Pakistan and launched into Jammu.

Far from heeding the Maharajah's protests, Pakistan capped its intervention by sending tribesmen from the North-West Frontier Province (NWFP) into the Kashmir Valley. On 22 October, the border town of Muzaffarabad was attacked and sacked, and the tribal raiders commenced their advance into the Valley. Reports of the increasing proximity of the tribesmen caused the personnel of the Mahura Power House, on which the Valley relied for its electric power, to abandon it and flee.

The Maharajah, finally realising the seriousness of the situation, sent the Government of India a desperate call for assistance. India could not, however, assist in repelling the tribal attack as long as the State did not accede to the Dominion. The Maharajah, who had evacuated Srinagar with his family on the night of 25 October, was contacted in Jammu. He signed the Instrument of Accession on 26 October, and Indian troops were thereupon ordered into the Valley. Sheikh Abdullah, the leader of the National Conference to whom the Maharajah had handed over the reins of the administration prior to departing from Srinagar, formed an interim Emergency Government.

Chapter 2

Did No Briton Know?

CAPTURED documents showed that the officer entrusted with organising and implementing 'Operation Gulmarg' for Pakistan's capture of Kashmir by force was Major General Akbar Khan, a Regular Officer of the Pakistan Army and a product of the Royal Military College at Sandhurst.

Adopting the pseudonym "General Jebel Tariq", the Moroccan name for Gibraltar, he established his Headquarters at Rawalpindi in the building occupied by Army Headquarters, Pakistan. He was an autocrat in so far as the operation was concerned, and was given free access to anything that he thought he should have in order to ensure that the operation was a success. His failure to produce the expected result led to his fall from favour, but being an individual of great ambition he decided to rehabilitate himself without undue loss of time.

This called for action of an abnormal type. He plotted to assassinate the Prime Minister of Pakistan, Liaquat Ali Khan. The plot was, however, detected a few days before the target date, and Akbar Khan found himself behind bars.

Akbar Khan must have been acutely disappointed at the failure of his Kashmir venture. On the face of it, the problem that faced him was a relatively simple one. All the communication factors presented him with a picture that few, if any, commanders have been lucky to have before them. There was no problem in the transportation of the formidable force of the Frontier tribesmen that had been lined up. As for opposition, it would encounter the Jammu and Kashmir State Force troops, who would be taken by surprise and who in any event were not high-grade troops. Moreover, Akbar Khan had taken steps to wean away a large percentage of officers and men of the Jammu and Kashmir State Forces from their loyalty to the ruler. The defection of these individuals at the moment of strike would embarrass the defenders of Kashmir. There was nothing that was not in his favour, and there was no reason for any qualms regarding the outcome of the operation. There could only be one result, and it could be achieved in a few days. He must have been a pleasantly excited and confident man as 22 October 1947 drew near.

Opposition by Indian troops was the only factor that could affect the successful outcome of the plan, but the raids against various State Force outposts in Jammu, which had been underway for some weeks, had drawn no reaction from the Indian Government. Active opposition from India could, therefore, be ruled out; and in any case, even if India did react, the time and space factors were predominantly in favour of the invading force. The Kashmir Valley would be Pakistan's before India realised what had happened. Any protests that might follow could be debated on political platforms, but possession was nine-tenths of the law.

The distance from Domel to Srinagar is about 100 miles, and Major General Akbar Khan must have been well aware of the fact that once the State Force unit at Domel was liquidated, the road to Srinagar would be wide open, there being no other units deployed along the route. It was merely a question of how quickly the tribal convoy could cover that mileage. Even at a slow rate of 10 miles in the hour, the leading elements of the convoy would be either in, or on the outskirts of, Srinagar in about 12 hours. The whole operation could, in fact, have been completed quite comfortably within 24 hours. And it would have been, but for a demolished bridge on the way at Uri. Even with this obstruction throwing the time schedule out of gear, had the invading force been composed of a disciplined and resolute body of men instead of rapacious tribesmen, the 62 miles from the demolished bridge to Srinagar could have been completed on foot, and three days would have been more than ample.

What had evidently not received attention during the planning stage was the tribal reaction to various situations that might be encountered. They had been tempted to undertake the operation with promises of loot and women, all theirs for the taking. They had no intention of settling down in the Valley permanently, nor for that matter would Pakistan have permitted them to do so. Their object was to get into the Valley, collect their booty, and to get home as soon as they could. Motor transport was essential in order to achieve this, and it is evident that the tribesmen were not prepared to be divorced from it. When a demolished bridge blocked the further passage of the vehicles, they sat back at Uri until such time as a diversion could be constructed. This took nearly four days, and there is no denying the fact that these four days played a vital role in saving the Valley.

As noted earlier, the Jammu and Kashmir State Forces were deployed for internal security, not defence of the State against attack from outside. The penny packets along the border, stretching from Gilgit in the north to Suchetgarh in the south, a distance of 240 miles, were garrisoned by units and sub-units ranging from a weak battalion to a platoon. This dispersal left the State Forces weak everywhere, and they did not have the backing of a readily available reserve. Once the thin crust of resistance along the border was overcome, there were neither plans nor units to form a second line of defence. Major General Scott, Chief of Staff of the State Forces, was not in the Valley when the tribal attack developed. Even had he been in the Valley, he would have found it impossible, in the short space of time available to him, to salvage the situation.

While military intelligence relating to the deployment of the Jammu and Kashmir State Forces was well known to Pakistan, that country having given it very serious attention over an extended period of time, India had not given the subject a thought. Military Intelligence Directorate of Army Headquarters, India, was fully engaged in trying to cope with the spate of reports dealing with the movements of troops and stores to and from India and Pakistan, in accordance with the plan to implement the partition of the Armed Forces and their assets which had been formulated by Supreme Headquarters, India and Pakistan. The internal situation, which necessitated reporting to Government on the progress of the refugee convoys threading their way into and out of the country, demanded constant attention. There was neither the time nor did it seem necessary to delve into the affairs of Jammu and Kashmir, a friendly autonomous State.

The Intelligence Bureau of the Government of India, manned by personnel of the Indian Police Service, were indeed expected to cover the State. They would naturally have been interested in keeping abreast of happenings within and along the border, in so far as they might have repercussions in India. But they were in a tragicomic state of helplessness. The Director of the Intelligence Bureau of undivided India, during the months preceding 15 August 1947, was an officer who was about to opt for Pakistani citizenship. This individual, who was earmarked for appointment as Director of the Pakistan Intelligence Bureau, took full advantage of his position to transfer across to Pakistan every file of importance dealing with Intelligence, leaving behind for his counterparts in India the office furniture, empty racks and cupboards, and a few innocuous files dealing with office routine. It is therefore no exaggeration to say that on 15 August, Pakistan came into being with a well-established Intelligence Service, while India had only a semblance of one.

The reticence of Maharajah Hari Singh about the hostile actions being launched against his State in Jammu, specially in the Poonch area, is understandable when viewed in the light of his ambition to retain his sovereignty. Moreover, he was perhaps unaware of the magnitude of the threat that was developing, and thought that his State Forces were capable of coping with what might have been assessed by him as minor border incidents. Whatever it was, his silence resulted in India's truncated Intelligence, both Civil and Military, remaining unaware of what was happening.

While the Indian Intelligence Services may have been blind, it is difficult to imagine that Pakistan's intention, preparation and plan of action could have escaped detection by the numerous British personnel who were holding key positions in both the Dominions. Strangely enough, Lord Mountbatten, the Governor General of India, and General Sir Rob Lockhart, the Commander in Chief of the Indian Army, apparently knew nothing about the attack on Kashmir until after the tribal raiders had sacked Muzaffarabad.

Before the division of the sub-continent into two Dominions, it had been suggested that the Viceroy of undivided India, Lord Mountbatten, should be the Governor General of both India and Pakistan. Jinnah, the architect of Pakistan, would not have it. He became the Head of the State of his creation, while India accepted Lord Mountbatten as its first Governor General.

That Jinnah disliked Lord Mountbatten is true, but surely Lord Mountbatten's British colleagues in service with the Dominion of Pakistan, the Commander in Chief of the Pakistan Army, General Sir Frank Messervey, in particular, would not have been swayed by Jinnah's animosity towards Lord Mountbatten so far as to withhold from him such vital information as Pakistan's intention to take Kashmir by force. They must have been fully alive to the fact that it would place Lord Mountbatten in a most invidious position if, as the Governor General of India and even more as the creator and pilot of the Mountbatten Plan, he knew nothing about it. Lord Mountbatten's ignorance of the plot that was being hatched against Jammu and Kashmir State can only point to one conclusion: his British colleagues in Pakistan did consider him an outcaste. What is even more amazing is the treatment accorded to Field Marshal Sir Claude Auchinleck.

In order to ensure that the partition of the Armed Forces and their assets was fairly and correctly conducted, both India and Pakistan had agreed to the formation of a Supreme Headquarters, with Field Marshal Auchinleck as the Supreme Commander. The Headquarters, staffed entirely by British officers, was located in New Delhi. As a neutral body, Supreme Headquarters owed its loyalty to both Dominions. In his role as a neutral, Auchinleck had free access to both Governments and their Armed Forces Headquarters, and was in constant touch with them, either by personal visits, on telephone or wireless, or through countries.

It would not have called for a great deal of thought on the part of the Supreme Commander to arrive at the inference that the induction of a large body of tribals into a Princely State that had yet to make its choice of accession could have serious repercussions, not excluding a clash between the two Armies of which he was the Supreme Commander. General Sir Frank Messervey, the C in C of the Pakistan Army, would also certainly have arrived at the same conclusion, and it is, therefore, difficult to believe that he did not brief Auchinleck fully on the events taking place in Pakistan, the intention behind them, and the serious repercussions that were bound to follow.

If Messervey did not keep Auchinleck fully informed, then one can only view the Supreme Commander as a rather pathetic figure, badly let down by one of his senior commanders. If Auchinleck was aware of what was happening, then he was not the neutral in whom India had placed its confidence and it was a case of clear betrayal of trust.

The bare fact is that at no time before 24 October did Field Marshal Auchinleck call the attention of the Government of India to any untoward developments in Pakistan or in the vicinity of the Pakistan-Jammu and Kashmir border. His report came after the tribal attack on Muzaffarabad.

The two Commanders in Chief, General Sir Frank Messervey of Pakistan and General Sir Rob Lockhart of India, were no strangers to each other, both having served in the undivided Indian Army for a number of years. Their Headquarters were linked by direct telephone and wireless circuits, and it was routine for them to have long telephone conversations during which they discussed matters of mutual interest to the two Armies and exchanged information. That Messervey knew what was happening and was about to happen can be taken for granted. It would be most extraordinary for the C in C of an Army to be kept completely in the dark about a large-scale operation such as the one that was being mounted, involving as it did a considerable amount of equipment and the posting of officers to the Headquarters of "General Jebel Tariq". This Headquarters was, in fact, located in the same building as Messervey's own Headquarters. Whether he informed his counterpart in India of what was brewing is not known, but if he did, General Lockhart did not pass the information to Military Operations and Intelligence Directorate.

An individual who was certainly fully aware of what was happening was Sir George Cunningham, the Governor of the NWFP. Thousands of tribesmen from across the Durand Line had appeared in Peshawar, the capital of the NWFP and were being heavily armed. Sir George was no stranger to the NWFP as he had served there in various capacities for almost his entire career, and this radical departure from the firmly maintained policy of containing the tribesmen must have shocked him. It is believed that he dropped a hint to General Sir Rob Lockhart, whom he knew well, the latter having been his predecessor as Governor of the NWFP. However the C in C of the Indian Army was apparently unable to grasp the full implications of it. Cunningham also knew Messervey and Auchinleck well, and it is more than certain that he must have warned Auchinleck.

Whether these individuals knew or did not know of the planned raid on Kashmir will never be firmly established. Suffice it to say that the Government of India, which had gladly accepted the formation of Supreme Headquarters for a period of four years, now demanded its dissolution. This was effected almost immediately. The services of the Commander in Chief, General Sir Rob Lockhart, who should normally have served for four years with effect from 15 August 1947, were dispensed with, General Roy Bucher replacing him on 1 January 1948.

What happened in Gilgit in 1947, prior to and during the tribal invasion, strengthens the inference of the involvement of certain British officers in Pakistan's plan.

It was the Treaty of Amritsar, concluded on 16 Mach 1846 after the First Sikh War, between Gulab Singh and the British Government, which resulted in Jammu and Kashmir being formed into a political entity. Gulab Singh became the Maharajah of the State comprising Jammu, Kashmir, Ladakh and Gilgit. On 23 September 1925, one of his descendants, Hari Singh, became the Maharajah. When Soviet Russia took over virtual control of Sinkiang in 1935, the British Government came to an agreement with the Maharajah under which a 60-year lease of Gilgit was executed. The sole responsibility for the administration and defence of Gilgit was transferred to the British Government, which raised an irregular force, the Gilgit Scouts, officered exclusively by British officers. With the announcement of the Mountbatten Plan on 3 June 1947, Gilgit was handed back to the Maharajah amidst much jubilation, and with it the Gilgit Scouts became a part of the Jammu and Kashmir State Forces.

The Maharajah despatched a Governor, accompanied by the Chief of Staff of the Jammu and Kashmir State Forces to take over Gilgit. When they arrived in Gilgit on 30 July 1947, Major General Scott and the Governor were informed that all the British officers of the Gilgit Scouts had opted to serve Pakistan. Scott returned to make a report to the Maharajah, but the Governor stayed on in Gilgit to administer the area. The Maharajah was taken aback by the information conveyed to him by his Chief of Staff, but worse was to follow. On 31 October 1947, soon after the tribal invasion of Kashmir had commenced, the Gilgit Scouts surrounded the residence of the Governor, and a Provisional Government was installed. On 4 November 1947, Major Brown, the British commandant of the Gilgit Scouts, hoisted the Pakistan flag in the lines of his command, and on 21 November, an official styling himself as Political Agent arrived from Pakistan and established himself in Gilgit.

The loss of Gilgit to Jammu and Kashmir State was the result of a piratical action. Major Brown was certainly not the chief conspirator.

He was a mere pawn in the game. The strategic value of Gilgit as a base was first realised in 1935, hence the 60-year lease. Its importance had not changed in 1947, and had in fact grown much beyond the earlier estimate because of the vastly increased power of the Soviet Union. India, it was realised, would never have agreed to Gilgit being used for spying on or mounting an attack on the Soviet Union. It is clear that the retrocession of the area to the Maharajah was no more than a gesture, and that Gilgit was firmly designed to become part of Pakistan.

Chapter 3

Delhi Caught off Guard

INDIA was far from a state of preparedness to answer the SOS call which came from the Maharajah of Jammu and Kashmir. As a result of the Junagadh Nawab's actions, it was not improbable that the situation in Kathiawar might explode if not tackled sensibly and expeditiously. Hyderabad was being difficult. But most pressing of all was the task of bringing back to normal the situation in the Punjab, Delhi and its environs, where communal riots had resulted in a breakdown of the local administration in certain areas. This was causing extreme anxiety. Kashmir had received scant, if any, attention, India being content to wait for Maharajah Hari Singh to make up his mind on the question of accession. The sudden and unforeseen happenings in the State therefore caught the Government of India off guard.

Jinnah's continuous harping on the two-nation theory, with constant references to the new Dominion of Pakistan that was about to be formed as the home of the Muslim, generated fears and tensions which resulted in clashes between Muslims and non-Muslims in the Punjab and Bengal, the two provinces that were to be partitioned. Mob violence increased as the date approached, and continued even after the partition. There ensued a mass exodus of minority communities from the Indian and Pakistani halves of the two provinces. They had to wrench themselves away from areas where they had lived for generations and which they had regarded as their homeland, selling at a loss or simply abandoning their agricultural land and property.

As the huge refugee columns crossed the border, the stories of the atrocities that they had witnessed and been subjected to spread like wildfire. In a short while, inflamed crowds, thirsting for revenge and egged on by the refugees, fell upon innocent citizens. A carnage such as undivided India had never experienced engulfed the divided Punjab. The refugee columns moving in both directions were subjected to attacks. The administration found itself paralysed by desertions of personnel belonging to the minority community who fled to join the refugee columns.

Whether the upheaval could have been avoided is debatable. There is, however, little doubt that Lord Mountbatten's accelerated time-table for partition and transfer of power contributed to the confusion. The 73 days allowed to execute the plan was far too short a span of time, considering the size of the problems. Perhaps it might have been more prudent to have phased the partition plan for implementation by stages and to have adhered to the original target of June 1948. The advancing of the date to 14 August 1947 was a gamble, and it had devastating results. Fortunately, however, the provinces of the newly born Dominion of India other than Punjab and Bengal remained unaffected, and no harm was done to the millions of Muslims residing there.

The Indian Army was able to bring the situation in the Punjab under control within a few weeks, though it had to face many other pressing problems. It was being split into the Armies of India and Pakistan, at the ratio of two-thirds to India and one-third to Pakistan. This was based not on the geographical dimensions of the two Dominions, but on the territorial origin of those enlisted in the undivided Army.

Demobilisation after the termination of World War II had proceeded apace. Of the infantry battalions, for example, only 152 remained. There was no infantry battalion consisting wholly of Pakistan-enlisted personnel. Pakistan's highest contribution was 50 per cent in 55 of them, and 75 per cent in 6. The composition of the rest was wholly or predominantly Indian. The situation was similar in the other combat units and in the Corps and Services. The movement of the sub-units to form the Pakistan Army was therefore in full swing. There were, however, many units composed of 100 per cent of Indian nationals which were garrisoning the North-West Frontier and other areas of Pakistan. These had to return to India to resuscitate the formations. In addition there were numerous sub-units composed of Indian nationals still serving in Regiments allotted to Pakistan. In order not to embarrass the fighting efficiency of the Pakistan Army, it was agreed that the Indian units and sub-units located in West Pakistan would remain in the Dominion for a few months till the Pakistan Army had organised itself and was in a position to assume its responsibilities.

Army Headquarters, India, was in a very unhappy state. While Pakistan Army Headquarters had established itself in the well-equipped Northern Command Headquarters in Rawalpindi, and was able to commence functioning without impediment, its analogue in New Delhi found itself engaged in an accommodation-cum-location battle with Supreme Headquarters. The Supreme Commander, Field Marshal Sir Claude Auchinleck, had decided that it would be incorrect for Supreme Headquarters and Army Headquarters, India, to be located in the same Secretariat building. This building, the traditional home of Indian Army Headquarters, was fully equipped. As it had accommodated a very large General Headquarters formed during World War II in the place of Indian Army Headquarters, it was more than large enough to meet the requirements of both the Supreme Headquarters and the Army Headquarters which was about to be resurrected. There were, in addition, a large number of wartime hutments, located close to the Secretariat, which had formed a part of General Headquarters and which were readily available to absorb sections which could not be accommodated in the main building. Supreme Headquarters, however, characteristically decided that Army Headquarters, India, should accommodate itself in the Red Fort in Delhi.

The Red Fort may be an imposing building, but it was neither designed nor does it lend itself to accommodating a major Headquarters. Besides, it was not wired for the extensive telephone communications necessary for an Army Headquarters to operate efficiently. Nevertheless, a sincere attempt was made by Army Headquarters to establish itself in the Fort, some Staff Officers with their Sections even being accommodated to the vehicle garages. Limited space, however, precluded the correct setting up of the various offices. Many files and documents had to be kept stored in boxes for security reason and could not be got at easily, causing delays and ruffled tempers. It soon became apparent that to continue to operate from the Red Fort would result in a major breakdown. Army Headquarters insisted that it return to the Secretariat in New Delhi before this happened. Supreme Headquarters vacated a small part of its accommodation, and, making use of the hutments, Army Headquarters established itself in its proper home and settled down to carry out its functions. Though subjected to a rocky start, it recovered quickly. It is well that it did so, as the unforeseen trouble in the Punjab was just around the bend. Had Army Headquarters remained in the Red Fort, it would have been incapable of coping with the situation.

With the Intelligence Bureau badly handicapped and the Civil Administration in the Punjab thrown out of gear, the responsibility for almost all types of Intelligence fell upon the shoulders of Military Intelligence. It was required to produce for the Government a comprehensive summary of the events taking place in the Punjab, on call, and consolidated summaries twice daily. In addition, Supreme Headquarters had to be kept briefed of the progress made by the railway trains carrying troops and stores to and from Pakistan. These requirements meant a tremendous load, and the Military Intelligence

Directorate had not been designed for work of these dimensions. The Staff Officers of the M.I. Directorate had to work a minimum of 16 hours per day.

In order to enable Supreme Headquarters to function effectively, the Indian Army Headquarters Signal Regiment provided it with all its communications, including those to Pakistan Army Headquarters. The links provided for Supreme Headquarters were for its exclusive use. With the breakdown of law and order in the Punjab, Supreme Headquarters found its traffic increased considerably, and began utilising the already overstretched channels of communications of Army Headquarters, India. This resulted in unacceptable delays in the submission of the various summaries and reports by Military Intelligence to the Government and to the Directorates of Army Headquarters. Some other channels of communication were desperately needed, and fortunately the Indian Navy and Indian Air Force found themselves in a position to assist. Their wireless sets while not linked to any specific stations were utilised as intercept sets, and any messages that they picked up were passed to Military Intelligence. In the majority of cases, the intercepted messages were those being passed between units and their formations giving the latest situation, and it was useful in that it enabled Military Intelligence to commence working on the various reports even if the messages from the formation headquarters were received late.

It was from some of these intercepts received via the Naval and Air Force channels that the first indication was received of something amiss in the Jammu Province of Jammu and Kashmir State.

Among the intercepts received early in October 1947 was one that read: "Gorkhas still holding out in Sensa". As Gorkha units were part of the Indian Army, and no message had been received that any unit was in trouble, a study was made of the Order of Battle of the Indian Army to ascertain the Gorkha Battalion located in Sensa. There was no such place. Then, to be quite certain, a meticulous study was made of the border of the NWFP and Baluchistan, but without success. Had a compendium of place names included in the maps produced by the Survey of India been available, it could have been referred to, but so ill-equipped was Military Intelligence that it lacked one. It was in fact in the same position as the civilian Intelligence Bureau, its legacy being a few files on routine office procedure and one file on a clandestine organisation that had operated in Burma during World War II and had been defunct since the termination of hostilities. This had been inadvertently left behind or had escaped the general destruction of sensitive records by the departing British officers.

To pass the half-baked information from the intercept to Military Operations would evoke the rejoinder, "Where is Sensa and which Gorkhas?", and the answer to neither question was available. It was therefore decided to shelve the matter and to attend to it only if further information came. This was received the next morning, one of the intercepted messages stating that Sensa was still holding out. The day after, another intercept stated: "Owen being attacked"; the same procedure as in the case of Sensa was undertaken to trace Owen, with the same result. Puzzled, Military Intelligence came to the conclusion that Sensa and Owen were probably the code names of two places, and as the Signal Regiment was unable to identify the station that had originated the messages, it was decided to file the Owen message too.

The following day a further intercept was received: "Commander to Commander. Owen captured. Wait until I join you then coordinated attack on Sensa." At about mid-day came another: "Commander to Commander. Have received one hundred Poonchies. Arrange rations."

The word 'Poonchies' at last gave a clue. It indicated that the area of operations was not the NWFP or Baluchistan, but Jammu and Kashmir State. As no maps of Jammu and Kashmir were available with Military Intelligence, a Staff Officer was sent to the Map Depot which handed him the necessary map sheets, but with a note to the effect that stocks of these maps were very limited, the main stock having been collected and taken to Pakistan. The Jammu-Pakistan border was scanned, and first Owen and then Sensa were located. They were both in the Poonch District of Jammu Province. From their locations it was obvious that they were both Jammu and Kashmir State Force border outposts. Only then was it realised that the Jammu and Kashmir State Forces enlisted Gorkhas.

As Military Intelligence was not required to cover Jammu and Kashmir, and Indian Army units were not deployed in the area, this information was not included in the Intelligence Summaries but a separate note, together with the map, was sent to the Director of Military Operations (DMO), who passed it on to the Commander in-Chief General Sir Rob Lockhart, through the Chief of the General Staff (OGS). Little interest was evinced in it by the DMO and the CGS, and the C in C returned it without comment. This was not unexpected, as what was taking place in Jammu was no concern of India, and in the absence of any information from the Maharajah of Jammu and Kashmir it was assumed that, as the Poonchies were subjects of the State, it was an internal security problem.

Further intercepts were received during the days that followed, each one relating to other outposts that were attacked and presumably forced into surrender or withdrawal. As neither the deployment of the Sate Forces nor the strength of the garrisons was known, the actual implications of the attacks could not be appreciated, nor was there any indication that Pakistan was involved in them.

Then came the attack on Bhimbar in the Mirpur District of Jammu. This evidently proved to be a hard nut to crack, and the attackers appeared to be experiencing difficulty in overcoming the stout resistance that faced them. There were many references in the intercepts to 'burning them out', but the implication was not realised until much later after the Maharajah had signed the Instrument of Accession and units of the Indian Army had moved into the State.

Survivors from the Bhimbar garrison stated that after they had beaten off a number of assaults launched by the enemy, soon after first light one morning, tanks approached their positions and engaged them with automatic fire and flame. Ill-equipped to withstand or neutralise such an assault, the defences were soon liquidated. Having completed their task, the tanks withdrew westwards to Pakistan territory. An aerial reconnaissance was made of the area to ascertain the authenticity of the survivors' statements, and the air photographs showed unmistakable signs of tank tracks leading to and from Bhimbar, from the west. Further investigations also revealed the fact that the assaults which had taken place along the Jammu-Pakistan border had been planned in Pakistan and executed by ex-soldiers armed by Pakistan, and reinforced by Pakistan Regular Troops who had been sent on leave and operated in civilian clothing. Fortunately for Pakistan, there were no questions asked when the attacks were being mounted, as there was no protest from the only source authorised to lodge one, the Maharajah. Still sitting on the fence, he had remained silent.

When the Maharajah of Jammu and Kashmir eventually acceded to India on 26 October 1947, the tribesmen were already at Uri, a mere 62 miles from Srinagar. The fate of the Valley hung by a slender thread.

Lord Mountbatten ordered the Indian Army to be despatched instantly to contain the raiders. That the tribal convoy had been halted by a demolished bridge was unknown at the time. Lord Mountbatten, who had been the Supreme Commander of the South-East Asia Command during World War II, must have been acutely aware of the communication problem when he gave the order. A powerful and mobile raider force of several thousands, with a tarmac road at its command, was poised to strike at Srinagar, and could do so in a matter of hours. The Indian Army, on the other hand, with an eleventh-hour warning, was required to be airlifted into the Valley in DC3 (Dakota) aircraft with their strictly limited payload and to land on a makeshift airstrip.

It was a hazardous task that few, if any, armies have been called upon to undertake. There had, however, been a definite violation by Pakistan of its Standstill Agreement with Jammu and Kashmir, and, on the State acceding to India, Lord Mountbatten had no option. It is to his credit that he did not hesitate to issue the order. The Indian Army accepted the challenge.

That the Valley was saved must be put down to two factors: the gallantry of the Indian soldiers, and Pakistan's error in choosing the frontier tribesmen as its cats'-paw.

When Pakistan decided to present the Maharajah of Jammu and Kashmir with a *fait accompli*, it chose to utilise the frontier tribesmen as a cover so as to avoid the impression of direct responsibility for violating the Standstill Agreement. These tribesmen were collected from the territory west of the Durand Line and assembled in Peshawar. It must have been a strange experience for them, as for decades they had never been permitted to cross the Durand Line in any numbers, and whenever small parties were given permission to enter the area to the east of the Durand Line, which was rare, their weapons were taken away at the border posts and handed back only when they were homeward bound. Now they found themselves being welcomed in Peshawar, presented with arms and ammunition, which in the past they had risked their lives to obtain, and transported across West Pakistan to a land that most of them had probably never heard of, in the role of 'liberators'.

To have attempted the *coup* with the Pakistan Regular Forces would have been very effective but much too blatant. Major General Akbar Khan, who was in charge of the operation, evidently calculated that the task could be successfully accomplished on these lines: following close on the heels of the tribals, soon after they had reached Srinagar, the Pakistan Infantry Brigade conveniently located near Kohala would have arrived, to persuade the tribesmen to return to their mountain homes with the loot they had amassed; this Brigade with an excellent motorable road at its disposal, could have been in Srinagar in a matter of hours; having achieved their object, the Pakistan leaders would then have announced to the world that they could not be held responsible for what had taken place—the tribesmen had flowed across the Durand Line and taken the law into their own hands, and had it not been for the speedy action taken by dispatching regular troops to contain them, the Valley would have been pillaged. The Maharajah's accession to Pakistan would have followed automatically, under duress.

In its selection of the tribesmen to consummate its plan, however, Pakistan made a blunder. The general impression about the fighting ability of the tribesman from the west of the Durand Line is a fallacy. That he is tall and powerful in appearance is true, and his haughty air of independence, coupled with the rifle and dagger with which he is invariably armed, makes him appear formidable. In actual fact he is chicken-hearted. He will only attack troops who are careless and present him with an easy ambush from which he can escape unscathed. He will attack isolated bodies of men when the numerical odds are greatly in his favour, closing in when the garrison has expended its ammunition, and overpowering it by sheer weight of numbers. If there is the remotest chance of a reverse, he will break action and withdraw, and he is allergic to having his flanks threatened or turned. His worst trait, however, is unreliability.

These characteristics of the tribesmen have been known for decades and are substantiated by numerous examples, the most important being that the British fought shy of enlisting the tribesmen into the regular Indian Army of the pre-Partition era. They had been enlisted at one period, but their lack of soldierly qualities and their untrustworthiness, especially during World War I when they indulged in mutiny and murder, accelerated their disbandment. During World War II, they were given another chance to prove themselves, but an Afridi unit raised as Infantry had to be relegated to the role of a Labour battalion and sent to Persia while the Mahsuds, enlisted and formed into a Rifle Company of the 4th Battalion 13th Frontier Force Rifles, behaved true to tradition when the unit was ordered overseas by deserting one night with its arms and ammunition. Recruitment of the tribals was, therefore, confined almost entirely to service in the Frontier Scouts, an irregular force located in their own tribal areas and utilised to keep their own people in check.

In arming and equipping the Mahsuds, Wazirs, Afridis and Mohmands, Pakistan scrapped in a matter of weeks what Britain had striven over a number of decades to prevent. In encouraging them to enter the territory to the east of the Durand Line, Pakistan nullified the very object of deploying three quarters of the pre-Partition Army of India, composed of British and Indian troops, in frontier forts, to contain the tribesmen.

Chapter 4

Lights Go Out in the Valley

MUZAFFARABAD, one of the three major towns of Kashmir, is located astride the Kishenganga River about two miles to the north of the Domel bridge over the Jhelum river. About seven miles to the west of Muzaffarabad is the West Pakistan-Kashmir border. The town was primarily a trade centre, most of the exports and imports of the State passing through the hands of its merchants. The sanctions imposed by Pakistan relating to the import of essential commodities into Kashmir, especially petrol, had begun to have a telling effect on the movement of merchandise, and was the subject of much adverse comment locally. Rumours of the raids against the State Force outposts in Jammu province had reached the townsfolk, but they were not unduly perturbed since one of the better battalions of the State Forces, the 4th Jammu and Kashmir Infantry (4 J&K Infantry), was located in the Muzaffarabad-Domel area.

This unit had seen service in Burma during World War II, and had done reasonably well. It was a mixed battalion, its composition being 50 per cent Dogra (Jammu Hindus) and 50 per cent Poonchie Muslims. It was commanded by a Dogra officer, Lt. Col. Narain Singh, who had spent most of his career with the battalion. As was normal, defensive positions had been constructed on the features that commanded the approaches into the State, and the Domel bridge in particular. But these were only required to be manned in an emergency, and, not apprehending any such type of threat, the battalion lived in its peace-time barracks. As is acceptable under such circumstances, the weapons were stacked in the Company armouries when not required. Although there had been incidents in Jammu, in which the State Force outposts had been assaulted and in some cases annihilated, there had been no such happenings on the borders of Kashmir. Kashmir State Intelligence sources had given no indication whatsoever that either Domel or Muzaffarabad was likely to be subjected to any form of attack.

With reports of continued assasults on the border posts in Jammu Province, Headquarters Jammu and Kashmir State Forces eventually became alarmed. It drew the attention of the Commanding Officer of 4 J&K Infantry to the fact that in certain cases the Poonchie Muslims had proved to be unreliable and had defected. It suggested, in fact advised him, that it might be prudent to return his Muslim troops to Srinagar in order to avoid the possibility of a similar occurrence. Dogras would be sent forward to replace them. Lt. Col. Narain Singh was furious when he received the proposal and rejected it. He stated that he had served with the battalion for many years and had more confidence in his Muslim troops than in the Dogras. To order half his command to return to Srinagar and have it replaced by Dogras would be to inflict a grievous insult on his Poonchie Muslim men. That he was not prepared to do under any circumstances. This laudable attitude of the Commanding Officer resulted in the battalion remaining intact, but Lt. Col. Narain Singh was to pay a very heavy price for his loyalty to his men.

In the early hours of the morning of 22 October, while their Dogra comrades lay sleeping, the Poonchie Muslim troops rose. They drew their weapons from the Company Armouries and trained light automatics and medium machine guns on the barracks occupied by the Dogras, and on their Armouries so that they would be incapable of reaching their weapons. They then moved in and killed their comrades, including Lt. Col. Narain Singh who had placed implicit trust in them. This accomplished, they made contact with the tribal convoy which had arrived and lay halted on the Pakistan side of the border. With the town of Muzaffarabad open to them, the tribals swarmed in. Rape, loot and arson engulfed the town. The tribesmen were only brought under control with the promise of even better booty ahead in the Valley. The tribal convoy, now led by the Poonchie Muslims of 4 J&K Infantry, moved up the road towards the Valley.

One might form the impression from these incidents in Jammu and in Muzaffarabad-Domel area that the Muslims of the State had risen against the Government and wished to join Pakistan. Nothing could be further from the truth. Thousands upon thousands of Muslims in the Government, the State Forces and in the National Conference, the political party led by Sheikh Abdullah, braved death in stemming the invasion. Many Muslim officers and men of the Jammu and Kashmir State Forces were later absorbed into the Indian Army. Their loyalty is beyond question. It was only a certain number who defected. The defection was primarily due to the subversive activities of Major General Akbar Khan and of a few other officers of the Pakistan Army whose domicile was in Jammu or Kashmir. These officers also took a leading part in the conduct of the operations both in Jammu & Kashmir.

Some of the Dogras of 4 J&K Infantry who had managed to escape the slaughter, slipped through the cordon thrown around them by the mutineers and moved back along the road to Srinagar. Reaching a telephone, they informed Headquarters Jammu and Kashmir State

Forces of what had happened in the Muzaffarabad-Domel area. The news was received with alarm and despondency. There were no State Force units of any description located between Domel and Srinagar, and the route to the Valley, and Srinagar the capital lay wide open to the tribals. With a mere 110 miles of good tarmac road to cover, the enemy could be at the gates of Srinagar in a matter of hours. There was not a moment to be lost in meeting the threat.

Brigadier Rajinder Singh, who had taken over as Chief of Staff from Major General H. L. Scott, decided to deal with the situation personally. Collecting some 200 men from the rear details of the State Force units in Badami Bagh Cantonment in Srinagar, he rushed down the road to Domel by motor transport. Realising that the only hope lay in delaying the enemy as much as was possible, he took with him sufficient explosives to carry out demolitions of the numerous bridges on the route. He reached Uri, 62 miles from Srinagar, before the raiders, and, deploying his small force on the features to the west of Uri, began preparing the large steel-girder bridge at the eastern exit of Uri, which spanned a deep seasonal river, for demolition. This completed, the defenders awaited the arrival of the tribal convoy.

It made its appearance soon after mid-day on 23 October, and was halted with long-range fire. The Brigadier was able to thwart the enemy attempts to outflank him, with a series of well-staged withdrawals. But as the pressure increased and further enemy bands were thrown in to encircle him, he decided to pull well back, and gave orders for the bridge to be blown. The Engineers had prepared it efficiently and the raiders were presented with a yawning gap which it was impossible to span without equipment and engineering skill, neither of which was readily available to them. The blowing up of the bridge at Uri was to make a difference more momentous than the gallant Brigadier Rajinder Singh could have anticipated. By immobilising for three to four days the tribal raides who would not let themselves be separated from motor transport, it saved Srinagar from the fate that had overtaken Muzaffarabad. With the only motorable route made impassable, the tribal convoy lay halted for as long as it would take to construct a diversion. With darkness falling, the raiders decided to postpone further action until the next day.

On the morning of 24 October, elements of the raiders engaged the small token force which had taken up a defensive position on the hills to the east of Uri. Unable to dislodge it with a frontal attack, they decided to hold it frontally and to cut off its withdrawal with a wide encircling movement. They crossed the Jhelum River by a footbridge which lay to the north of Uri, and advanced along the north bank in the direction of Mahura. Here lay another bridge across the river, and having crossed it they would have been in a position to occupy the features behind the State Force party. Their movement was, however, spotted. Brigadier Rajinder Singh had no option but to evacuate his defensive position and withdraw. A running battle across the hills now took place until, at Diwan Mandir, Brigadier Rajinder Singh fell, mortally wounded. Realising that any attempt to evacuate him would only hamper his men, he ordered them to leave him behind and to continue the withdrawal. His men placed him under a culvert, hoping that he might escape detection. That was the last that was seen or heard of brigadier Rajinder Singh.

In Srinagar, the electric power supply failed at about mid-day. Those in authority drew the only possible conclusion. The Mahura Power House had fallen to the raiders.

That Brigadier Rajinder Singh's action was gallant in the extreme is unquestionable. It disrupted the planned time-schedule of the enemy and gave the Valley the hope of survival, but there is one point in connection with his action which is inexplicable. Available to him in Badami Bagh Cantonment was a total of 1,850 officers and men of the Jammu and Kashmir State Forces of whom 500 were Poonchie Muslims. In view of what had taken place, he may have lost faith in the latter and decided not to put their loyalty to the test. The remainder were either Sikhs, Dogras or Gorkhas—all trained soldiers who were the Depot parties of the battalions deployed in both Jammu and Kashmir or personnel who had returned from leave and courses of instruction who were awaiting movement orders. This sizeable number of 1,350 officers and men could have been formed into two relatively able battalions. They might not have had the full complement of light automatics and mortars, but they were all equipped with rifles and there was no shortage of ammunition or grenades. These two *ad hoc* units would certainly have offered stiff resistance to the tribals in the country that lends itself to defence. Yet, well aware that half the 4 J&K Infantry had joined hands with the enemy, and knowing that the tribal force was of several thousands, he rushed forward with only 200 men.

It is possible that the petrol supply situation in Srinagar was bad, severely limiting the motorised element that could be rushed to Uri. The Brigadier probably felt that the task of demolishing the bridge could be accomplished with a small force of 200 men. But in taking over personal command of this party, he demoted himself to the role of a Company Commander. It is difficult to understand why he did not place a junior officer in command of the token force, and, as Chief of Staff and the virtual Commander of the State Forces, keep himself free to organise the resources at his disposal and deploy them to man various defensive positions. His disappearance with his small force evidently left his Headquarters rudderless, as no one made any effort to move troops forward or in fact do anything to meet the serious situation. The officers and men sat tight in their barracks and even kept their existence a secret from the Indian Army which commenced arriving on 27 October. Had the raiders succeeded in capturing Srinagar, they would have been butchered in their barracks.

The fall of Muzaffarabad and Domel, the death of his Chief of Staff, and the stoppage of electric power from Mahura at last brought home to Maharajah Hari Singh the grimness of the situation.

He had, some time previously, appealed to a brother Ruler, the Maharajah of Patiala to send him military aid. This request had been complied with. An infantry battalion of the Patiala State Forces moved to Jammu presumably to bolster up the garrison after the fall of Bhimbar, and a Mountain Battery from Patiala arrived in the Kashmir Valley. But, in view of the raiders' strength and the extraordinary deployment of the Jammu and Kashmir State Forces, these reinforcements were a mere token and their presence could not materially alter the situation.

With the possibility of the tribesmen reaching Srinagar any moment, Maharajah Hari Singh was strongly advised to evacuate the capital with his family and to proceed to Jammu. This he did by motor convoy over the Banihal Pass, leaving a Srinagar plunged in darkness on the night of 25 October. His dreams of an independent sovereign State of Jammu and Kashmir had been shattered.

Chapter 5

On Wings of Courage

It is a basic military tenet that, in training during peace, all units of an Infantry Brigade should be "married up" with one another, the armour, artillery, signals, infantry and the Corps units being exercised together until very close liaison between them has been achieved and they get to know one another like members of a large family. When committed to the battlefield, such cohesion ensures team work, smooth cooperation and *esprit de corps*. Commanders must know their units and the men, and have a shrewd knowledge of their strong points and limitations, while the men must know their commanders and have confidence in them. Only then will a unit or a formation operate like a well-oiled machine. The situation prevailing in India at the time when the first troops were despatched to the Kashmir Valley denied to both commanders and the men these essentials. Contrary to normal expectations, however, 161 Infantry Brigade moulded itself, almost overnight, into one of the hardest hitting Brigades of the Indian Army.

This Brigade was one of the formations of the Fifth Indian Division which was located on the Ranchi Plateau in Bihar Province. The Divisional Commander was Major General Russell, known affectionately throughout the Army as 'Russell Pasha' because of his exuberant moustache which likened him to a famous Turkish military commander. Consisting as it did of both Indian and others who were about to become Pakistanis, the main effort of the Division was directed towards dispatching the Pakistani element to its new country. By 15 August 1947, this task had been completed and the Fifth Division, now down to 60 per cent of its authorised strength, was no longer an effective battle formation. The only training that could be carried out was individual training, until such time as its formation and units could be built up to their normal establishment.

The sudden deterioration in the internal situation in the Punjab, and the calm that prevailed in Bihar and the adjoining United Provinces (now known as Uttar Pradesh) caused Army Headquarters to order the Fifth Division to move certain units to Delhi immediately to assist the civil power in and around the capital. All that was required to move was a skeleton Divisional Headquarters, an element of the Divisional Signal Regiment, Brigade Commanders with a small Brigade Staff, a few Infantry Battalions and the Motor Transport Companies. The remainder of the Division and Brigade Headquarters, the Artillery, the Engineers, Signals, Infantry, the Corps units, and the rear parties of the units were to remain behind in Ranchi. It was stressed that the move to Delhi was purely temporary.

The journey from Ranchi to Delhi, about 600 miles, was carried out by road and rail, and on arrival units and sub-units were detailed to various trouble spots in order to instil confidence in the population and to deal with any situation that might arise. As the heavier infantry weapons such as three-inch mortars are not used in internal security duties, they were left behind. Major General Russell was appointed Commander, Delhi and East Punjab Area (DEP Area), and set up his Headquarters in New Delhi. His role was to coordinate the activities of all the units deployed in his area for internal security duties. The Fifth Infantry Division element that had moved from Ranchi now became DEP Area troops. 161 Infantry Brigade found itself deployed in the Gurgaon District area under a newly promoted commander, Brigadier J. C. Katoch, the previous one having been taken away and posted to a Staff appointment.

It was while the units of DEP Area were fully committed and operating in penny packets ranging from a Platoon to a Company that the Maharajah of Jammu and Kashmir's accession to India was received. It was accepted by Lord Mountbatten, the Governor General, and, following a decision taken in a Cabinet meeting, orders were issued to Army Headquarters to move troops immediately into both Jammu and Kashmir.

Under normal circumstances, Lord Mountbatten's order would have presented few difficulties, but at that particular moment the order entailed re-forming nearby units by hastily assembling their scattered sub-units, some of which were operating in out-of-the-way places and were not easily contactable by wireless or telephone, and moving them to New Delhi. The task was closely interlinked with other major problems. In order not to denude inflammable areas of troops, reliefs had to move in and take over before certain withdrawals could be effected. This called for innumerable adjustments to the deployment plan and rapid movement of motor transport from one area to another. Time was of the essence, as the Governor General issued his order on 26 October 1947 and required the first troops to arrive in the Kashmir Valley by the next day.

A few hours after Lord Mountbatten's order had been received, a second one followed, this time from the British Government. It stipulated that no British officer would accompany the troops moving into either Jammu or the Kashmir Valley. This order could have had a devastating effect, as at that time almost every unit of the Indian Army had a high percentage of British officers commanding units and sub-units. Some of these officers had served with their units for a number of years preceding World War II and then throughout the war. Many of them had family connections with the Regiments in which they were serving, in some cases dating back to nearly one hundred years. They knew their men and held their confidence. Yet, in this crisis, as a result of the British Government's ruling, they were to be divorced from the men they knew so well, and the men were to be placed under leaders who would be strangers to them. It cut against the grain of the teaching which is accepted in almost every Army in the World. While it could not have quite paralysed the Indian Army, it could cause a delay which the situation would not brook.

The reason advanced for the issue of the order forbidding British officers to accompany troops into Jammu or the Kashmir Valley was that Britain did not wish her nationals to be pitted against one another in battle. This is understandable, and would have been valid had Pakistan Army troops been the invaders. But that was not the case. Tribesmen, apparently unknown to Pakistan, had invaded the Valley and Pakistan denied for many months that her regular Army was also involved. There were, at the time, British officers serving in units of both the Indian and Pakistan Armies in the NWFP of West Pakistan, units which were located there for the express purpose of keeping in check the remainder of the tribesmen from the same clans that had invaded Kashmir. If the British Officers could perform that role in the NWFP then why not in the Valley? Ironical though it may seem, Indian units were also guarding Pakistan's NWFP and preventing the tribesmen from surging into that newly born Dominion, while their comrades were sacrificing their lives to save Kashmir from the ravages of tribals from the same area. Those Indian units, as mentioned already, only returned to India after Pakistan had reorganised its Army from the various sub-units that it inherited.

The most accessible unit for movement into the Kashmir Valley was the 1st Battalion the Sikh Regiment (1 Sikh), which was deployed in Gurgaon District, not far from New Delhi. It was commanded by a very capable Indian officer, Lt. Col. Ranjit Rai. Orders were issued to Ranjit Rai to withdraw immediately the sub-units of his battalion from the areas in which they were operating and to assemble them in Gurgaon town. He was then to move to Delhi with whatever troops he had managed to concentrate and to arrive by the evening of 26 October. Lt. Col. Ranjit Rai was able to assemble enough sub-units to form the equivalent of three Rifle Companies. Leaving instructions for the remainder of the battalion to follow him in Delhi as soon as they had arrived in Gurgaon town, he sped to Delhi with his Battalion Headquarters and the three Rifle Companies, arriving soon after four o'clock. He reported to DEP Area and was directed by Major General Russell to report to the Director of Military Operations at Army Headquarters.

The initial responsibility for the command and control of the units being deployed in the Valley lay with Army Headquarters, the administration resting with DEP Area. This peculiar set-up was dictated by the conditions that prevailed. The undivided Punjab had been the responsibility of Headquarters Northern Command, but after partition this Headquarters, which was located at Rawalpindi in West Pakistan, ceased to be responsible for East Punjab which had become a part of India, and in fact became Headquarters Pakistan Army. DEP Area had to be established almost overnight, its foundation being the element of Headquarters Fifth Infantry Division which had moved up from Ranchi. This newly formed Headquarters had its hands full in coping with the internal security situation in Delhi and East Punjab, and confined its activities to those areas. When an operation in Kashmir suddenly presented itself, it was necessary for someone to command and control it. It was illogical to expect DEP Area to take on a commitment of which it knew nothing—not that Army Headquarters was any wiser. DEP Area was therefore made responsible for marshalling the units to be despatched to Kashmir and administering them, while Army Headquarters issued orders regarding their induction and controlled the operations.

If the movement of Indian Army units into the Valley was to be effective, with the main raider force barely 62 miles away from Srinagar, speed in transporting them was paramount. The only land route available to India was untarmacked and unbridged, and more than 300 miles in length, of which about two-thirds ran through mountains. There was no alternative to an airlift.

The holding of Srinagar airfield and ensuring its immunity from enemy action was of vital importance. The orders to Lt. Col. Ranjit Rai were therefore short, simple and to the point. He was first given an Intelligence briefing, which merely amounted to being informed that thousands of raiders, well armed, were in the area of Uri and perhaps beyond it. Their target was obviously Srinagar, but when they would reach it was unknown. He was then ordered to report at Safdarjung airport in New Delhi the next morning with whatever troops he had available, for an airlift into the Valley. On arrival at Srinagar airfield, he was to organise its defence and ensure that it was kept free from enemy interference. Further troops would be flown into the Valley as and when they became available.

There were, at the time of the partition of the sub-continent of India, a number of civil airline companies operating the DC3 (Dakota) aircraft. These had been purchased after the termination of World War II, in which they had done magnificent work. Quite a number of these Companies were fully employed in lifting evacuees from one Dominion to the other. The Government of India requisitioned all these aircraft for flights into the Valley. Though the Indian Air Force utilised all aircraft it possessed, and even with the requisitioning of civil aircraft, there was need for many more. Had they been available, the induction of men and stores into Srinagar could have been much faster.

To ask the pilot to land a fully loaded plane on an airstrip that he has never seen before, which offers less than the requisite length of runway, and which is devoid of any type of navigational aids and airfield safety precautions, would normally bring a flat and merited refusal. He would risk it only in an emergency, after first jettisoning a large quantity of his fuel and perhaps a high percentage of his load. In the present instance, however, he had to reach the airstrip after flying over a treacherous range of mountains. With the limited ceiling capability of the Dakota, he must cross at the lowest point, which is 9,300 feet, and which is more often than not shrouded in clouds or mist. Having negotiated this hazard he is required, with a full load, to land on an airstrip which, because another aircraft has landed just before him, has pillars of dust reaching high and seriously affecting visibility. Being one in a relay of aircraft, the pilot's decision to land is dependent entirely on what he can see through the haze of dust, for there are no instructions from the airfield. Nor is there time for him to dawdle, as there are aircraft following him at short intervals, and he is required to hasten back to Delhi to return with a fresh load. Any error of judgment, whether in landing or taking off, would be disastrous as it would make the airstrip unusable and perhaps prejudice the whole operation.

Despite all these dangers and normally unacceptable hazards, the pilots of the civil airline companies cheerfully undertook the flights into the Kashmir Valley with aircraft loaded with troops, stores and ammunition. They judged the loads of their aircraft visually, and they were lavish in their load acceptance. In almost every case, the aircraft were loaded to a point which would have confounded the manufacturers.

The courage and devotion to duty displayed by the civilian pilots and their crew played a decisive part in saving Kashmir from the ravages that threatened it. Nor were these qualities displayed for just one day. Day after day, these gallants flew flight after flight from New Delhi to the Valley, commencing from first light and only ceasing when darkness made yet another flight quite impossible. It speaks volumes for their skill that there was not a single accident. The Dakota aircraft also earned unstinted praise. It flew hour after hour and day after day with little or no maintenance. Its performance will probably never be equalled by any other aircraft.

Army Headquarters Movement Control Units are usually located in major railway stations and at the ports. It is not normal in India, in peacetime, to move troops by aircraft, and Safdarjung airport in New Delhi had no such unit. A Movement Control Unit is essential in any large-scale transport operation such as the one that was to be mounted from Safdarjung, to enable close personal contact with the airport authorities, ensure smooth working and avoid frayed tempers when working under stress. When Lt. Col. Ranjit Rai arrived at Safdarjung airport with the leading element of his battalion, there was no such unit to assist him, but the urgency of the situation overcame the normal difficulties. The airport officials and the air crew rallied magnificently, and the Battalion Headquarters and the three Companies were ferried expeditiously into the Valley. At half past nine on 27 October, the first aircraft landed at Srinagar. With others following at periodic intervals, the initial body of 1 Sikh was in position in the airfield area by mid-day.

Having formulated a plan for the defence of the airfield and allotted roles to his sub-units, Ranjit Rai made contact with Headquarters Jammu and Kashmir State Forces and was provided with some transport by the State Force and the civil administration. He obtained the latest Intelligence reports and learnt that the raiders had not reached Baramula, but as the State Force had no patrols out, it was not possible to treat the information as being wholly reliable. With neither a telephone nor a wireless link with New Delhi, this information was carried back by a returning pilot and passed on to Army Headquarters. It was disturbing not to know where the raiders had reached, but it was consoling at least to know that the airfield was firmly in our possession.

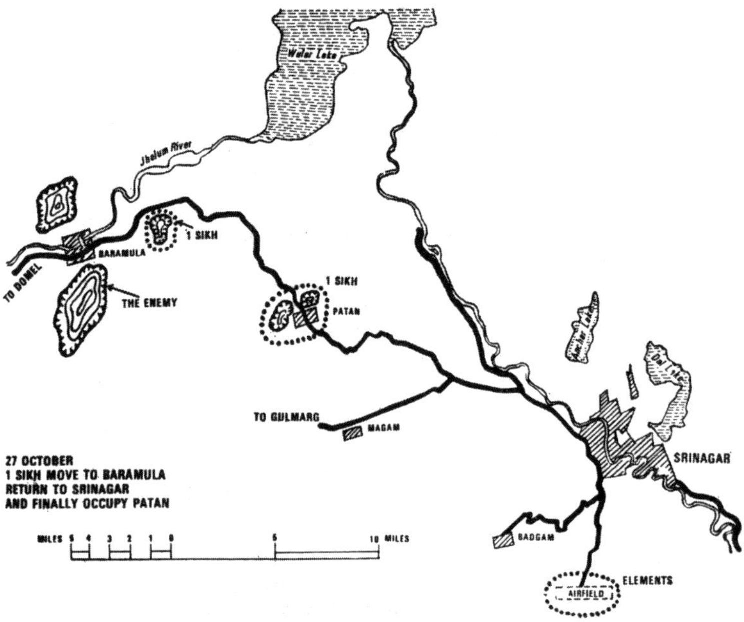

Further sub-units of 1 Sikh continued to arrive in New Delhi from Gurgaon during the day, and were immediately despatched to Safdarjung airport for ferrying into the Valley. By the afternoon of 27 October, 1 Sikh was almost a complete battalion in strength. Planning, meanwhile, had proceeded apace and it was decided to build up the strength in the Valley to an Infantry Brigade. The units to form the Brigade were obtained by relieving those units that could most easily be spared from their internal security duties, and the skeleton Headquarters of 161 Infantry Brigade, which was also located in the Gurgaon area, was ordered to move to the Valley and take over the operational role. The Brigade that had moved from Ranchi was not, therefore, the one that flew into the Valley, but an improvised Brigade made up of units and sub-units collected at random, the principle adopted being the ability to release them from their role and their capability of concentrating without undue loss of time.

With almost his whole battalion now available for operations, Lt. Col. Ranjit Rai decided to hand over the protection of the airfield to a part of his command, and collecting a further assortment of vehicles from the Emergency Government of Kashmir, he embussed 1 Sikh and moved forward to Baramula. He probably considered that if he could reach Baramula before the raiders, and from the intelligence reports in his possession this was a live possibility, he would be able to deploy his battalion on the hills in the vicinity of the town. If he succeeded in achieving this, he would be in an advantageous position to check any further enemy advance, and with further units under orders to proceed to Srinagar, prevent them from debouching into the Valley.

1 Sikh moved from the airfield, through Srinagar and on to Patan, which is 17 miles from Srinagar, and from there to the hills to the east of Baramula, a distance of 34 miles from Srinagar, without incident. Debussing his unit, Ranjit Rai placed it in a defensive position on the hills, and taking a small escort headed for Baramula town which lay about a mile and half away. The enemy was already in Baramula, having got over the problems of the broken bridge at Uri by constructing a diversion down and up the banks of the stream and taking the motor convoy across. When the party reached a point about half way to the

town, the enemy engaged it with a medium machine gun located on a hill to the south of the town and at the entrance to the Valley. Ranjit Rai had to beat a hasty retreat, but his jeep was struck and put out of commission. Abandoning it, he started to make his way back to his battalion across the fields, those who had been wounded also hobbling back. It was while he was following his wounded that he was struck in the face by a burst of automatic fire from a hill on the flank and was killed, as was the platoon commander who was by his side. The well intentioned gamble had failed, perhaps by a few hours.

1 Sikh, now without a Commanding Officer, embussed and returned to Srinagar airfield. Here they were met by the Second in Command of the battalion, Major Sampuran Bachan Singh, who took over command and led the battalion back the 17 miles to Patan. Here the unit debussed and went into a defensive position. Patan, the only hilly terrain between Srinagar and Baramula, lends itself to forming a reasonably strong defensive position. The hills command the road, and if held, deny the use of the road to traffic. Having established itself at Patan, 1 Sikh awaited the expected advance by the raiders and a possible attack. Neither, however, materialised. Perhaps the raiders were surprised at the sudden appearance of 1 Sikh, and being uncertain of the strength that lay behind 1 Sikh, decided that caution was necessary. They left 1 Sikh well alone that night and in the days that followed, merely probing the position. Reluctant to assault the Patan defences, the tribals finally decided to bypass it and to fan out all over the Valley.

The news of Lt. Col. Ranjit Rai's death came as a shock. There were the arguments that normally follow such a tragedy, as to why he had ventured forth to Baramula when his orders had been limited to the protection of the airfield. A commander of troops placed to the position of Ranjit Rai always leaves himself vulnerable to such remarks and questions. It is true that he had left his prime responsibility, the safety of the airfield, in the hands of an extremely weak force, and had sallied forth 34 miles to Baramula. Had his battalion become involved in a dog fight and been pinned to the ground, or perhaps even surrounded by the enemy which was known to be many times its superior in numbers, it would have presented quite a problem to extricate it. On the other hand, had he not moved forward and made contact with the enemy at Baramula, and kept his battalion in the airfield area, the raiders' convoy could have been in the city within two hours through an open and unprotected road, 34 miles in length, that lay between Baramula and Srinagar. With the airfield seven miles away from Srinagar, it is difficult to visualise what 1 Sikh could have done to salvage the situation. With the city in his hands, it is fair to assume that the enemy commander would have taken steps to seal off the Valley, and to do so was a relatively easy matter. A strong party, probably formed mainly from the defectors of the 4 J&K Infantry, would have been rushed in the Banihal Pass to hold it, while another strong party would have moved to the airfield and engaged the troops manning its defences with small arms and mortar fire, ensuring that no further aircraft made a landing.

Lt. Col. Ranjit Rai's action in moving forward to Baramula was bold, but certainly not foolhardy. If, as was said by some at the time, he strayed from the orders given to him, it was extremely fortunate that he did so, although it cost him his life. He deserves full credit for having had the initiative and the courage to do what he did. It was a sound move by a very gallant soldier.

When Jinnah heard, on 27 October, that Indian troops had landed in Srinagar, he ordered General Messervey, the Commander in Chief of the Pakistan Army, to rush troops into Kashmir. Messervey contacted the Supreme Commander, Field Marshal Auchinleck, on the telephone, having informed Jinnah that he must have the approval of the Supreme Commander before issuing such an order. On 28 October, Auchinleck flew to Lahore and informed Jinnah that as Kashmir was now a part of India, if Pakistan troops moved into it every British officer serving in the Pakistan Army would be immediately withdrawn. This would have crippled the Pakistan Army, which could not function without the British officers. Jinnah stormed, but had no option but to rescind his order.

Pakistan's Regular troops, however, did move into Kashmir soon enough, early in 1948. General Sir Douglas Gracey had meanwhile succeeded General Messervey as C in C, Pakistan Army, in which there was a very large percentage of British personnel serving as staff officers and commanding formations and even units, a percentage much higher than in the Indian Army. The threat of withdrawing every British officer proved empty and Jinnah had his way when, on it becoming evident that the 10,000 tribal raiders could not overwhelm Kashmir by mere numbers, regular troops of Pakistan entered Kashmir.

The United Nations Commission for India and Pakistan, established by the United Nations Security Council by its resolution of 9 November 1948, had this to say on Pakistan's belated admission that three regular Pakistan Army Brigades had been fighting in Kashmir: "The statements of the Foreign Minister of Pakistan to the effect that Pakistani troops had entered the territory of the State of Jammu and later his reply to the Commission's questionnaire that all forces fighting on the Azad side were under the overall command and tactical direction of the Pakistan Army, confronted the Commission with an unforeseen and entirely new situation.... The presence of Pakistan troops in J & K, however, constitutes a material change in the situation inasmuch as the Security Council did not contemplate the presence of such troops in that State, nor was it apprised thereafter by the Government of Pakistan." (UNCIP First Report, S/1100).

Chapter 6

Command of 161 Brigade

In the absence of a direct wireless link with the troops in the Valley, it was extremely difficult to form any reliable picture of what had actually happened in the region of Baramula and thereafter. The wounded, who had been evacuated to the General Hospital in Delhi Cantonment, related varying versions of the incident and the situation. I therefore suggested to the DMO, Brigadier Thapar, that I fly into the Valley the next morning, 29 October, in the first outgoing aircraft and return by the last incoming plane. This would enable me to spend about six hours in the Valley and I would be able to obtain an accurate and comprehensive picture. Although Brigadier Thapar was the Director of Military Intelligence, on my assuming the appointment he had decided that as he would be fully occupied on the operational side, Intelligence would be left entirely to me and

I would in fact function as the Director of Military Intelligence. He was, at first, somewhat reluctant to let me leave New Delhi for a whole day in view of the spate of work, but eventually agreed that it would be the best course of action.

Arriving at Safdarjung Airport at six o'clock in the morning of 29 October, I met a Brigadier waiting to emplane and introduced myself. He informed me that he was Brigadier J. C. Katoch, the Commander of 161 Infantry Brigade, and introduced me to his Staff Officers. We flew into the Valley in the same aircraft, and on arrival went into conference with the officers commanding the sub-units at the airfield. 1 Sikh, we learnt, was still at Patan and had not been engaged by the enemy, while the airstrip was being guarded by a Rifle Company of 4 Kumaon. Bits and pieces of other units had, meanwhile, started arriving in the following aircraft, and they were ordered to remain in the airstrip area until further orders.

By the time the conference concluded, the Brigade Signal Section reported that wireless communication with Delhi had been established, and a message was despatched to the DMO giving him a factual account of the 1 Sikh action of the previous day. Returning to operational matters, it was decided that the first essential was to deploy all the arrived and arriving sub-units for the protection of the airstrip. With the aid of a map, all roads and tracks leading to the airstrip were noted, and a plan was formulated to cover them. This completed, a ground reconnaissance was carried out to choose suitable positions and to determine the minimum force required to hold them. By mid-day, the sub-units that had arrived were moving into position and, by four o'clock that afternoon, were reasonably well dug in and ready for action. It was by no means an impregnable defensive layout, the paucity of troops precluding that, but unless attacked in strength it was capable of beating back small bodies of the enemy and ensuring the airstrip immunity from small arms fire.

A quick visit to 1 Sikh at Patan was planned, but had to be dropped because the only available vehicle was a jeep that was firing on two cylinders and its guage indicated that there was little or no petrol. Communication with the battalion was, however, good and a very detailed report of the situation facing the unit was received. 1 Sikh and enemy patrols had been active but there had been no clashes. The enemy had not debouched from Baramula in strength, but had visited nearby villages in small parties, setting alight the houses if any resistance was offered by the villagers.

With what was the most comprehensive picture of the situation available so far, I emplaned on the last aircraft leaving for Delhi and arrived at Safdarjung Airport at eight o'clock. The DMO arrived at the office about half an hour later, and was given a complete briefing and an assessment of the situation. I stressed that from what I had seen and heard during my few hours in the Valley, the situation could be summed up as being extremely dangerous. If we were to bat back the thousands of raiders and save the Valley from destruction, many more troops would have to be flown in and very quickly. It was a time and space problem and both factors favoured the raiders. They had thrown many golden opportunities to the winds, but it was much too much to hope that they would continue in this strain.

This final assessment of the situation seemed to shatter the DMO. He informed me that another senior officer, deputed by the Prime Minister, Pandit Jawaharlal Nehru, had also visited the Valley, flying in on a later aircraft, and had returned about three hours earlier. His assessment of the situation was totally different from mine. He had painted a picture of complete calm, and of the situation being more than well in hand, and had suggested that the number of troops in the Valley were adequate and could easily cope with what was no more than a band of ill-trained hooligans. His report to the Prime Minister had been delivered in the evening, and now, a few hours later, had come an entirely different picture.

I informed Brigadier Thapar that I had not met this officer in the Valley and that he might have arrived and departed while I was on reconnaissance in the airfield area with Brigadier Katoch. His assessment of the military situation was certainly not arrived at as a result of consultations with Brigadier Katoch, because Katoch and I were together the whole time that I was in the Valley. After a great deal of persuasion, Brigadier Thapar agreed to send the latest assessment of the situation to the Prime Minister. A conference was called that night, and after a stormy session, with the Prime Minister in the chair, it was eventually agreed that further units would be called to Delhi and inducted into the Valley.

In our discussion prior to the meeting with the Prime Minister, Brigadier Thapar had argued that though at present only one full strength battalion was in the Valley, it had been agreed that the strength would be built up to an Infantry Brigade and two more battalions would therefore be positioned there. My contention was that three infantry battalions would be inadequate to deal with the task. The area was much too large, the enemy was very much superior in numbers and would employ will-o'-the-wisp tactics, and with numerous routes leading to Srinagar, three battalions would not be capable of preventing them from infiltrating into the city and doing tremendous damage. Quite apart from this, the ultimate aim was to evict the tribesmen from the whole of Kashmir, not only the Valley, and that meant past Domel which was well over one hundred miles away. The pursuit to Domel and the holding of the territory recaptured would require one Infantry Division. I suggested that we make a bid for a Division right away. Although Brigadier Thapar agreed that the arguments advanced were sound, he said it would be quite useless putting it up, as Government would never give its assent, not with the Internal Security situation in the country being what it was and requiring even more troops to bring it under control.

The Prime Minister's anger during the conference was justifiable. To receive two diverse reports on the situation in the Kashmir Valley over a matter of hours was more than he could tolerate. The establishment of a Boundary Force, composed of units of the Indian and Pakistan Armies, had certainly assisted in controlling the situation in the divided Punjab, and law and order was slowly but surely being restored in the trouble spots. Further troops if required for Kashmir would have to be found by denuding some of these areas, and the chance of fresh outbreaks of hooliganism could not be ruled out. There was, however, no other immediate solution, and the risk of sending some more troops was accepted.

Arrived in Delhi, and arriving from Pakistan, were Rifle Companies of Sikhs and Dogras from the Regiments that had been allotted to Pakistan. These Rifle Companies were held in Delhi and a few were, in due course, despatched to the Valley and attached to the battalions there. In addition, some Sikh Artilery personnel, about 160 in number, who had served in a mountain Artillery Regiment that had been allotted to Pakistan, and were to form part of a Medium Artillery Regiment in India, were also held up in Delhi and were despatched to join 1 Sikh as a Rifle Company.

On 30 and 31 October, the airlift into the Valley went on apace. Conditions were becoming more and more difficult with each landing at Srinagar airstrip, which showed definite signs of crumbling under the abnormal traffic. Thick walls of dust now filled the air with each take-off and landing, and without sufficient quantities of water or the means of spraying the strip, it was impossible to arrest the deterioration. All one could hope and pray for was that it would not reach a stage where further landings of aircraft would be either dangerous or impossible.

In the evening of 31 October came further bad news. Brigadier Katoch, while proceeding to visit 1 Sikh at Patan in a jeep, was hit in the leg by a bullet. Fortunately, it had been fired at long range and did very little damage. It was assumed that he would be able to carry on, but at mid-day on 1 November, a signal was received stating that he was suffering from shock and was being evacuated. Once again, the troops in the Valley were being left without the appointed commander.

At five o'clock that evening, the Military Secretary, Brigadier Rudra, accompanied by Brigadier Thapar, entered my office. Assuming that they had come in for a briefing, I gave them the latest situation report and awaited any questions that they may have wished to ask. After a silence that must have lasted at least one minute, Brigadier Rudra asked me to go and see the C in C immediately. When I inquired what it was all about, I was informed that the Chief would tell me. As I walked down the corridor to the Chief's room, I wondered what I had done. I could only guess that it had something to do with the Press briefing I had given that morning, in which I had perhaps divulged more than I should have.

General Lockhart received me almost immediately, and his opening remark was, "Well, I suppose you know why I have sent for you?" I informed him that I had no idea at all. "I have selected you," he replied, "to go to Kashmir to command 161 Infantry Brigade. I want you to leave first thing tomorrow. You will be given the temporary rank of Brigadier, but it will only be until Katoch returns, which will be in about ten days. You will then revert to your rank as Colonel and return to your present appointment. Go and see General Russell right away, and he will tell you the latest regarding the troops he has earmarked for Kashmir."

I went from the Chief's room to the DMO's and informed him of what I had been told, and asked to whom I was to hand over Military Intelligence. He informed me that Col. Chand Narain Das would be taking over and was already on his way to my office. The handing over to Chand Narain Das took only a few minutes as my Staff knew as much about everything as I did. I borrowed a couple of stars from one of my Staff Officers, rearranged by badges of rank to conform to those worn by a Brigadier, and set off to meet General Russell.

General Russell was having tea in his drawing room when I reported to him. He congratulated me on my promotion, and then glancing at my shoulder said that he was very glad to see that I had put on the badges of rank as it was essential that on my arrival everyone should be well aware of who the Commander was. He informed me that a new formation, to be designated Jammu and Kashmir Force, or Jak Force for short, was being raised and Major General Kulwant Singh had been named as the Commander. 161 Infantry Brigade would, eventually, come under the command of Jak Force. Then he told me what units would move into the Valley. When I asked him for advice as to how I should go about my task, he thought for a few moments and then replied : "You know much more about what is happening than I do, and I am not allowed to enter the Valley. You will have to find your way about when you get there. The only advice that I can give you is that if you get a chance of hitting them, hit hard with all you have got, and don't let up."

Vague though General Russell's words may sound, it was in fact advice of solid worth. A practical commander and a veteran of many campaigns, he made no vain or rash statements. There was no attempt to hedge the issue, a failing of many less brilliant soldiers, with the cliché "when you get there, send me your appreciation of the situation and your plan," thereby giving the impression that he would vet them and advise one accordingly. With his wide experience of warfare, he knew that it was not possible to fight a tactical battle in Kashmir off a map pinned on boards in Delhi, and he made no attempt to do so. What he did do, in a short chat as we had a cup of tea, was to raise my morale and confidence to the ceiling.

As I was leaving General Russell's house, I received a message to the effect that Brigadier Thapar would be awaiting me at the southern entrance to South Block of the Secretariat. When I arrived he informed me that Mahatma Gandhi wished to see me and be given an Intelligence briefing. We drove to his residence and I told him everything that was known to us. He listened most intently and when I finished and asked whether he had any questions he would like answered, he replied "No, no questions." After a few seconds of silence, he continued: "Wars are a curse to humanity. They are so utterly senseless. They bring nothing but suffering and destruction." As a soldier, and one about to be engaged in battle in a matter of hours, I was at a loss to know what to say, and eventually asked him: "What do I do in Kashmir?" Mahatma Gandhi smiled and said, "You're going in to protect innocent people, and to save them from suffering and their property from destruction. To achieve that you must naturally make full use of every means at your disposal." It was the last time that I was to see him alive.

On the morning of 2 November when I arrived at Safdarjung Airport at six o'clock, I found the place buzzing with rumours. Some individuals asserted that the raiders had entered Srinagar during the early hours of the morning. Others said the airstrip was in enemy's hands, and even if it was not in their physical possession, enemy mortars and light automatics were raking the area making it impossible for aircraft to land. These rumours had apparently been set afloat by enemy agents in order to arrest the airlift into the Valley but it was not possible to trace the source of the rumours. The statements however had no visible effect on the officers and men loading aircraft and awaiting emplaning orders. Nor did they appear to affect the civil airline crews who went about their work calmly and showed no concern. They had received their orders to fly into the Valley, and fly they would.

I phoned Military Intelligence Directorate and asked for the latest information from 161 Brigade. I was informed that nothing further had been received since the report that had been sent to me at 8 o'clock the previous night.

The aircraft in which I was travelling was the first to taxi out to the runway, and in course of time the Banihal Pass lay below us. As we crossed it, the co-pilot came into the cabin and asked me to come to the cockpit. On reaching it, the Captain of the aircraft beckoned me to come forward. "That's the airstrip down there," he said, pointing in its direction. "Some people in Delhi were saying that it is in enemy hands and that the enemy is firing at it. What's the answer? Shall I land?" "I've got to get down," I replied. "That's good enough for me," he said. "I'll land."

The aircraft touched down at five minutes past nine. The airstrip was neither in enemy hands nor under enemy fire. I deplaned and walked to the Control Tower, and on inquiry was led to Headquarters 161 Infantry Brigade. It was an apology for a Brigade Headquarters. It was one small room, located in the Control Tower Building, and around a small table were seated the Brigade Major, the Staff Captain and Brigade Intelligence Officer, each trying to do his work without disturbing the others. I announced that I was the new Commander of the Brigade, and would be such until Brigadier Katoch returned. I then asked for the latest situation, and Major Dilbagh Singh, the Brigade Major, had barely started briefing me when the next aircraft from Delhi flew in. A thick cloud of red dust swept through the room making visibility impossible, while outside the room people started shouting to one another to do this or to do that, and in order to make themselves heard above the noise of the aircraft engines they did not

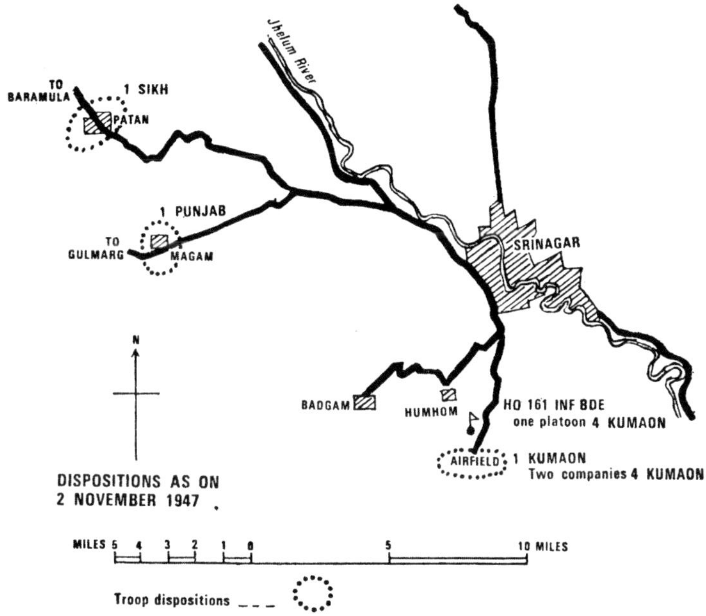

spare their lungs. Further landings made matters even worse, until it was impossible to see, hear or think. To attempt to plan under such conditions was out of the question. Taking up the situation map and accompanied by the Brigade Staff, I moved to a relatively quiet corner of the airstrip.

I gave first attention to the deployment of the units and sub-units that had arrived in the Valley, the infantry in particular. 1 Sikh was still at Patan, and had been reinforced by attaching to it two independent Rifle Companies. One was a Sikh Company from a battalion of the 12th Frontier Force Regiment, that Regiment having been allotted to Pakistan, and the other was an ad hoc Rifle Company formed from the Sikh personnel of the Mountain Artillery who had arrived in Delhi from Pakistan. It was, therefore, a very strong battalion, nearly 1,200 in strength.

The 1st Battalion The Kumaon Rifles (1 Kumaon) was a Parachute Battalion, 650 in strength and commanded by Lt. Col. Pritam Singh.

This unit and two Rifle Companies of 4 Kumaon were manning the airfield defences. An adjustment was made here. 1 Kumaon was made responsible for all the airfield defences, and the two Rifle Companies of 4 Kumaon were brought inside the airfield perimeter and held as the Brigade reserve.

The 1st Battalion The Punjab Regiment (1 Punjab), commanded by Lt. Col. G. I. S. Kullar, however, received much more attention. It was under-strength, totalling 450 all ranks, the result of its Pakistani element having left for that Dominion. Being a parachute unit, and with no surplus para-trained personnel available, it had not been built up to its normal strength. This unit was deployed astride the road at Magam, which is about 12 miles from Srinagar, on the road to Gulmarg. I asked the Brigade Major whether there were any particular reasons for locating the unit at Magam, and was informed that its role was to deny to the raiders' convoy the use of the road, to protect the left flank of 1 Sikh at Patan, and to prevent the enemy infiltrating to Srinagar from the west. I told him that in my opinion it was most unlikely that the enemy convoy composed of about 200 large passenger buses and load carriers would use the road via Magam. In order to reach it from Baramula, the convoy would have to move across country in many places since, although there was a road marked as 'motorable in the dry season', it was not designed for the movement of a large number of heavy vehicles. The denial of the road was therefore, I considered, a sheer waste of effort. Regarding the protection of the left flank of 1 Sikh, there was a gap of nearly 5 miles between 1 Punjab and 1 Sikh, and the protection angle could therefore be discounted. Finally, the presence of 1 Punjab at Magam would not arrest the enemy infiltration tactics. They could move to Srinagar by by-passing 1 Sikh from the north, pass through the 5 mile gap between the two battalions and even by-pass 1 Punjab's southern flank. The movement might be spotted by day, but not by night. I therefore informed the Brigade Major that while I would not disturb the deployment at that moment, I would find a more useful role for 1 Punjab within the next 48 hours. I asked him to give the battalion an indication that it might have to move at short notice.

What had to be disturbed immediately, however, was 3 Light Field Ambulance. This unit of the First Armoured Division had been sent to the Valley to provide medical cover. On arrival, the Commanding Officer had asked where he should locate his unit, and had been told to choose any nice spot. He had selected an untenanted house on a hill to the north-west of the airfield, but it was about 3,000 yards distant from the perimeter of the airfield defences. Here his unit lay completely unprotected and liable to be scuppered during the hours of darkness. Although the Medical Officers protested and advanced the valid argument that the airfield was much too full of dust, the unit was brought inside the perimeter defence.

The airfield itself required quite a bit of clearing up. As aircraft landed, the troops unloaded them and stacked the stores on the sides of the runway. There were many such stacks, and in the absence of labour to move them, they had lain there ever since the first aircraft landed, growing in size every day. The small Ordnance and Service Corps detachments that had arrived were instructed to collect them, with the assistance of troop labour, and to take them on charge. This required careful coordination, as some troops were inclined to take a short cut across the runway, unaware of the arrival of incoming aircraft. By last light, however, the stores and equipment were stacked and put in the custody of a Corps detachment.

While the airfield now looked neater, the road leading from the airfield to Srinagar resembled a graveyard for vehicles. Many people who had come to the Valley in their private cars for a holiday found themselves stranded in Srinagar. The route back via Domel was blocked by the raiders and there was an acute shortage of petrol. It started with requests from a few for transportation back to Delhi in the returning aircraft. This was agreed to and they were told to present themselves at the airfield at a specified time. Contrary to what was agreed to, they arrived, not as small families with a little luggage but with their entire household staff and enough baggage to fill half a Dakota. This was due to the fact that it was customary to come to the Valley for periods ranging up to six months and setting up house at Gulmarg or other camping site. It was understandable that the owners wished to take back with them all their household goods. Their attitude towards their cars, however, was extraordinary.

They arrived in motor vehicles of all shapes and sizes, mainly of 1936–39 vintage and piled up with enough luggage to make the springs reach breaking-point. Because of the lack of personnel to porter for them, they were permitted to drive the vehicles to the aircraft. Having heaped his luggage in the aircraft, the vehicle owner would inform a Staff Officer that he was handing over his vehicle to the Army and request a receipt for it. When it was explained to him that the Army could make no use of the vehicle and he was asked to have it removed immediately from the airfield, he would throw the ignition key on the front seat and step into the aircraft. Troops had to be utilised to clear the airfield of the abandoned vehicles and to park them in a site that did not interfere with the field of fire of the defence positions. Orders were issued that no further vehicles would be permitted to enter the airfield. The pattern had, unfortunately, been set and further batches of returning vacationers, while not abandoning their vehicles on the airfield, left them on the road leading to the entrance. Since this affected the movement of military transport, the cars were removed to a site earmarked for them. Over a period of a week, they totalled nearly one hundred.

The news that seats were being provided on aircraft returning to Delhi spread like a forest fire, and Headquarters 161 Infantry Brigade found itself overwhelmed by hundreds of individuals, of all types and descriptions, pleading to be allotted seats in the aircraft. Two officers from an already understaffed Brigade Headquarters had to be struck off their normal duties to deal with the problem. As any delay of the aircraft returning to Delhi would have resulted in their inability to make the necessary number of flights to the Valley each day to bring in desperately needed troops and stores, the evacuation by air was limited to the afternoon flights, when it was certain that the aircraft could not make another trip from Delhi to the Valley.

It must have been very frustrating for those awaiting evacuation to watch empty aircraft taking off without them, but nothing could be allowed to prejudice the operational situation. By and large, the greater majority of those awaiting instructions to emplane were patient, but a few individuals, asserting that they were Government of India officials and that their presence in Delhi was necessary without delay, created unpleasant situations. They not only demanded immediate evacuation for themselves, but also for their families and other individuals whom they claimed were office personnel. One individual, in particular, was extremely truculent and went so far as to say that he would stand in front of an aircraft and see what we would do about it. A quiet warning that if he made any such move he would be treated as an enemy agent and be dealt with accordingly, brought him to his senses, and he returned to take his place in the queue that had formed outside the airfield gate.

To add to the difficulties, the Government of India readily agreed to a request from Britain that Royal Air Force aircraft be permitted to evacuate British families who had come from Pakistan to holiday in the Valley. This imposed an extra strain on the airstrip which was fast breaking up, and affected to some extent the landing and taking off of our own aircraft. The task was, however, completed over three days, with only one unpleasant and unnecessary incident. In order to maintain contact with Rawalpindi, the RAF established a ground wireless station on the airfield. In charge of this station was an RAF Sergeant who kept up a constant conversation with his station at Rawalpindi, and in doing so caused serious interference to 161 Infantry Brigade's communications. He was asked to change his frequency or limit his communications, both of which he refused to do. There was no option but to give him a firm order to close down his set, which he did. The situation was explained to the Captain of the next RAF aircraft to land, and he rectified matters.

The constant commotion in the airfield area made it impossible for Headquarters 161 Infantry Brigade to conduct operations from its small room in the Control Tower Building. There were far too many demands from civilians to interview the Brigade Commander if the decision made by a Staff Officer did not meet with approval. Headquarters 161 Infantry Brigade was in fact rapidly deteriorating from an Operational Headquarters into an Information-cum-Travel

Bureau. I summoned Major Kak of the Jammu and Kashmir State Forces, who had been assigned to me as Liaison Officer, and asked him whether he knew of any place nearby to which I could move the Headquarters. He said there was a small bungalow, about one and a half miles from the airfield on the road to Srinagar, which belonged to the Forest Department and was unoccupied. He was certain that there would be no objection to my using it. Although it meant moving the Headquarters away from the protection that it was being afforded by remaining within the perimeter of the airfield defence, and creating a situation that had enforced my bringing back the Field Ambulance from its original location, I gave orders for the Headquarters to prepare to move. The skeleton Headquarters and its small Signal detachment did not take long to get ready. With one platoon of 4 Kumaon as the Headquarters Defence Platoon, we arrived at the Forest Bungalow and by four o'clock that evening 2 November, were well established and operating.

At my initial meeting with Major Kak, which was soon after my arrival, I had inquired of him whether there were any State Force units deployed in the Valley, and how many men, by Arms and Services, with particular reference to infantry, were in Srinagar. As he was an officer of the State Force Veterinary Corps, he was unable to give me a ready answer, and suggested that he go to Srinagar and obtain the details. To this I readily agreed, and climbing into a jeep he drove to the city. Returning after about an hour, he informed me that the information he had received was that there were no State Force units deployed in the Valley, and the small number of men in Badami Bagh barracks were either hospital or convalescent cases. He had been unable to obtain the actual figures, but had been informed that they were unfit for any type of service. All fit personnel had been despatched to rejoin their units in Jammu and elsewhere. There were, however, about one hundred troopers of the Maharajah's Bodyguard, but as this unit was utilised purely for ceremonial purposes, its fighting value was negligible. Bitterly disappointed that there were no State Force troops available to assist in manning the extremely lightly held defensive positions, I told Major Kak that something was better than nothing, and instructed him to order the Maharajah's Bodyguard to be ready to move at short notice should I require them.

No sooner had Headquarters 161 Infantry Brigade settled down in its new location in the Forest Bungalow than I asked the Brigade Major to hand me the latest patrol reports together with the patrol programme for the night and at dawn the next morning. The patrol reports from 1 Sikh and 1 Punjab showed no contact with the raiders, who appeared to be avoiding these two battalions, but the information collected from the villagers had clearly indicated that they were fanning out all over the Valley. The patrols that both units intended sending out during the night and next dawn were then studied on the map and found suitable. There were, however, neither reports nor petrol programmes from any of the units deployed in the airfield area, and it transpired that there had been no patrol activity by the troops located in this area at any time. This had come about because the sub-units which had manned the airfield defences had been located there temporarily, and moved out to join their parent units. Therefore the troops available on the airfield, normally the last to arrive during the day from Delhi, had been utilised to man the defence and were only able to settle into their defensive positions before darkness set in. The Rifle Companies of 4 Kumaon, which had remained in the airfield area, had also been fully employed in multifarious duties on the airfield. This was much too dangerous a state of affairs to be allowed to continue, as it was inviting the enemy to take the defences by surprise. With 1 Kumaon now made responsible for the airfield, the Brigade Major was ordered to contact the Commanding Officer of the unit immediately and ask him to produce for me a patrol programme within an hour.

Major Kak was then instructed to order the Maharajah's Bodyguard to report at the Forest Bungalow as quickly as was possible and not later than in one hour. It arrived just before five o'clock, and with the light failing, it was only possible to give it a very limited task. It was ordered to move at the trot in a westerly direction from the airfield for a period of 45 minutes and then to retrace its steps. As its role was purely reconnaissance, the commander was instructed that should any enemy forces be encountered, he was not to get involved in a battle but was to fall back on the airstrip immediately. Pointing to a small hillock about 800 yards off the main road, I informed the Bodyguard Commander that I would meet him there on his return, this vantage point giving me an opportunity of watching the Squadron operating. As the Bodyguard moved off, I set out for the hillock with my Intelligence Officer and a small escort.

On nearing the feature, I was astonished to find a Battery of Mountain Artillery deployed for action. It was in a fold of the ground which made it invisible from the main road. The gun pits had been dug and the gun crews were relaxing beside their guns. As I stood watching them, with an equally surprised Intelligence Officer, the Battery Commander came forward to meet me. As a result of our conversation, I learnt that it was the Patiala Mountain Battery which had been sent to the Valley in answer to the request made by the Maharajah of Jammu and Kashmir to the Maharajah of Patiala, and had been in Kashmir about ten days. When 1 Sikh had landed in the Valley, the Battery had been given orders by Headquarters Jammu and Kashmir State Forces to move out of Badami Bagh barracks and to deploy itself near the airfield. It was being administered from Badami Bagh, but had received no further orders. This was a most welcome bonus and I immediately informed the Battery Commander that from that moment his Battery would form part of and be under command of Headquarters 161 Infantry Brigade, and would act on orders received only from my Headquarters. Stuck outside the defences and with no infantry protection, the Battery was in a very vulnerable position, but with darkness fast approaching, it was not possible to effect a change in location. The Battery was, therefore, ordered to remain in situ for the night and to be ready to move to a fresh location by eight o'clock the next morning.

Then came a shock and the bonus, acquiring wings, flew away. I asked the Battery Commander what targets had been registered and whether it had been done through silent registration or actual ranging. He informed me that he had not been given any targets, and even if he had been given any, he would not have been able to engage them as his guns were without dial sights. That the guns were without this essential part of their equipment was known before the Battery had left Patiala, but he had been informed that on arrival in the Valley the Jammu and Kashmir State Forces would supply them. On arrival, he had asked for the dial sights but had been told that none were available; nor had any effort been made to get them. It was not difficult to see that the gunners were completely frustrated. Their artillery pieces were in fact hindrances instead of being assets.

While I stood talking to the unfortunate gunners, the Bodyguard returned from its reconnaissance and reported no sign of any enemy. It was ordered to return to Srinagar and to be prepared for another mission early the next morning, the orders for which would reach it that evening. As the troopers trotted away, I ordered the Battery Commander to cock up the barrel of one of his guns and to fire two rounds of smoke and one round of high explosive into the blue, in order to give any enemy in the area the impression that a target was being registered. We had guns that could not hit any given target, but it was worth announcing to the raiders that we did have guns. If nothing else it might impose caution and even act as a deterrent. On arrival back at my Headquarters, a signal was despatched to Delhi asking for dial sights to be flown in as quickly as was possible.

A Brigade patrol programme for the next day and following night was then drawn up. Patrolling had so far been uncoordinated and it was essential that it be brought on a sound basis. Those that affected 1 Sikh and 1 Punjab, both these units being out on their own, were first dealt with and liaison patrols between the two units established. Then the Maharajah's Bodyguard was given the role of establishing standing patrols in the area of Gandarbal to watch the approaches to Srinagar from the north. This Squadron was to move out at first light and to remain in position until last light. The territory due west of the airfield and in-between it and 1 Punjab at Magam, had, however, been totally neglected except for the rather hurried patrol undertaken by the Bodyguard a few hours earlier. This required immediate remedying as it was an extremely sensitive area so far as the security of the airfield was concerned, and although there had been no indication that the enemy was operating in that area, it was more than likely that he might, if he learnt that it was being neglected.

I therefore decided that a patrol, planned and controlled by Brigade Headquarters, must search the area the next morning. Earmarked to carry out this role was the newly formed Brigade reserve of two Rifle Companies of 4 Kumaon. Orders were issued for the senior Company Commander of the two 4 Kumaon Companies and the Company Commander of the 1 Kumaon Company to report to me at Brigade Headquarters at eight o'clock on the morning of 3 November, the three Rifle Companies to follow and be concentrated in the Brigade Headquarters area by a quarter past eight.

The plan for the patrol operation was for the two Companies of 4 Kumaon, the platoon taken as the Brigade Headquarters Defence Platoon rejoining its Company on arrival, to move to the hills overlooking the village of Badgam which lay three miles to the west, and to establish a firm base. When this had been effected, the Rifle Company of 1 Kumaon was to pass through the firm base and, moving cross country, make contact with 1 Punjab at Magam. As the distance to be traversed by the 1 Kumaon Company was about 8 miles, it was given four bounds, each of approximately 2 miles, on which it was to halt prior to proceeding to the next one. On reaching the second bound, which was the half-way mark, the Company's firm base would change from the 4 Kumaon held position at Badgam to the 1 Punjab position at Magam. Until it reached the second bound, one of the 4 Kumaon Companies was earmarked to rush to its assistance should it encounter any difficulties. On moving forward from the second bound, the role of reinforcing it was made the responsibility of 1 Punjab, the two 4 Kumaon Companies to be withdrawn from Badgam only on orders from Brigade Headquarters. With command and control of the 1 Kumaon Company changing half way through its operation, very close coordination supported with sound communications had to be ensured between Brigade Headquarters, 1 Punjab, 4 Kumaon and the 1 Kumaon Company.

While these orders were being prepared for despatch, I walked out of the Forest Bungalow and looked towards the west. The sky was lit up by a red glow of burning huts and houses, the flames licking their way up to the skies. It was obvious that the raiders had moved out of

Baramula in large numbers and were announcing their entry into the Valley by setting fire to village after village. Then, suddenly, flames shot high up from what could only be a house or a hut on a prominent feature in Gulmarg. This was senseless destruction, as Gulmarg, a summer holiday resort, was at that time completely unoccupied. The firing of the house on the highest feature could only be interpreted as a grim warning to the people of Srinagar as to what awaited them. Except for the flames, and a flicker of lights from kerosene lamps and candles, the Valley, deprived of its electricity, remained in darkness.

With the patrol programme checked and ready for despatch, I decided to go to Srinagar to make contact with Sheikh Abdullah and Bakshi Ghulam Mohammed, the Leader and Deputy Leader of the National Conference who were now controlling the Emergency Government in Jammu and Kashmir. Events throughout the day had precluded my doing so earlier, but now that matters had been more or less tidied up, it was an opportune moment. Taking Major Kak with me, I set out in a jeep. We had barely proceeded two miles towards Srinagar when we were faced by a long stream of men, women, children, hand-carts and pack ponies. It was virtually impossible to make headway. Inquiries revealed that they were proceeding to the airstrip in order to be first in the queue for the airlift to Delhi the next day. As it was impossible to use the road, the jeep was left with the driver to make his way back to Headquarters as best he could, and Major Kak and I went back on foot.

The movement of civilians towards the airfield after dark had almost resulted in an unfortunate incident the previous night, and on learning of it I had conveyed to the authorities concerned, through Major Kak, a very special request that after four o'clock in the evening, all civilian movement from Srinagar towards the airfield must be stopped. I had been assured that my request would be given immediate attention and strict measures would be taken to comply with it. In my letter I had explained very carefully and clearly that it was quite impossible for the troops to distinguish friend from foe in the dark, and that the troops had been told that any movement outside their perimeter, after darkness had set in, would be automatically treated as being hostile. The advance of the civil population towards the defences, after dark, would therefore draw fire. I had also stressed that it presented a very live danger to the troops, as parties of the enemy might intermingle with the civilians in the dark and attempt a surprise attack.

Rapid orders were now sent to the airfield to warn the troops to hold their fire and a section of the 4 Kumaon platoon with Brigade Headquarters was rushed down the road to halt all persons and to make them spend the night where they were. To have attempted to make them return to Srinagar would probably have resulted in even greater chaos. The halting of the civilian column was successfully achieved, and the danger of moving forward to the airfield in the dark carefully explained to the entire column. Only then was the order to the troops to hold their fire rescinded, and we settled down to face the night, which passed quietly.

Having been inducted into the Valley by air, the units had been deprived of their own motor transport. The Emergency Government did its best to assist by placing local passenger buses and load carriers at the disposal of the Brigade, but these were limited in number and their running had to be strictly controlled as the petrol stock in the Valley was at a very low mark. The State Forces also handed over a few jeeps and 15 cwt trucks but stated that the petrol stock was almost finished. Apart from the petrol required for the motor vehicles, there was the problem of refuelling the few Harvard aircraft which the Indian Air Force had stationed on the Srinagar airstrip and which, armed with machine guns, were being used for reconnaissance duties. An unorthodox method had to be adopted for refuelling them. As each civil airlines Dakota arrived in the Valley, with troops or stores, it would be met by a jeep with a barrel in the trailer. The Captain of the Dakota would be asked if he could spare any petrol, and not a single Captain refused, a receipt being handed over to the Captain for the approximate amount of petrol decanted into the barrel.

The petrol thus obtained kept the Harvards airborne, and saved the diversion of aircraft, already taxed to the limit in ferrying men and supplies, for fuel-carrying duty. Later some Spitfires were also positioned in Srinagar and were refuelled in the same manner. When, in due course, the airline companies submitted their bills for the payment of the fuel supplied to the Air Force, there was an uproar from the finance authorities of the Government of India at petrol having been acquired in this unorthodox manner. They demanded explanations as to why it was not carefully measured on receipt and recorded on the correct forms. That the method employed was unorthodox is undeniable, but the conditions prevailing at the time were also extraordinary. Had the petrol been lifted into the Valley in aircraft, which was the only method open at the time, air freight would have meant quite a sizeable bill. What is more important, had the civil airline Captains refused to supply the petrol, the Harvards and Spitfires would have been grounded, and the battle of Badgam, which was just around the corner, might have taken an entirely different turn with disastrous consequences for the Valley.

Chapter 7

Anxious Vigil at the Airfield

At eight o'clock on the morning of 3 November, Major Somnath Sharma of 4 Kumaon and Captain Ronnie Wood of 1 Kumaon reported to me at my Headquarters. We went over the patrol plan on the map and discussed the action to be taken by the 1 Kumaon Company if it encountered the enemy, and the possible action by the 4 Kumaon Company if it had to rush to its assistance. Meanwhile, the three Rifle Companies had arrived from the airfield, and Sharma and Wood, having briefed their men, reported that they were ready to move. Major Somnath Sharma was a seasoned soldier who had seen much of the bitter fighting in the Arakan during World War II. His right arm was heavily plastered, the result of a fracture sustained in a fall on the hockey ground. Although advised to remain behind until the fracture had set and the plaster was removed, he had insisted on accompanying his Company into the Valley. He had argued that he knew his men better than anyone else, and if they were going into action, they were not going in without him. Captain Wood came from far-off Assam, and was also a very experienced Company Commander.

The two Companies of 4 Kumaon moved towards Badgam, followed after a short interval by the Company of 1 Kumaon. Soon after half past nine, Major Sharma reported on the wireless that his command was in position on the hills in the vicinity of Badgam and had established a firm base. Captain Wood was then ordered to pass through the firm base and to head for Magam and make contact with 1 Punjab.

The Rifle Company of 1 Kumaon had an uneventful patrol to Magam, and having made contact with 1 Punjab, returned to the airfield just before one o'clock. Captain Wood reported that there were no signs of the enemy and that the villages that had been skirted en route were undamaged. With the patrol successfully accomplished, Major Sharma was ordered to commence thinning out from the Badgam position from half past one. At two o'clock, Major Sharma reported that one Company had moved back towards the airfield, and I told him that I would like the second Company to stay on the position for another hour and to commence withdrawing from three o'clock. He said that everything was very quiet and that the villagers of Badgam were going about their business in the normal way. He then confirmed that he would start thinning out, commencing at three o'clock. There was no indication whatsoever of what was going to happen within the next thirty minutes.

At twenty-five minutes to three, Major Sharma came up on the wireless and informed me that his Company was being shot at by people located in the houses in Badgam. He said that the firing had been ineffective, but it was most unpleasant and he had not answered it for fear of killing or injuring women and children.

While we were discussing this awkward situation and how to cope with it, Major Sharma suddenly said that a large force of the enemy had appeared from a depression to the west of his position and was engaging his Company with mortar and automatic small arms fire.

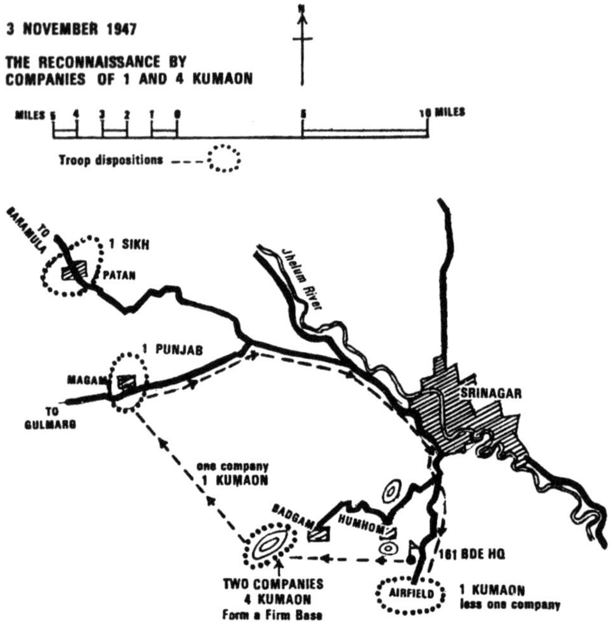

With the road blocked against them at Patan by 1 Sikh, a group of the raiders had moved across the country in an obvious bid to put the Srinagar airfield out of action. Major Sharma appeared to be worried about the firing from the houses in Badgam which had intensified, but it was obvious that this was to distract his attention from the main attack which was developing from the west. He then reported that the enemy from the west had advanced, that his Company was engaging him with everything that it had, but as he was heavily outnumbered the enemy was gaining ground. No sooner had he made this report than I heard a loud explosion, and the wireless set went off the air.

A Liasion Officer (LO) with the Indian Air Force was with me at the time, and he was ordered to rush back to the airstrip and to inform the Air Force of what had happened and ask for aircraft to strafe the raiders in the Badgam area. The LO said that he did not have a 1 inch to 1 mile map, nor did the Air Force. Taking up a razor blade, I immediately cut out from the one and only map with Brigade

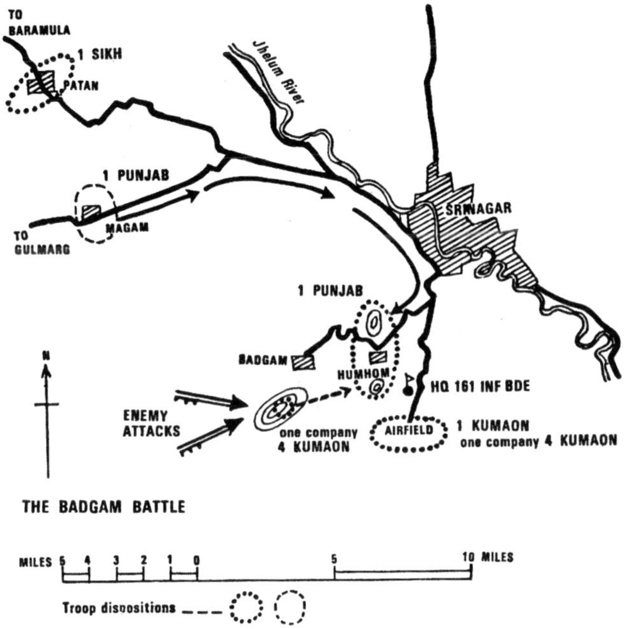

THE BADGAM BATTLE

Headquarters the squares that included Badgam, and handing it to him asked that it be returned to me the moment the Air Force had finished with it, as I would require it for the land battle. In a few minutes, fighter aircraft were over Badgam and strafing the area. With only one map between two aircraft, the form used was for the leading aircraft to strike the target and the second one to watch and then attack the same area. As the aircraft returned to the airstrip, the piece of map was handed to the pilot waiting to take off. The last sortie completed, the strip of map was rushed to me and pasted back on its original position. It is probably the only occasion when the commander of the ground troops and the Air Force pilots have had to share the same map to fight a battle.

Meanwhile, 1 Punjab was ordered to move immediately from Magam to the Badgam area and to occupy a defensive position on any suitable feature in the area of Humhom-Badgam in order to seal off the route to Srinagar. It was not possible to give the battalion commander, Lt. Col. G. I. S. Kullar, any specific position to occupy as it was unknown what enemy was in the area and how far he had advanced. He was told that he would have to judge the situation for himself on arrival. 1 Punjab moved with great speed, and when I visited it just before last light, it had taken up positions in the Humhom area and had taken under command the men of the 4 Kumaon Company which had fallen back under the heavy enemy pressure. There was peace and quiet in the area, the position having stabilised as quickly as it had erupted, but then peace and calm had also prevailed shortly before the 4 Kumaon Company came under enemy fire.

It was impossible to arrive at any conjecture as to the enemy's future intentions. His route to Srinagar was blocked by 1 Punjab. This battalion was considerably under-strength, in strange terrain with neither the chance not the time to survey the country and formulate a sound defensive plan. While it would be hard-pressed if attacked by an overwhelmingly strong enemy force, it would put up very stiff resistance and take a heavy toll of the enemy. The chances were, therefore, that the enemy would now turn his attention to the airstrip. If he did so, the initial opposition that he would encounter would be a Brigade Headquarters, about twenty-five all ranks in strength and armed only with rifles and pistols, and bereft of its Defence platoon. With Brigade Headquarters over-run, as it certainly would be, command and control would be lost. Even if he did not assault the airfield defences, the fire from his automatic weapons and mortars would make the airfield unusable. But with light fading fast, there was no alternative for Brigade Headquarters other than to stay put, present the stoutest defence possible if attacked, and hope for the best.

Brigade Headquarters stood to all night. The long vigil seemed interminable. Eventually when dawn broke, patrols which moved out reported that the area was clear. The enemy had failed to exploit his success at Badgam, and with it had missed the chance of a lifetime. Why he failed to move towards the airfield is unfathomable. Just three miles from Badgam lay features from which he could have commanded the airstrip, which, if denied to us, would have swung the balance to a marked degree in his favour. Just one aircraft hit and damaged on the airstrip, or hit in the air and forced to crash-land, would have made it unusable.

One can only make a guess and ascribe the reason to the bullet wound suffered by their leader, Kurshed, in his leg. The Pathan without a leader is like a rudderless ship. With Kurshed wounded, the tribesmen probably decided to retrace their steps and get him back to Baramula. Or was it Kurshed's miscalculation of the strength that faced him? On return to Karachi, he made a statement to the Press that he had engaged an Indian Army Brigade and had routed it, while all he had actually engaged was one Rifle Company. Perhaps it was the reported arrival of 1 Punjab in the Humhom area which gave the impression that he was facing great strength, and, worried by the wound in his leg, he thought it prudent to withdraw. Whatever the reason, the answer will never be known, as he died a few months later.

Major Somnath Sharma was killed in the battle of Badgam, and a number of his men were killed and wounded. The crash heard on the wireless set before it went off the air was the bursting of a mortar bomb which had landed near him. He and his Company had fought a great battle against tremendous odds and their engagement with the enemy had disclosed an unknown and dangerous threat. What would have happened if the 4 Kumaon Company had been given orders to withdraw at two o'clock, in accordance with the original intention, and had not been ordered to remain in position until three o'clock, or if Kurshed and his large band of raiders had held their attack for another half an hour and allowed the Company to withdraw undisturbed? 161 Infantry Brigade would in either event have settled down for the night quite oblivious of the fact that within three miles of the airfield, and with the route from Badgam to Srinagar wide open, was a large body of the enemy who could have presented it suddenly with an extremely serious situation. With 1 Sikh at Patan, 1 Punjab at Magam, and 1 Kumaon and 2 Companies of 4 Kumaon on the airfield, the Brigade would have been splintered into three pieces and would have lost its effectiveness as a fighting formation. If, in addition, the tribesmen had liquidated the isolated Brigade Headquarters, the confusion would have been complete.

The deficiency of dial sights with the Patiala Mountain Battery was most unfortunate, indeed tragic. Had this Battery been properly equipped and operational rather than a liability, it would certainly have been utilised to give covering fire to the 4 Kumaon firm base at Badgam. It would have been presented with a wonderful target to shoot at and would have done considerable damage to the enemy, including neutralising the enemy mortar fire to answer which 4 Kumaon had not. On the other hand, if the dial sights were not available in Patiala the Battery must have been completely untrained, and its firing could have been as erratic as was the decision to send it to the Valley in a non-operational state.

In the morning of 4 November, while engaged in reviewing the grim situation that had faced the Brigade the previous evening and during the night, and making the necessary adjustments to the troop dispositions, I received a message that Sardar Vallabhbhai Patel, the Deputy Prime Minister of India, and Sardar Baldev Singh, the Defence Minister, had arrived in the Valley and were on their way to my Headquarters. On arrival, I led them into the Operations Room and briefed them on the situation. I explained what had happened at Badgam and stressed that it was only sheer good fortune that had seen us through the crisis. I then emphasised that Srinagar must now be viewed as being very definitely threatened. Sardar Baldev Singh was wide awake and had taken in all that I said. Sardar Patel had, however, closed his eyes soon after I had begun the briefing and I assumed that he was feeling the effects of the air journey and had fallen asleep. The briefing completed, I therefore looked at Sardar Baldev Singh and asked him a direct question: "Am I expected to eject the tribesmen from the Valley regardless of the fate that may befall Srinagar, or is the town to be saved?"

Sardar Patel stirred. The Tiger had not been asleep, and had heard every word of the briefing. A strong and determined man, and one of few words, "Of course Srinagar must be saved," he snapped.

"Then I must have more troops and very quickly," I answered, adding: "And if it is possible, I would like some artillery."

Sardar Patel rose. "I'm returning to Delhi immediately," he said, "and you will get what you want as quickly as I can get them to you."

On reaching the vehicle park, I called forward my jeep and asked him whether I could drive him to the airfield. "No, Brigadier," he replied, "don't bother to come to the airport to see me off. You have got more important things to do than wasting your time doing that." He then climbed into his own vehicle and, with a wave of his hand, was off.

That evening I got a message that two Battalions of Infantry, one Squandron of Armoured Cars and a Battery of Field Artillery were being despatched to the Valley by road. The Engineers had bridged the numerous culverts on the road from Pathankot to Jammu, and the Valley could now receive large bodies of troops by surface transport. This was heartening news, as the airstrip was beginning to look like a ploughed field. Sardar Patel lived up to his reputation as a man of action.

Sheikh Abdullah and Bakshi Ghulam Mohammed, who had gone to the airfield to see Sardar Patel off, apparently decided to visit Brigade Headquarters on their way back to Srinagar. Having been denied the opportunity of meeting them the evening before, because of the road being blocked by people heading for the airstrip, I had no idea what they looked like. They arrived when I was busy on a wireless set, and Major Kak, the LO, had led them into the Brigade Operations Room and had proceeded to explain the situation to them, pointing out the deployment of the Brigade. When I entered the room and was greeted with the sight of two unknown civilians carefully studying the map, I was furious. I did not ask who they were, but ordered them to leave the room immediately and never to set foot in it again. They left hurriedly. It was only when their vehicle had disappeared into the distance that Major Kak told me who they were.

Chapter 8

The Battle of Shalateng

During the day—4 November—information poured in from all sorts of sources to the effect that the enemy was here, there and everywhere. With the limited number of troops available, it was quite impossible to engage them and in any case, as they had split into parties of trying strength and were constantly on the move, it would have been tactically unsound to have attempted to do so. It was clear that to bring the tribesmen to battle and to defeat them, it was essential that they concentrate. Unless some method could be evolved to achieve this, they would inflict immense damage with hit-and-run raids. I therefore decided that the best way to effect such a concentration would be to give them the incentive to do so, and this could only be achieved by giving them a very attractive bait.

The bait, I felt, could only be the road—freedom to use which, I was convinced, would act like a magnet. The tribesmen had been tempted to come to the Valley because of the loot that they would be able to take back, and with the use of the main road denied to them they could not move the vehicles which were so essential to carry back their booty. 1 Sikh at Patan was the stumbling block, and I decided to withdraw this battalion and throw open the road to the tribals. The withdrawal from Patan, coming in the wake of the Badgam battle, would, I hoped, give the tribal leaders the impression that we had taken a crippling knock at Badgam and were pulling in our horns.

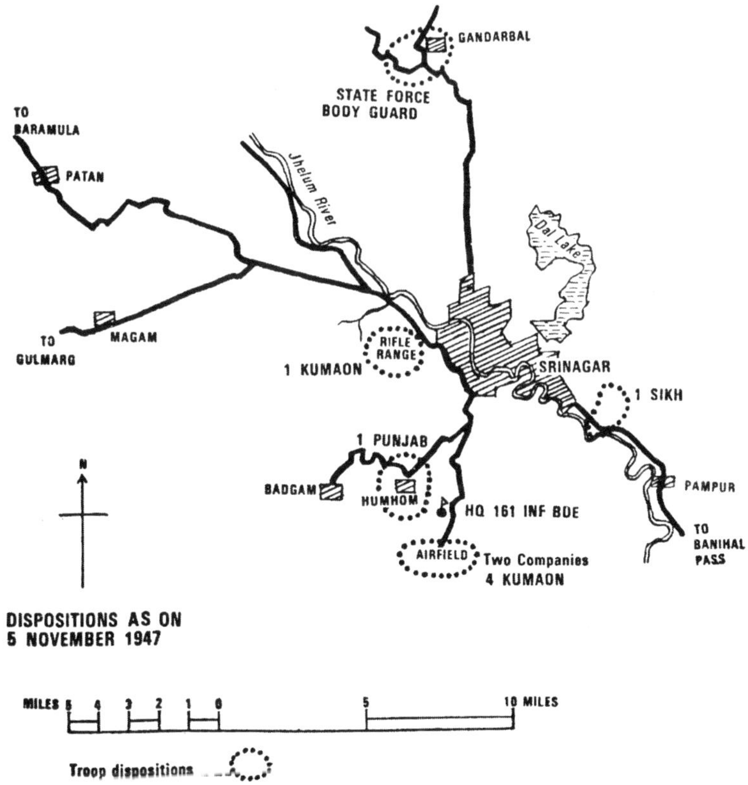

Before rushing headlong into an action based on a hunch, the relevant factors had to be given serious consideration. There was a live possibility that 1 Sikh might be segregated from the rest of the Brigade by the enemy, who could very easily interpose himself in-between 1 Sikh and Srinagar. If this materialised, the maintenance convoys to 1 Sikh at Patan would either have to run the gauntlet of enemy fire or face ambushes. It was also not improbable that the enemy would pin down 1 Sikh in the Patan area and move past the flanks of the battalion and on to Srinagar, thereby reducing the attacking potential of 161 Infantry Brigade to just one battalion, 1 Kumaon, or if a risk was to be taken and 1 Punjab removed from Humhom, to two battalions. This would be totally inadequate to ensure the safety of Srinagar. Although there was never any doubt that 1 Sikh, a strong battalion with two extra Rifle Companies, would be able to hold Patan, its withdrawal and with it a temporary loss of territory which could be recovered in a matter of hours was accepted as a justifiable gamble on the chance of the enemy biting the bait and presenting us with a concentrated target. Orders were issued to 1 Sikh to evacuate Patan and withdraw to Srinagar.

The Commanding Officer of 1 Sikh, Lt. Col. Sampuran Bachan Singh, was most unhappy when he received the order to withdraw to Srinagar. He stated that he would find it very difficult to break contact with the enemy, who were now active along his front and possibly in his rear. But firmness was employed and 1 Sikh evacuated Patan after darkness had set in, and withdrew to Srinagar without any interference from the enemy.

The gamble worked like magic. Penny packets of the raiders disappeared from our front and information poured in throughout the next day that they were all heading back towards Baramula. That evening, while 1 Sikh was preparing to evacuate Patan, I went to call on Sheikh Abdullah. He had taken up residence in a small house next to Nedous' Hotel, and Bakshi Ghulam Mohammed and D. P. Dhar were closeted with him in a room lit by candles. Major Kak introduced me, and I apologised for the rough treatment that I had meted out to them that morning, explaining that an Operations Room is more or less a "holy of holies", access to which is strictly limited. In the flickering light of the candles, we then studied a map that had been laid out on the table and discussed the situation. The National Conference Volunteers, carefully chosen individuals from the political party headed by Sheikh Abdullah, who volunteered to carry out reconnaissance missions many of which were very dangerous, had brought in a great deal of information relating to the movement of the tribesmen. I was shown on the map the concentrations that had been located and were stated to be obvious targets for attack.

I listened patiently, making notes and stating that I would do what I could. What I did not say was that with the limited number of troops at my disposal I could do nothing at the time to engage the concentrations, nor did I mention that I had, only an hour previously, ordered 1 Sikh to withdraw from Patan. I knew they would learn of it sooner or later, but to have mentioned it at that moment, when I was being urged to move out and engage the raiders, would have been catastrophic. During the conference, I had noticed a definite tinge of bitterness in the hearts of the three men in the room, and it was Bakshi Ghulam Mohammed who, unable to restrain himself, brought the reason to the surface. "Brigadier," he said, ,"may I ask you a question?" I answered in the affirmative. "What," he continued, "would you do to a commander who left his troops and ran away?"

"Court-martial him," I replied, "on a charge of cowardice."

"Well, that's just what our Maharajah has done," he said slowly. "He is the Commander in Chief of the State Forces, and when the tribesmen arrived at Mahura he collected all his valuables, loaded them into all the trucks he could lay hands on, and bolted with his family to Jammu."

Bakshi Ghulam Mohammed's statement was not wholly accurate. The Maharajah might have been the C in C of the State Forces, but he was the titular head and not the executive commander. That position was held by the Chief of Staff, who, unfortunately, had been killed at Diwan Mandir. Nor had the Maharajah "bolted" as Bakshi had put it. He had been persuaded for political reasons to leave Srinagar and take up residence in another part of his State. Had he remained in

Srinagar and fallen into tribal hands, his functions as the Maharajah would have been dictated to him.

There was very little movement along the roads and no motor vehicles were operating as I made my way back to my Headquarters. Srinagar, with the dull glow of candles behind the windows of the houses, gave the impression of a city that knew it was doomed but was trying to postpone the dreaded fate by hiding itself under a blanket of darkness. The streets were deserted, but not due to any curfew or other order warning people to remain indoors after dark. At no time were such restrictions placed on Srinagar, as doing so might create panic which anti-social elements and fifth columnists would exploit to embarrass the Emergency Government.

As I expected, my signal to Jak Force Headquarters—it had meanwhile been established at Jammu—that I had withdrawn 1 Sikh from Patan created a furore. Major General Kulwant Singh sent a message that he would be arriving by air early the next morning, 5 November and wished me to meet him at the airfield. He arrived a ten o'clock, and having driven him to my Headquarters, I explained to him in detail my reasons for having ordered the move. He was not in a receptive mood, and not one bit impressed with my arguments. He told me in no uncertain terms that he entirely disagreed with me, that the tribals would never move towards Baramula but would surge forward to Srinagar, and that my opinion was not a calculated risk but sheer suicide. He made it very clear that as Jak Force Headquarters had not been approached before the order was issued, I must accept full responsibility for what I had done. Further, he insisted that I give it to him in writing, and in triplicate, that I had withdrawn 1 Sikh without his approval and without consulting Jak Force Headquarters. This I did, and having placed the three copies in his pocket he stormed out of Headquarters and drove to Srinagar to make a courtesy call on Sheikh Abdullah.

Major Kak, who accompanied Major General Kulwant Singh, returned to Brigade Headquarters after a short while and stated that neither Sheikh Abdullah nor Bakshi Ghulam Mohammed were present. They had received information about the withdrawal from

Patan, and had left to visit various areas to ascertain for themselves the effect that it had on the population. D. P. Dhar was, meanwhile, in an aircraft heading for Delhi. It was he himself who, six weeks later while lunching with me at Uri, apologetically told me the object of his flight to Delhi. It was to interview the Prime Minister personally and to request him to despatch another Brigadier to command the troops in the Valley. Pandit Nehru had immediately agreed, but Sardar Patel, who was also present, was adamant that no change of commander was called for, regardless of the merit or demerit of withdrawing from Patan. Sardar Patel's view prevailed.

With the road link from Pathankot to the Valley now available, I considered that I could afford to take a risk with the safety of the airfield. Sardar Patel had been emphatic that Srinagar must be saved, and so I decided to redeploy the troops with the accent changed from the security of the airfield to the security of Srinagar. There were numerous approaches to Srinagar from almost every point of the compass, and to cover all of them was impossible. The risk of infiltration into the city by small bodies of the tribesmen would, therefore, have to be accepted, although if it did materialise it would be very difficult to flush them out. The only course open was to occupy certain nodal points on the outskirts of the city, to patrol vigorously, and to switch to the offensive as soon as was possible after the arrival of the reinforcements that were already on their way to the Valley.

As 4 Kumaon were still in the process of being built up, whatever had arrived of the unit was made responsible for the defence of the airstrip. 1 Punjab was left in its position in the Humhom area astride the road leading from Badgam to Srinagar, and 1 Kumaon was moved forward from the airstrip and deployed in the Rifle Range area, locally named Chandmari, with orders to deny to the enemy the approaches to the city from the west. 1 Sikh, on return from Patan, was deployed on the south-eastern edges of Srinagar and covered the road running from Pampur to the city. This was essential as there had been persistent reports that the enemy had by-passed the airfield, moving south of it, and was heading towards that suburb of Srinagar. The Kashmir State Force Bodyguard was located in the Gandarbal area with the role of covering the approaches to the city from both the north and the west. This defensive layout, planned to save the threatened city, was light by any standards, there still being many loopholes, but with the limited number of troops available it was as much as one could do.

What was particularly worrying was the fact that there was no Brigade reserve. If any sector of the front came under heavy enemy pressure and necessitated rapid reinforcing, it could only be achieved by withdrawing a sub-unit or unit from another sector. This would result in the already slender Brigade defensive layout being still further embarrassed. An infantry battalion, no matter how weak in strength, or even two reasonably strong Rifle companies, would have been worth their weight in gold. They would have shifted the bias from what was not short of extreme peril to a position which, although dangerous, could have been held in check without placing in jeopardy other equally sensitive areas. Unfortunately, they were not available, or, to be strictly accurate, they were not known to be available.

Strange though it may appear, a very large number of Jammu and Kashmir State Force troops, fully trained and equipped, with Officers and Non-Commissioned Officers, were, unknown to Headquarters 161 Infantry Brigade, concealing themselves in Badami Bagh Barracks in Srinagar. What made this crime even more heinous was the fact that 1 Sikh was deployed south-east of Badami Bagh Barracks and was in fact covering the route to the Barracks. The reason for Headquarters Jammu and Kashmir State Forces adopting this attitude is unfathomable since, if 161 Infantry Brigade had suffered a serious reverse, the tribals would have slaughtered them in the Barracks. It was only towards the end of the first week of December, just over a month later, and after 161 Infantry Brigade had attacked and hurled back the tribals and was consolidating its position at Uri, 62 miles to the west of Srinagar, that the existence of over 1,850 fully armed, trained and equipped officers and other ranks of the Jammu and Kashmir State Forces in Badami Bagh Barracks came to light. The State Force had run out of rations and had submitted a ration indent to Rear Headquarters 161 Infantry Brigade which was located in Srinagar. This request was relayed by telephone to Main Headquarters 161 Infantry

Brigade at Uri, and permission sought to issue 2,000 rations. As the Maharajah's Bodyguard had been despatched to Jammu towards the end of November, and I had been originally informed by Major Kak that there were only a small number of State Force troops in Badami Bagh Barracks, hospital or convalescent cases, I assumed that the request was for 200 men for ten days. The rations were sanctioned, but Rear Headquarters was instructed to ensure that the State Forces realised that the rations were being issued for that period. I was, however, informed that the State Force indent gave the figure of 2,000 all ranks, which included the non-combatants enrolled.

Rear HQ was ordered to check back with the State Forces, it being more than probable that an extra '0' had slipped into the indent through a typist's error. The reply was received about ten minutes later. The figure of 2,000 was confirmed as correct by the State Force, that being the actual strength of the State Forces personnel in Badami Bagh. Wondering whether the rations were to be utilised to feed unauthorised personnel, I instructed Rear Headquarters to issue just 2,000 rations, and to inform Headquarters Jammu and Kashmir State Forces that I would be arriving at Badami Bagh at ten o'clock the next morning and that all Officers and men, including the non-combatants enrolled, were to be paraded on the barracks square in full field service marching order. Only the sick and convalescent cases would be excused from the parade, but their numbers and exact location would be included on the Parade State.

I arrived at Badami Bagh Barracks at ten o'clock the next morning and was led to the Parade Ground. I was greeted with a sight that was quite shattering. Lined up on the Parade Ground was a mass of armed personnel, equipped with light machine guns, sten guns and rifles. The Parade State showed 1,854 all ranks present on parade and 146 in the hospital or in the barracks. I inspected the parade and noticed that almost every man was wearing a campaign or other medal issued during World War II, establishing the fact that they were not raw recruits. Meanwhile, two of my Staff Officers were making a head count and confirmed that the number 1,854 was correct. I ordered the parade to be dismissed and taking the officers aside, I asked them where they had been during the last two months. There was a grim silence. On an answer being demanded from the senior officer present, he informed me sheepishly that everyone had been in Srinagar the whole period. My further question as to why they had concealed their existence from 161 Infantry Brigade, and done nothing to assist in the grim days that the Brigade had had to face, remained unanswered. I went away from Badami Bagh Baracks thoroughly disgusted.

I telephoned Major General Kulwant Singh at Jammu and asked him to come to the Valley to see a very interesting sight. He arrived the next day, was presented with an identical parade, and was as stunned as I had been. I informed him that I did not want these personnel in the Valley and requested orders for their immediate despatch to Jammu. They were merely consuming rations that were still being built up, were nothing more or less than a liability, and would never win my confidence. He agreed, and orders were issued immediately. I was, however, persuaded to retain 600 Dogras and to form them into an *ad hoc* battalion. The battalion, when formed, was moved to Baramula to garrison that town and patrol the area. It proved, however, to be such a nuisance, upsetting not only the civilians but also the troops of 161 Infantry Brigade, that I had to pack it off to Jammu after a week.

Having spent the morning and afternoon of 5 November visiting all units and ensuring that the Commanding Officers had no doubts that needed clarifying, I went to see Major General Kulwant Singh at his residence in Srinagar, in order to brief him on the latest situation. He had calmed down quite considerably, accepting the withdrawal of 1 Sikh from Patan as a *fait accompli*. I gave him the latest tactical picture, informed him of the progress of the reinforcements which were expected to reach the Valley on the evening of 7 November, and explained to him my future plans.

The date I had selected for the attack, I informed him, was 10 November, and the plan, in brief, was to hold the enemy with the troops already in position, and to make a wide encircling movement with the two battalions due to arrive, from their concentration area, which would be the airfield, to Patan via Magam. The approach march to Patan would be carried out in the dark, commencing in the early hours of 10 November, and the rate of the advance so timed as to enable the column commander to launch his attack on Patan at first light. Reliable guides, who knew every inch of the ground, were already with me at my Headquarters, and this would ensure that although the units moving to Patan would be strangers to the ground, they would not lose direction. Further, a Company Commander of 1 Sikh, who knew the Patan position well, would be attached to the Column Commander and would be readily available to assist him with advice relating to the quick deployment of the units into defence on the Patan feature. As soon as Patan had been consolidated, the enemy sandwiched in-between Patan and Srinagar would be subjected to attacks from both the front and the rear. When enemy resistance had been broken, the units from Srinagar would advance to Patan, which would be held as a firm base, and move forward to assault Baramula. This, I estimated, if things went according to plan, would be on 11 November.

Major General Kulwant Singh agreed that it was a sound plan, but inquired whether it would be possible to speed it up by one day, that is, to capture Baramula by 10 November. I said that I would try to do so, but it was dependent on the actual date and hour of arrival of the reinforcements, and also the physical condition of the troops. They were scheduled to arrive in Srinagar by about last light on 7 November, but the Banihal Pass had to be surmounted, and it was not impossible that the loaded vehicles might feel the strain, and the overheating of their engines might result in enforced stoppages and consequent delay in arrival. Moreover, the troops would have been on the road, cooped up in vehicles, for possibly 72 hours, and with lack of sleep, cramp and hill road sickness, which would certainly affect a number of them, time would have to be allowed for them to find their land legs and regain their fighting efficiency. It was finally agreed to leave the 'D' Day to my discretion and I returned to my Headquarters, still in the Forest Bungalow, to finalise the plan.

The leading vehicles with the reinforcements actually arrived more or less on schedule, soon after last light on 7 November, and the whole column was in the airfield area just before midnight, but the plan incorporating them was not to see the light of day.

On the night of 5 November, an unfortunate incident took place involving a party of National Conference volunteers. Returning to Srinagar from a patrol in the Badgam area, it approached the positions held by 1 Sikh after darkness had set in. It was challenged, but instead of answering the challenge, it started to run. The 1 Sikh sentry opened fire at the fleeing personnel, firing more at the sound than any specific target. The next morning, the bodies of two men were found about fifty yards from the 1 Sikh outpost. The unit could not be held to blame for this incident, as it was impossible to see the intruders in the dark and they might well have been the enemy. Where the unit did err was that the bodies having been recovered were buried in slit trenches in the unit's position, and Brigade Headquarters was not informed.

The news that two of his volunteers had been killed reached Sheikh Abdullah first thing the next morning, and he asked me to meet him. I had, fortunately, been informed by Major Kak of the reason for the meeting, and having obtained the details from 1 Sikh, I arrived at Sheikh Abdullah's house to be greeted by an infuriated individual. I offered him my deepest sympathies that such an unfortunate incident should have cost two lives, but impressed on him that it was the result of a genuine mistake, which could have been avoided had the volunteers answered the challenge and not run away. He was very upset and it took some time to get him to accept the explanation, whereupon he calmed down. Dissident elements decided, however, to make capital out of the incident. I was left no option but to move 1 Sikh away from its position at the south-eastern end of Srinagar. The battalion was redeployed in the Rifle Range area, to the north of 1 Kumaon and with its right flank resting on the Jhelum River and astride the Srinagar-Baramula road.

No sooner had 1 Sikh evacuated its positions and moved to the Rifle Range area than certain locals dug up the two bodies and carried them in procession through the main roads of the city. Major General Kulwant Singh, who had also gone to see Sheikh Abdullah, to offer his condolences, was present when the procession reached the latter's residence, and not all his efforts prevented Sheikh Abdullah from relapsing into a most morose state. It was then that Bakshi Ghulam

Mohammed rose to the occasion. Going to the head of the procession, he explained to the people what had happened and told them that it was nothing but an unfortunate accident. They listened to him, and having accepted his statement dispersed quietly. While it lasted, however, it was a most explosive situation.

The morning and afternoon of 6 November was spent in tidying up the defences, and in briefing the unit commanders on the latest situation and the proposed plan of action. It was a quiet day, disturbed only by the demonstrations in the city, with no signs of the enemy. All the reports that flowed in indicated that he had abandoned his harassing of the villages, and after wandering about the area in parties of varying size, was hurrying back in the direction of Baramula. The gamble in withdrawing 1 Sikh from Patan, in the hope that it would tempt the tribesmen to concentrate, had paid off. Now it was merely a question of when they would debouch from Baramula towards Srinagar in their thousands and engage 161 Infantry Brigade in what would be a critical battle, on the result of which depended the fate of Srinagar and the Valley. There was a possibility that the enemy might dawdle and postpone his advance towards Srinagar for another 48 hours, that is, not commence his move until the morning of 8 November. In that case, the arrival of the reinforcements on the evening of 7 November would halve the numerical advantage that he possessed at the moment, which was in the region of five to one. 161 Infantry Brigade's chances of scoring a decisive victory would then be greatly enhanced.

If, however, he advanced before the arrival of the reinforcements, and that meant during the early hours of the morning of 7 November, he would meet two battalions holding a thin red line, with nothing in the shape of a strong reserve behind them. If he succeeded in breaching the line held by 1 Sikh and 1 Kumaon, a Rifle Company of 4 Kumaon could be rushed up from the airfield, but it would be faced with a task quite beyond its capabilities. It was fully expected that the enemy would make his approach march from Baramula to Srinagar during the hours of darkness. It was appreciated that the enemy commander would not be so foolhardy as to attempt a motorised advance along the main road during the hours of daylight. He would realise from the air attack that struck the raiders attacking Badgam, that such a column would be subjected to similar treatment. There was a danger inherent in the enemy's advance in the dark, as having debussed, he might have probed the position held by 161 Infantry Brigade and eventually found the left flank of 1 Kuamon. Had he done so, and moved around it in strength, it could have been disastrous. It was, therefore, hoped that he would confine his activity to the area near the road and attempt to bulldoze his way through the position. This course if adopted by the enemy also had its disadvantage in that it would probably result in the two front lines being so close together that it would have been impossible to use aircraft for strafing purposes, thereby neutralising our air superiority.

Last-light reports on 6 November, from all sources, still indicated bodies of the tribesmen weaving their paths back to Baramula, and gave rise to the hope that although the advance might commence during the early hours of the morning of 7 November, it was more likely that it would be 8 November, or perhaps even later. This assumption, which was a fair one, was based on a number of reliable reports that the enemy commander was having a spot of bother with his various tribal clans as to who should lead the way. Each tribal leader evidently felt that someone else should be in the forefront, and was not prepared to allow the rest of the column to move on unless all his men had returned to Baramula. This attitude could only cause delay which eminently suited 161 Infantry Brigade.

In order to cater for the possibility of an attack developing before the reinforcements were ready to carry out the encirclement move to Patan, an alternative plan was also prepared and kept ready. This plan provided for one of the battalions rushing forward from the airfield and being placed in depth in the Rifle Range area, the other battalion being held close to Srinagar and in reserve. That the tribesmen would not appreciate a frontal slogging match against Regular troops, deployed in what would be Brigade strength, gave much confidence and strength to this plan. While the alternative plan was receiving its finishing touches and I was trying to pry into the mind of the enemy commander, an officer walked into the Operations Room and announced that he was Major Inder Rikhye. He told me that he was the Squadron Commander of a Squadron of Armoured Cars of 7 Cavalry, and had been leading the reinforcement convoy. As the bridge at Ramban was not in a very sound condition, the passage of vehicles across it was being limited to one at a time, thereby causing quite a bit of delay. He had left the remainder of his Squadron to accompany the main convoy, and had come ahead with a Troop of Armoured Cars and a Rifle Troop. The main convoy, he estimated, would arrive late the next evening, 7 November, on schedule. As the four Armoured Cars with him had been subjected to considerable strain, he requested that he be given the next day free for the maintenance of the vehicles.

I explained to Major Rikhye the situation as a it faced us, and told him that his unanticipated arrival had virtually been a gift from the gods, and asked him whether it was humanly possible for him to produce something, no matter how small, to assist with the next day's reconnaissances. Sheikh Abdullah had constantly requested me to send troops to Bandipura, a town lying to the north of Wular Lake, since the people were panicking although the tribesmen had not approached the town. I was unable to accede to the Sheikh's request, but now we had the ideal troops for the task. If he could carry out a reconnaissance to Bandipura, which would mean a turn-round of 74 miles, it would relieve Sheikh Abdullah of his anxiety and also establish whether there was a threat to Srinagar from the north. Major Rikhye left the room and returned after a short time with Lieutenant Noel David, the Troop Commander. He informed me that all hands would be turned on to two Armoured Cars to get them ready for the task, and they, together with the Rifle Troop, would be ready to move at first light the next morning.

Lt. David was then briefed. He was to move from Brigade Headquarters through Srinagar to Zinyimar and on to Gandarbal. Here he was to contact the local Police Station, liaise with the Maharajah's Bodyguard, and obtain any information that they might possess. Leaving Gandarbal, he was to proceed via Krahom, Camping Ground at point 5250, to Tsiyu and on to Bandipura. After spending about an hour at Bandipura and having obtained the latest information from all sources, he was to return to Brigade Headquarters by the same route. From the moment he left Brigade Headquarters on his outward journey, and until he reported back, he was to keep in constant touch with Major Rikhye by wireless and report his progress. The briefing over, I finished the plan that I had been working at, and we had dinner and settled in for the night. Not one of us had any idea of the very vital part that this reconnaissance was going to play in the events that were going to strike us the next morning.

No contact was made with the enemy during the night of 6 November, nor in the early hours of the 7th morning. This was exactly what had been hoped for. At half past six, two Armoured Cars and the Rifle Troop of 7 Cavalry, under the command of Lt. David, started out from Brigade Headquarters to carry out its reconnaissance. A guide led them through the city and having placed them on the road to Gandarbal, returned and reported that he had done so. David's reports commenced coming in almost immediately, relating mainly to the expressions on people's faces as they saw the Armoured Cars. It was while we were receiving these reports, and having a laugh at some of them, that 1 Sikh came on the air soon after seven o'clock. The Commanding Officer reported that his forward Companies were being heavily sniped at by the enemy, and then, a few moments later, that the Rifle Company which was covering the bridge in the vicinity of milestone 4 was being heavily engaged by light automatic fire. Rushing to my jeep with a Rover wireless set in it, I streaked off to the Rifle Range area, with Major Rikhye following in the jeep in which had been installed a wireless set linked to Lt. David. As I flashed through the city, I did not hear the sound of firing, this presumably being dimmed by the somewhat thick mist. The people were moving about unconcerned and apparently unaware of the fact that the enemy was at their doorstep.

As I neared the Rifle Range area, the sound of firing was distinctly audible, and by the time I had reached the Headquarters of 1 Sikh, the volume of firing had increased quite appreciably. It was apparent that the enemy was opposite us in strength, but whether we were in

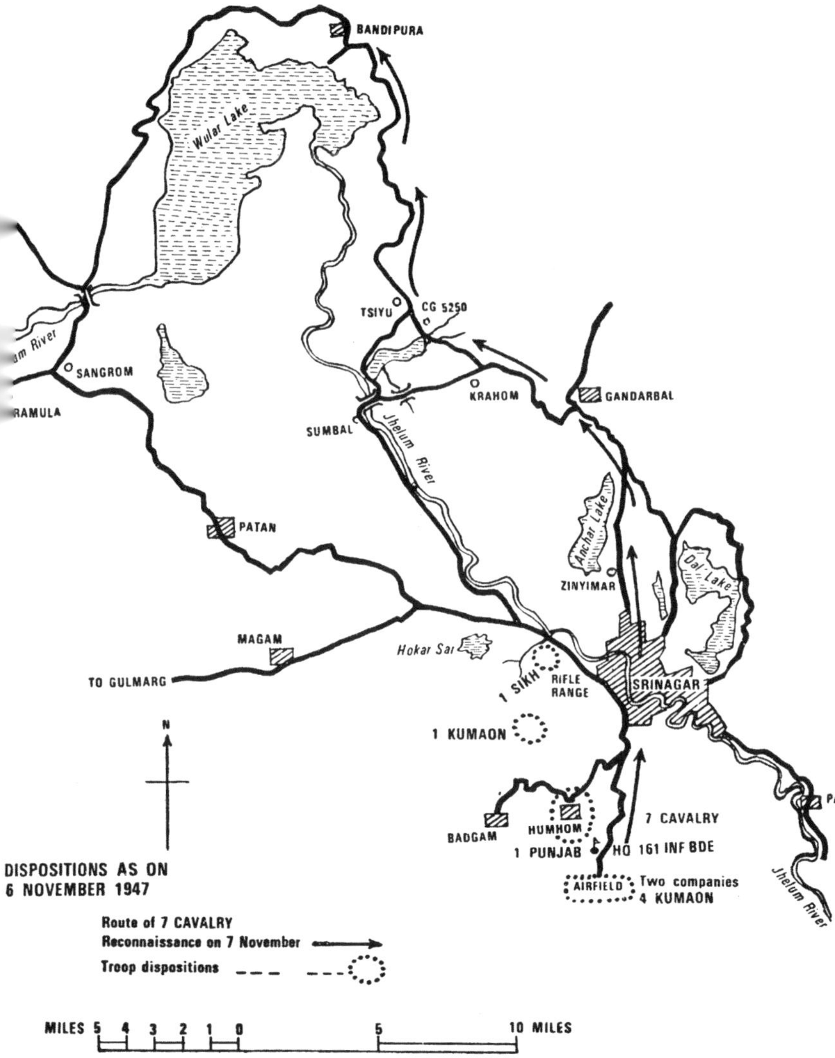
BANDIPURA
Wular Lake
SANGROM
TSIYU
CG 5250
KRAHOM
GANDARBAL
SUMBAL
Jhelum River
PATAN
Anchar Lake
ZINYIMAR
Dal Lake
MAGAM
Hokar Sar
TO GULMARG
1 SIKH
RIFLE RANGE
SRINAGAR
1 KUMAON
N
PAMPUR
7 CAVALRY
BADGAM
HUMHOM
1 PUNJAB
HQ 161 INF BDE
AIRFIELD
Two companies 4 KUMAON
Jhelum River
DISPOSITIONS AS ON 6 NOVEMBER 1947
Route of 7 CAVALRY
Reconnaissance on 7 November
Troop dispositions
MILES 5 4 3 2 1 0 5 10 MILES

contact with a strong leading element or the whole body of them was impossible to guess. I contacted my Brigade Major on the wireless set and having explained the situation to him, ordered him to rush to the airfield and request the Air Force to carry out an immediate reconnaissance of the road linking Srinagar and Patan, and the area to the north and south of it. I wanted answers to the following questions as soon as possible:

(a) What is the approximate strength of the enemy facing us in the milestone 4 area?
(b) What other strength, if any, is moving down the road towards us?
(c) Are there any vehicles on the road, and if so, how many and where is the head of the convoy?
(d) Is there any large-scale movement towards the Humhom-Badgam area?

The mist had lifted and visibility was good when a Harvard flew over the Rifle Range heading westwards, and the first report was received a few minutes later. It stated that the enemy was in front of us in their thousands, that no further strength was moving down the road and that about 150 lorries were parked almost nose to tail on the road, facing east, with the head at about milestone 6. The second report stated that there was little movement north of the road, but extensive movement to the south of it, and trenches were being dug. There was no movement towards Humhom or Badgam.

A medium machine gun now opened fire and this was closely followed by two rounds of smoke from a three-inch mortar. The MMG fire coming from the enemy right flank established the fact that the defectors of the 4 J&K Infantry were in that area. Meanwhile, the volume of rifle and automatic fire increased steadily, covering almost the entire frontage of the Brigade. The situation that I had played for had been presented to me, but unfortunately 24 hours too early. We were heavily outnumbered both in manpower and weapons, having no medium machine guns and only a very few three-inch mortars. If only the Patiala Mountain Battery had been equipped with dial sights, here were perfect targets, and targets that could have been struck so effectively that the enemy concentration would probably have been broken up. Even if the Patiala gunners were untrained, it would have made no difference, as I would have made them swap places with the well-trained Mountain gunners now being used by 1 Sikh as a Rifle Company. Unfortunately, the dial sights so urgently signalled for on the evening of 3 November had not yet been received.

What was very disturbing was the thought that, in the course of the next hour or so, the situation prevailing at milestone 4 would become known in Srinagar and it would perhaps result in panic setting in. This would suit the tribals, but would seriously embarrass the Brigade's lines of communication and nullify any chance of moving forward 1 Punjab from Humhom, should it be absolutely necessary, and cut off the replenishment of our ammunition from the airfield. There was no option, however. Even if we were outnumbered by five to one, and also outgunned, this concentration had to be tackled immediately and routed, and that meant within the next hour, before the enemy had had a chance to consolidate his position. Once he was well established, he would probably pin down both 1 Sikh and 1 Kumaon to the ground, and during the hours of darkness sweep round the left flank of 1 Kumaon and stream into Srinagar.

Thus came about the battle of Shalateng, fought in the morning of 7 November, seventy-two hours before the proposed 'D' Day. It had been forced on 161 Infantry Brigade before it had been geared to face it, and was, therefore, fought with a plan that I had to formulate on the spur of the moment. In view of the fact that it was vital that the attack be launched with minimum loss of time, it was simple in the extreme.

The troops available for the battle were 1 Sikh and 1 Kumaon, both deployed in the Rifle Range area, two Armoured Cars and a Rifle Troop of 7 Cavalry, and one Rifle Company of 4 Kumaon which had been rushed forward from the airfield and located in the rear of 1 Sikh as the Brigade reserve. The withdrawal of 1 Punjab from Humhom and its deployment in the Rifle Range area was given serious consideration, but in view of the behaviour of certain elements of Badgam on 3 November, it was decided to leave that battalion in its position. It was also thought that the withdrawal of 1 Punjab would become known to the enemy and would perhaps encourage him to work his way around the left flank of 1 Kumaon, and threaten not only Srinagar but also endanger the security of the airfield. An immediate air strike was also considered, but with the two front lines so close together, it would have had to be delivered at the rear elements of the enemy, and this might have resulted in their surging forward into 1 Sikh and 1 Kumaon, and a hand to hand battle might have resulted, which, with the numerical odds against us, was not acceptable until we were ready for it.

I decided, therefore, to hold the enemy with 1 Sikh and 1 Kumaon until such time as I could bring Lt. David and his small element from 7 Cavalry into the battle. Taking Major Inder Rikhye to a sheltered spot where we could open out a map and study it without attracting the enemy's attention, we discussed the situation. Rikhye had already made inquiries regarding the state of the other two Armoured Cars undergoing maintenance, but they were unfortunately already being worked upon and could not be made ready for some considerable time. The map showed an unmetalled road taking off from Krahom to Sumbal on the Jhelum River. From Sumbal a road ran south, through Shadipur until it joined the main Srinagar-Baramula road at the village of Shalateng. This stretch of road was metalled, and while this would present no problems we were uncertain about the unmetalled portion from Krahom to Sumbal, as it had some bridge which might or might not be capable of withstanding the weight of an Armoured Car. If, however, the bridges could be crossed by the Armour, David could get his cars down to Shalateng , and would arrive in the rear of the enemy. The surprise he would create among the tribesmen, when he opened up with his automatics, would be quite devastating. It was a gamble well worth taking, and Rikhye rushed to his Rover-set jeep to guide David on to Sumbal and Shalateng, while I called in the Commanding Officers of 1 Sikh and 1 Kumaon to my Command Post.

Lt. Col. Pritam Singh of 1 Kumaon and Lt. Col. Sampuran Bachan Singh of 1 Sikh sat grim-faced as I explained the plan. 1 Sikh was ordered to remain in its position and to continue to answer the enemy

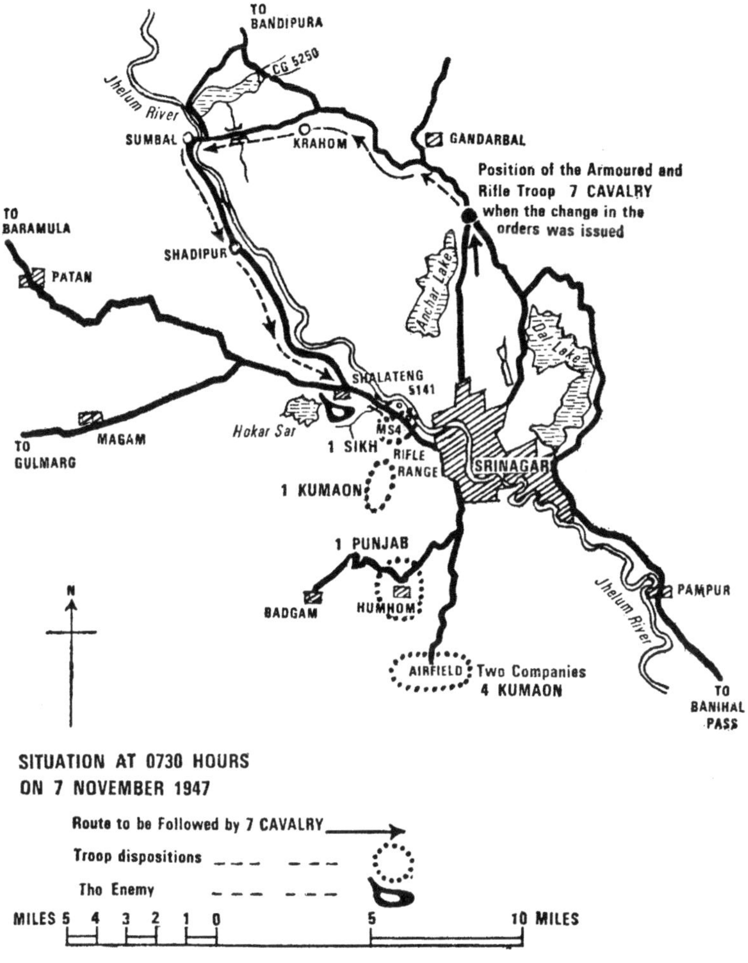

fire lightly. 1 Kumaon was to get ready to move, and when I gave the executive order, it was to work its way forward to the west, in small parties, as surreptitiously as possible, for about a mile, and then to form up facing north. This would place the battalion on the right flank of the enemy. When Lt. David and his command were in position in the region of the road junction near Shalateng and ready for action, I would give the order GO. On receiving this order, the Armoured Cars would engage the enemy with their automatics and 1 Sikh would open up with rapid fire. At the same time, 1 Kumaon would advance and deliver a bayonet assault on the enemy right flank. I impressed on the two battalion commanders that the plan was based on the ability of the Armoured Cars to reach Shalateng, and if they found it impossible to cross the bridges that lay in their path, I would whip them back to Srinagar and bring them in behind 1 Sikh, and formulate another plan. Meanwhile, they were to brief their units regarding the plan that had been formulated, and I would keep them informed of the progress of the Armour. Finally, I informed them that I was quite certain that neither they nor I had any doubts in our minds that there could only be one result to our attack, it just had to be a complete success.

The two battalion commanders having left, I walked across to Rikhye's jeep. He informed me that he had halted the Armoured Cars just short of Gandarbal, had given David his new route and task and that they were already on their way to Krahom. Good progress was made until David, soon after passing through Krahom, announced that he had come to a wooden bridge which he didn't think would take the weight of the Armour.

Further, it appeared to be too narrow and had railings. When Rikhye inquired whether there was a diversion that could be used, David, who had dismounted, said that he would have a look, but soon reported that there was none, and said that he would examine the bridge. After about five minutes, which seemed a very very long time, he came on the air and said that the bridge was groggy but might possibly stand up under the weight of the Armour. But its width, with the railings including inwards slightly, was too narrow to permit the safe passage of an Armoured Car. The Rifle Troop was at the moment knocking down the railings, and when that had been completed, he would have another look. The railings were removed without much difficulty, but on measuring the bridge for width, David found that there would only be about two inches of freeboard on either side of the wheels, which called for extreme skill in driving, there being no margin for error. Despite this, he said that he would take the risk. It took ten minutes to get each Armoured Car across the bridge. At the end of twenty minutes, which seemed a lifetime, we were immensely relieved on hearing David announce that he was across with the Armour and the Rifle Troop. He added that he would never like to try doing it again.

Rikhye and I waited as the Armour moved towards Sumbal, hoping that David would not meet another such bridge: getting the Armour back to Srinagar would present a serious problem. Fortunately there were no hazards, and David reported eventually that he had reached Sumbal and had turned on to the road leading to Shalateng. This was great news as now it was an easy run. When this report was received, I ordered 1 Kumaon to start infiltrating forward. The battalion did a wonderful job and arrived on the right flank of the enemy undetected, and reported that it was ready to attack.

When he was well clear of Sumbal, David was ordered to halt, to receive an operation order and to brief his command. This I had jotted down on the back of a message pad and handed to Rikhye, who communicated it to David. The gist of it was:

(a) On reaching the cross roads of Shalateng, he would see thousands of armed individuals—they were the enemy. Appearing from the rear, it would be assumed by the tribals that his Armoured Cars and Rifle Troop were part of their own forces.
(b) In order not to disturb this thought or to attract attention to his command, he was to approach Shalateng very slowly, and the general behaviour should incline towards being casual.
(c) If approached by any of the enemy, the attitude towards them must not be hostile.
(d) His Armoured Cars and Rifle Troop must, before proceeding any further, be ready for immediate action.
(e) On arrival near the cross roads of Shalateng, he was to deploy his Armour and Rifle Troop facing east, as if he was a part of the tribal force and in support of it.
(f) The roles allotted to 1 Sikh and 1 Kumaon were then explained to him, and he was ordered to open rapid fire on the enemy on receipt of the word GO.

(g) The subsequent switching of his fire would have to be decided by him, but he was warned to be careful that he did not shoot up 1 Kumaon.

Asked if he had any doubts or questions to ask, David said that he had none and that his role was clear. He was then wished the best of luck. After he had briefed his men, the 7 Cavalry sub-unit made its way down to Shalateng, arriving almost at the same moment that 1 Kumaon reported itself in position on the enemy flank.

David was asked what he could see and replied that there were masses of armed men moving about, some of whom had approached his Armoured Cars and, touching them, had smiled at him and his men and said to one another that they were their Cars. The Rifle Troop, he said, had dismounted and taken up a position on a bank quite close to the Armour, and he was ready for action. With 1 Sikh also reporting its readiness, I gave the word GO and hell broke loose.

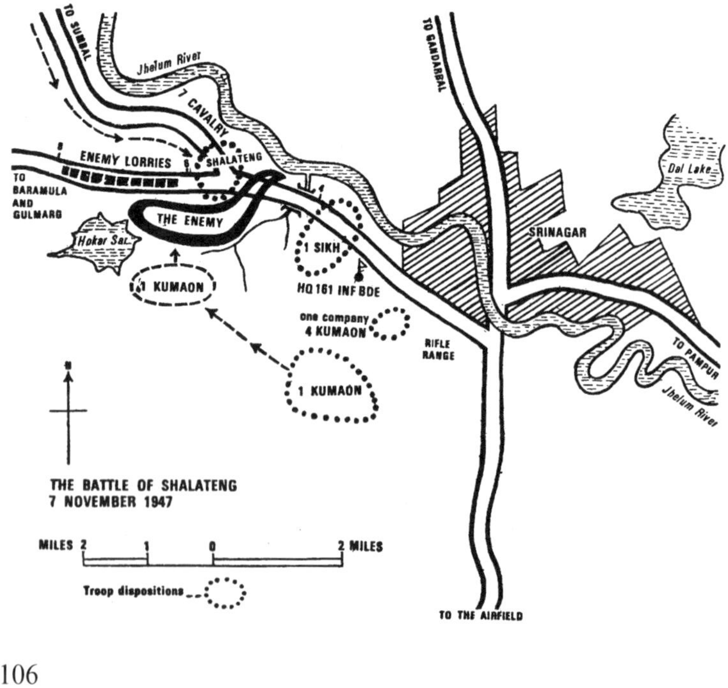

Shot up in the rear by the Armour and frontally by 1 Sikh, the stunned enemy was wondering what was happening, when suddenly 1 Kumaon burst in on his right flank, its automatics blazing as they were fired from the hip, and bayonets flashing. There was complete confusion in the enemy positions. The defectors of 4 J&K Infantry, the Mahsuds, Wazirs, Afridis and Mohmands, in trying to escape the fire that was hitting them from three sides, and seeing the bayonet charge descending on them, rushed in all directions and, crashing into one another, turned and fled westwards. As they broke, 1 Sikh was ordered to attack and the Rifle Company of 4 Kumaon was thrown into battle on the right flank of 1 Sikh. An immediate request to the Air Force to strike the fleeing tribesmen was answered with some telling blows. The disorganised enemy streaked across the fields towards Baramula, while the Armour, switching its fire to the west and supporting 1 Sikh, hurried him on his way.

The battle of Shalateng had been won, in twenty minutes from the word GO. It was a major disaster for the tribesmen. Apart from leaving behind 472 dead on the battlefield and a further 146 in-between Shalateng and Baramula, they had to abandon one hundred and thirty-eight civilian buses and load carriers which had transported them from the NWFP almost to the gates of Srinagar. Scattered all over the Shalateng area were a large number of weapons, including medium machine guns which were very acceptable, boxes of ammunition and grenades. Two freight carrying lorries and one passenger bus formed the Field Ambulance and were well equipped with medical stores, making it clear that the tribals had not expected to return to their homes unscathed, while the other lorries and buses were full of rations, kit and beddings.

Orders were immediately issued to pursue the enemy, 1 Sikh to lead the advance, and to make for Patan. This involved searching the villages on both sides of the road, and flushing out any enemy party that might have hidden in them. It was slow work, but essential. Prior to moving forward with my Tactical Headquarters, I sent an officer into Srinagar to inform Major General Kulwant Singh that I had fought a battle, had routed the enemy, and was pursuing him. He came to the area of Shalateng after about an hour, and I explained to him what had happened. I was surprised to learn from him that Srinagar had no idea that a major battle was being fought, but it was not long before the news spread and there was jubilation. I informed Major General Kulwant Singh that I intended attacking Baramula the next morning, 8 November, and then moved forward to join my advancing troops.

An attempt was made to use the vehicles captured from the tribesmen, but many of them were short of petrol, while others had various mechanical idiosyncrasies, knowledge of which was essential to make them run. As their drivers had fled, and like untrained horses many would not answer to the normal aids, the few that did were taken over by reserve drivers with the units, and utilised for the carriage of supplies and ammunition. The remainder were handed over to the Emergency Government who were very happy to receive them.

1 Sikh occupied Patan at eight o'clock that night, the remainder of the Brigade arriving about two hours later, having cleared up small pockets of tribesmen who had eluded 1 Sikh. There was a short halt, and the advance to Baramula commenced at midnight. The approach march to Baramula met with no opposition. We were happy to be moving as it was very cold, and our thin olive-green cotton uniforms were quite inadequate for weather that demanded woollen clothing. Halting the column behind the hills about a mile and a half to the east of Baramula, I made a quick plan for the assault on the town. 1 Kumaon, supported by the Armoured Cars, was to move forward and capture the features to the south of the town. When that had been effected, 1 Sikh was to move forward and, with the Armoured Cars joining the unit, was to enter the town.

Chapter 9

Baramula Retaken

1 KUMAON reached its objective unopposed and was ordered to change direction and to move on to the town. Meanwhile, 1 Sikh was also ordered to move forward and enter the town together with the Armoured Cars. At half past seven in the morning, Baramula was in our possession. It had been captured without firing a shot, the tribesmen having passed through it and continued their flight westwards. So, evidently had their senior-most commanders, as one of the platoons of 1 Sikh, which had been operating to the south of the road when advancing to Patan, had found an abandoned Chevrolet Station Wagon in the vicinity of Hokar Sar. This was a duck-shooting preserve of the Maharajah, and only he and his selected guests were permitted to use it. The enemy commanders were evidently at Hokar Sar shooting duck while their tribesmen and the defectors were being

smashed at Shalateng. It was only when they streamed past them, in full flight towards Baramula, that the officers must have realised what had happened and, considering it too dangerous to try retrieving their car, had abandoned it and joined in the race. Apart from the shot-gun cases in the car, there were a number of love letters written to one of the officers and some very inferior poetry. A map, marked with the dispositions of 161 Infantry Brigade, showed one Rifle Company in the area of milestone 4, and the rest of the battalion further south in the Rifle Range area. This, in fact, was the layout when 1 Kumaon was the only battalion in the area.

The fortunes of war are strange and unpredictable. In the case of the battle of Shalateng, the markings on the enemy commander's map would have been completely accurate, had two incidents, both unforeseen, not changed the Order of Battle of 161 Infantry Brigade. The first was the enforced move of 1 Sikh from its location in the south-east approaches to Srinagar, owing to the unfortunate incident involving the killing of two members of the National Conference volunteers. The second was Major Inder Rikhye's decision to leave the column at Ramban and to make a free run to Srinagar with a Troop of Armoured Cars and a Rifle Troop. It was even more fortunate that the Squadron of 7 Cavalry sent to the Valley was a Jat Squadron and not a Sikh Squadron. Had it been a Sikh Squadron, while the Armoured Car crew might have escaped detection, the Rifle Troop could never have done so. It would have blown the gaff that the Armour was from Pakistan. Had neither of these incidents taken place, the enemy would have found his path to Srinagar held by only one battalion, 1 Kumaon.

As the 1 Kumaon move towards the hills south of Baramula was under way, a group of people was observed running towards the hills to the east of Baramula from the northern part of the town. A Rifle Company of 1 Sikh was immediately deployed to cover them, and not knowing whether they were the enemy or friendly, a burst of light machine gun fire was aimed in their direction but well away to their right, whereupon the whole group went to ground. While we were watching them, a white piece of cloth attached to a stick was raised and waved. A platoon of 1 Sikh was therefore sent forward to contact them and escort them forward. On arrival, the leader of the group introduced himself as Captain P. R. Dewan of the Indian Army, and the Staff Captain of an Infantry Brigade located at Ferozepore in the Punjab. He looked anything but an Indian Army Officer. He was wearing a khaki Service cap which looked as if it had been extracted from a dust bin, a fawn mackintosh which showed unmistakable signs that it had been buried in the ground, grey flannel trousers and a pair of sandals. As 1 Kumaon was nearing its objective, I told him to take his group to the side of the road and to relax.

Later, when I had a chance to talk to him, I asked him to tell me what had happened. He said that he was on leave in Baramula, and everything was peaceful until the afternoon of 27 October, when the tribesmen suddenly appeared in their lorries. They took control of the town and an orgy started. Anyone who attempted to argue with them or showed any signs of resistance was shot immediately. This resulted in those residing in the southern portion of the town fleeing to the northern part which lay across the Jhelum River. Almost throughout the night there were signs of arson and bursts of firing. The next day, 28 October, groups of tribesmen entered the northern part of the town and abducted women whom they dragged back to the southern part. They warned the people to stay in their houses on pain of death if they stirred out. He had hid his uniform and had escaped detection, his Muslim friends sheltering him, or else he would have been despatched like hundreds of others. Hearing that the tribesmen had retreated, he had ventured out and made contact with us.

The sight that greeted us in Baramula is one that no period of time can erase from the memory. It was completely deserted, as silent as a tomb, with not even a whimpering pie dog. Everywhere one looked, whether it was a house or a shop or a shed, there were signs of pillage, arson or wanton destruction. The well equipped Mission Hospital, the most modern in the Valley, looked as if it had been hit by a tornado. Nor had the Mission Church escaped the wrath of the savages. The lovely images had been mutilated with axes and riddled with bullet holes. There were unmistakable signs that the patients in the hospital had been slaughtered in their beds or dragged out to meet the same fate in the compound. The battle-seasoned World War II veterans of 161 Infantry Brigade shuddered at the sight, and my thoughts drifted back to Srinagar and the fate that it had so narrowly escaped.

It was a lovely little liver-coloured cocker spaniel that led to the discovery of the spot where the Mother Superior and the nuns lay butchered. They had evidently rushed out to save the patients in the Mission Hospital and had drawn the wrath of the tribesmen. Where the little dog emerged from no one knew, but he approached the Armoured Car Troop, which was resting in the Mission Hospital area, very slowly and obviously very frightened. Lt. David whistled to him and called him to come over, but the spaniel appeared doubtful and decided to keep his distance. David walked over to him and patted him as he lay cowering on the ground. The pat and a few kind words, and his confidence was soon restored. Moving back to the Armoured Cars, David called to the spaniel to follow him, but it did not move Then it made a sharp move in the opposite direction, stopped and looked at David. A few more steps by David towards the Armoured Cars, however, brought a reaction. The spaniel ran to him, and then whipping round ran back and stopped.

One of the men of the Armoured Troop then suggested to David that perhaps the dog wanted to show him something, David agreed that it was possible, and taking a few men of the Rifle Troop as an escort, moved towards the little dog, who wagged his tail and bounded forward, looking back frequently to see that he was being followed. He led the party to the spot where his mistress and her companions had been dumped. David, tough soldier that he was, was overcome by the sight and wept unrestrainedly. His escort was equally stunned. The spaniel was immediately adopted and, in view of the move forward from Baramula to Uri, was sent to Srinagar. Even though affection was showered on him, he continued to pine and one day disappeared, never to be found.

On Baramula being taken, a wireless message was flashed to Srinagar to inform Major General Kulwant Singh and the Emergency Government that the town was in our possession. Bakshi Ghulam Mohammed came to Baramula within an hour and immediately got down to calming the local population. Doubtful at first whether it was really true that they had been liberated, they were chary of venturing across to the south bank of the Jhelum River. But when the news got round that Bakshi had arrived, they flowed across the bridge and rushed to meet him. Most of them were weeping, and denounced the quislings who had been responsible for much of their suffering. Bakshi's very presence had a wonderful effect on the people, who soon went about trying to rehabilitate themselves.

That afternoon Press correspondents, some of whom had remained in Srinagar and others, who in view of the inactivity had returned to Delhi on 6 November, arrived in Baramula to view and judge the situation for themselves.

Chapter 10

To Uri, but not on to Domel

A QUICK reorganisation of the Brigade was now necessary in order to absorb the reinforcements who had arrived on the evening of 7 November. The 6th Battalion The Rajputana Rifles (6 Rajrif), commanded by Lt. Col. S. S. Kalaan, M.C. was allotted to the airfield. The 2nd Battalion The Dogra Regiment (2 Dogra), commanded by Lt. Col. U. C. Dubey, was located in Srinagar, and 4 Kumaon, now complete and commanded by Lt. Col. Man Mohan Khanna, was ordered to move from the airfield and to garrison Baramula. 1 Punjab, its presence at Humhom no longer being necessary, was ordered to move forward and join the Brigade at Baramula, together with one troop of Field Artillery, the Battery less this Troop having arrived at Baramula as the attack on the town was being mounted. With the dial sights for the Patiala Mountain Battery having arrived, the

Sikh Mountain gunners who had been acting as a Rifle Company with 1 Sikh were withdrawn from the battalion and ordered to take over the guns from the Patiala Mountain Battery, the personnel of which were returned to their State. On taking over, the newly formed Mountain Battery moved up from Srinagar and joined the Brigade at Baramula.

A hitch in the rank structure of two officers enforced a small change in the locations of 4 Kumaon and 2 Dogra. Lt. Col. Harbakhsh Singh had been given the local rank of Colonel and sent into the Valley to assist with the administration of the Brigade. Although not given that designation he was more or less the Administrative Commandant at the airfield. With the capture of Baramula, it was decided to move all administrative units located on the airfield, and those about to arrive, to Srinagar. An 'Administrative Commandant Srinagar', it was considered, should therefore be appointed. General Kulwant Singh, however, felt that as there were two infantry battalions located in Srinagar, the title 'Commander Srinagar Garrison' (Sri Garrison) would be better, as the Commander could then use the two battalions to deal with any situation that might arise. It was, however, very clearly laid down that all troops located in the Valley, and Sri Garrison, would form part of and be under the command and control of Headquarters 161 Infantry Brigade, and that the responsibility for all operational commitments in the Valley would rest with the Commander 161 Infantry Brigade. The change of the designation to Commander Srinagar Garrison resulted in Lt. Col. U. C. Dubey, who was many years senior to Lt. Col. Harbakhsh Singh, being placed under the command of his junior. To rectify this, 4 Kumaon which was under orders to move to Baramula was ordered to remain in Srinagar, and Lt. Col. Dubey's unit, 2 Dogra, which was to remain in Srinagar was ordered to move to Baramula.

The reorganisation completed, 161 Infantry Brigade moved out of Baramula at seven o'clock on the morning of 10 November and headed for Uri and on towards Domel. With the Brigade, at the start of the move, was one Troop of Armoured Cars of 7 Cavalry, two infantry battalions, 1 Sikh and 1 Kumaon, and a Troop of Field Artillery. 1 Punjab which was engaged in handing over Baramula to 2 Dogra was ordered to join the column as quickly as possible, and did so at ten o'clock, soon after the Brigade had entered mountainous terrain. The road to Domel, down which the Brigade was advancing, follows the south bank of the Jhelum River, and is overlooked for almost its entre length by heavily forested spurs of the Pir Panjal Range of Mountains. This forbidding mountain range runs from east to west on both the north and south banks of the Jhelum River. The terrain, which lends itself admirably to defence and ambushes, necessitated the piquetting of the heights that overlooked the road and the searching of the hills, and in consequence the rate of advance was severely curtailed. To have rushed down the road without taking the essential steps to ensure security would have been to invite disaster. These operations were being conducted against enemy fire, from light to moderately heavy, aimed at the column by odd bodies of the tribesmen who were wending their way back on foot, having failed to reach Baramula in time to move along with their comrades.

THE ADVANCE FROM BARAMULA TO URI

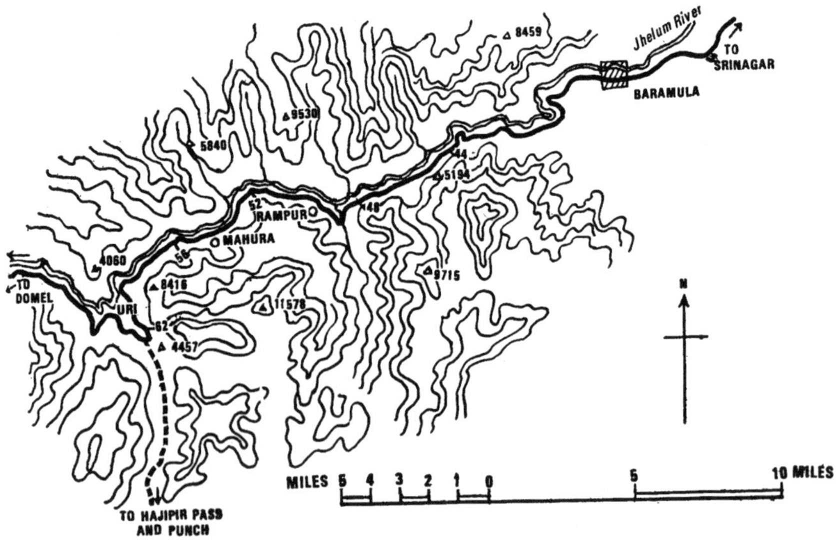

It was at this juncture that I received a staggering signal message from Major General Kulwant Singh. I was ordered to return 1 Punjab to Srinagar immediately. Assuming that there was some mistake, I signalled back that it was not possible to do so, as it would totally unbalance the Brigade which had now entered mountainous terrain, and I could only do so if a relief battalion from Srinagar was first rushed forward. I further stressed that, if anything, more units should be sent forward rather than anything being moved back. In reply, I received a curt message ordering me to comply with the order immediately. It further stated that as 1 Punjab was a parachute battalion, it was necessary to send it to Jammu to join 50 Parachute Brigade. I insisted that Major General Kulwant Singh speak to me on the wireless. Despite my arguments that to take the unit away from me at that moment would seriously affect the advance towards Domel, that 1 Punjab was unlikely to be used in a para role in Jammu, and that there was easy access to an infantry battalion in the Punjab or elsewhere to build up 50 Para Brigade, I failed to convince him that the need of 161 Infantry Brigade was greater than that of 50 Para Brigade. I was ordered to return 1 Punjab immediately, and in consequence had to call a halt to the advance.

1 Punjab, which was already on its way to occupy certain features, had to be stopped and 1 Sikh, which was deployed on other features, withdrawn to take over the 1 Punjab task. It was time-consuming and resulted in at least three hours of daylight being wasted. In addition, the complete operational plan had to be recast and modified to suit the capabilities of the two infantry battalions that remained with the Brigade. The advance became a slow and laborious affair. With the enemy taking full advantage of the situation, and darkness fast approaching, I decided to call a halt and to take up a defensive position for the night. It had been a most frustrating day. At five o'clock, after Brigade Headquarters had tucked itself into a small re-entrant, I asked the Brigade Major to check whether 1 Punjab had reported back in Srinagar, and was surprised to be informed that the unit had halted in Baramula. I spoke to the commander. Lt. Col. Kullar, and asked the reason. He told me that not long after

receiving my signal ordering him to return to Srinagar, he had been handed another one by his Signal Section cancelling the order, and ordering him to return to his last location. Assuming that the move back to Srinagar had been cancelled, he had halted in Baramula. As the signal message had been passed in clear to 1 Punjab, only the code word for Srinagar being used, the enemy had obviously intercepted the message and not knowing which place the code word for Srinagar referred to, had sent a signal message changing the code word to 'last location' and cancelling the previous order. Our security measures were immediately tightened up and all units warned to be careful regarding conversations in clear.

1 Punjab returned to Srinagar in the transport that had lifted 2 Dogra to Baramula, and was then despatched to Jammu by road to join 50 Para Brigade. The battalion was numerically weak, as mentioned earlier. It was given the task of holding Jhangar, which was well beyond its capabilities, only to be heavily attacked and mauled by the enemy operating in the Jhangar area. Perhaps the theory that a formation fights better with units that are known to it prompted the removal of 1 Punjab from 161 Infantry Brigade to 50 Para Brigade. It was certainly not because 161 Infantry Brigade was entering mountainous terrain, in which a para battalion would find itself placed at a disadvantage, since in that case, 1 Kumaon, also a para battalion, should have been removed and sent back from the Valley to rejoin its parent formation, 77 Para Brigade. Whatever may have been the reason, the removal of 1 Punjab violated a cardinal principle: instead of reinforcing success, exactly the opposite was done.

With 161 Infantry Brigade's striking force reduced to two infantry battalions, and the task in front of it demanding a third battalion, I signalled Srinagar to order 4 Kumaon to move forward and to join the Brigade as soon as was possible after first light the next morning, 11 November. In return, I received a message from Major General Kulwant Singh stating that he had formed 4 Kumaon, 6 Rajrif, the Squadron 7 Cavalry less the Troop with me, and one Troop of the Field Battery into an *ad hoc* force, and had placed it under Lt. Col. Harbakhsh Singh, the Commander Sri Garrison. As such, 4 Kumaon was not available to join 161 Infantry Brigade, and I must make do with the three battalions that I had.

I replied to this signal and stated that one battalion, 2 Dogra, was deployed in Baramula which had to be firmly held and as such could not be moved forward. I had also sent back the Troop of Field Artillery with me as the terrain was totally unsuitable for field guns and the newly formed Mountain Battery had joined me. The infantry strength was, however, extremely light, especially as the terrain was mountainous, and was placing a very great strain on the two battalions. The inclusion of a third infantry battalion in the striking force was neither a bonus nor over-insurance; it was a pressing necessity.

Major General Kulwant Singh's reaction to this request was to inform me that although the enemy had been defeated at Shalateng, he was of the opinion that odd parties of the tribal raiders were still in the Valley, and as such he wished Srinagar airfield to be well protected, Srinagar and its environs to be patrolled, and the Srinagar-Baramula road to be vigorously patrolled by a mixed force of armour, artillery and infantry. As such, he could not send anything forward. Even the suggestion that he postpone 1 Punjab's move back to Jammu and retain it as Sri Garrison's second battalion for a few days, or until such time as Uri was captured, and then review the situation and troop allocation, was rejected. I did not consider it prudent to inform him that his fears of tribal parties operating in the Valley were unrealistic, as I felt that it would act as an irritant. Consequently, 161 Infantry Brigade, seriously weakened when it should have been strengthened, advanced to Uri, being engaged by enemy parties the whole way, while Sri Garrison, with equality in infantry but stronger in armour and artillery, patrolled a Valley completely devoid of the enemy.

161 Infantry Brigade spent the night of 10 November in the area of milestone 44. It had advanced ten miles from Baramula, and, considering the enemy opposition and the thickly wooded mountainous terrain which had to be searched, the progress was reasonable. In order to retard the advance of a motorised column that might be pursuing him, the enemy had destroyed every wooden bridge on the road. This did not present any insurmountable problem as it

was possible to construct diversions around the bridge site without much difficulty. Hostile fire had on occasions been heavy but tended to be wild and inaccurate. The Brigade suffered only one casualty, unfortunately from our own fire. The Company Commander of an Independent Rifle Company, attached to 1 Sikh, lost his way in the dark and approached his command from the wrong direction. He failed to answer the whispered challenge of the sentry and was shot in the leg. The wound was not serious, but necessitated his evacuation the next morning. Apart from this incident, the night passed quietly.

The advance was resumed early the next morning, 11 November, and almost immediately came under heavy enemy fire from light machine guns sited on the hills overlooking the road. An attack was mounted to dislodge the enemy, but before the attacking troops could close with him, he withdrew. This was the typical pattern of a rearguard action by the enemy which persisted throughout the day. With the Mountain Battery unable to engage any targets, because of the lack of suitable positions for deployment, the Armoured Cars provided the supporting fire, the Humbers being particularly useful. The Daimlers also did some useful shooting, but there was no suitable target for their main armament, the two-pounder gun, until they were presented with one at Mahura. With the progress of the vehicles retarded, the Brigade reached Rampur at four o'clock that evening, having covered only six miles.

With about one and a half hours of daylight left, I was about to call a halt in order to enable the units to carry out reconnaissance and take up their dispositions for the night, and also to give the cooks a chance to prepare a hot meal for them, when the sound of an explosion was heard. A quick glance at the map left no doubt that it had emanated from Mahura, and it was realised that the enemy was employed in destroying the Power House machinery. Leaving 1 Sikh to protect the transport and escort it forward, the Troop of Armoured Cars and the Rifle Troop 7 Cavalry were ordered to throw caution to the winds and to rush to Mahura, and 1 Kumaon to follow them as fast as it could on foot. It was about five miles to Mahura, but it was only possible to do four of them, as the enemy had demolished the bridge at milestone 54. On reaching the bridge, the Armoured Cars were engaged by light automatic fire to which they replied, and in about half an hour 1 Kumaon joined them. As it did so, the sound of a second explosion rent the air. The enemy light automatic fire now increased in volume, being switched towards 1 Kumaon, but as in the previous cases it was erratic and did no damage.

There were only two alternatives, a frontal attack by 1 Kumaon, supported by fire from the Armoured Cars, which would enable us to attain speed which was so vital, or an attack from the left flank which would entail climbing a steep hill and would be time-consuming. Despite the fact that it would take much longer, the flanking attack was decided upon, as the frontal attack might have resulted in severe casualties being inflicted on the unit. The move by 1 Kumaon to climb the hill was spotted by the enemy, who increased his rate of fire. But it had little effect, and realising that a strong attack was developing against him, he prepared to evacuate his position. As he did so, five uniformed individuals, three of whom were officers, appeared on the main road from the Power House site. Rushing to a khaki-coloured Staff car which was parked on the road, facing west, they opened the doors hastily and started leaping in. Unfortunately for the occupants of the car, a Daimler Armoured Car had already trained its two-pounder gun on it, and the gunner was waiting for it to move. As it did, he pressed the trigger and scored a direct hit and the wrecked car burst into flames.

1 Kuamon reached its objective to find that the enemy had fled, and sent a platoon to search the Power House area, which was found to be clear of the enemy. An inspection of the interior of the Power House showed slabs of gun cotton, primers and fuse wire littered over the floor. One generator appeared to be damaged, one was being prepared for destruction when the enemy was disturbed, and the others appeared to be unharmed. Sand had also been lavishly thrown into the working parts of the generators. The arrival of the Brigade had, however, saved the Power House from extensive and possibly irreparable damage. It was able to commence functioning in a few weeks, and to provide Srinagar with the electric power it so badly needed.

With the dawn patrols of 12 November morning reporting the area clear of the enemy, the task of constructing a bridge at milestone 54 was taken in hand. But there was not the remotest possibility of constructing a diversion without the use of a bulldozer, as it involved cutting away a large portion of the hillside. Without Field Engineers to assist or guide us, nor any type of equipment available to bridge the 15 feet gap, the only solution was to throw boulders and branches of trees into the dry bed of the hill stream until road level was reached. This was quite a formidable task as the dimensions of the gap to be filled were 15 feet in length, 10 feet in depth and 8 feet in breadth, and the filling had to take the weight of Armoured Cars and loaded supply lorries. It was very slow work, but was completed by the afternoon of 13 November. The 'bridge' that was constructed was certainly unorthodox. It swayed gently as vehicles crossed it, but it held, and was in constant use until a Company of Field Engineers constructed a proper bridge about three weeks later.

While the 'bridge' was under construction, a Company patrol of 1 Sikh moved forward towards Uri, and reported it free of the enemy. With the vehicles across, the Brigade moved forward and occupied Uri. The diversion built by the raiders in the vicinity of the bridge demolished by Brigadier Rajinder Singh was well made, and of great assistance to us. It was in constant use for nearly six months until a Bailey bridge replaced the demolished bridge.

With the capture of Uri, 161 Infantry Brigade—composed of a skeleton Brigade Headquarters, a Troop of Armoured Cars and a Rifle Troop of 7 Cavalry, 1 Sikh, 1 Kumaon and a newly formed Mountain Battery formed after the capture of Baramula—had advanced 62 miles from Srinagar, and had been engaged in battle with the enemy almost the whole way. It was no mean achievement, and for this the credit must go entirely to the unit commanders and their men who accepted every difficulty willingly and with enthusiasm. Although still clad in cotton uniforms, and with one blanket to be shared by three men during the cold nights, they braved the enemy and the elements and got the better of both.

Uri, until the raiders razed it to the ground, leaving one brick house and two wooden ones to indicate that the area was once inhabited, used to be a flourishing little town. Situated almost half way between Domel and Srinagar, it was a most convenient halting point for the tourist and other traffic to and from the Valley, and its residents were engaged mainly in the running of wayside restaurants and cafes. At its eastern approach, a road takes off to Poonch, winding its way through the steep climb to the Haji Pir Pass on the Pir Panjal Range and then dropping towards Poonch. The Uri area is shaped like a cup, with what used to be the town at the base and encircled by high hills. To defend it is both difficult and easy—depending on the availability of a sufficient number of infantry units to man the heights, the effectiveness of medium and light automatic weapons being severely limited by the folds in the ground. With only two battalions available, 1 Sikh was deployed on the heights, the Independent Rifle Company being kept in the bowl as the battalion reserve, while 1 Kumaon was made responsible for the lower slopes and the road entries into Uri.

As soon as the capture and consolidation of Uri was signalled to Major General Kulwant Singh, who was still in Srinagar, a message was received to stay and further advance along the road to Domel, and for me to return to Srinagar the next morning for a conference.

Arriving in Srinagar at ten o'clock on 14 November, I immediately put in my logistical requirements, emphasising that winter clothing and extra issue of blankets were urgently required. A signal had already been received from Delhi that these items had been despatched, and they arrived about three days later. I also asked for the remainder of Headquarters 161 Infantry Brigade, which was still located on the Ranchi plateau in Bihar Province, to be moved to the Valley as it was no longer possible to continue to operate with a skeleton Headquarters. The party arrived in Srinagar about ten days later and, after certain adjustments, the Main Headquarters of the Brigade was established in Uri, and the Rear Headquarters at Srinagar. With the logistical problems sorted out, I was given my next task. I was ordered to hold Uri and to prepare to advance to Poonch, over the Haji Pir Pass.

This order took me completely by surprise. I explained to Major General Kulwant Singh that I had the enemy on the run, and unless I kept up the pressure he would recover and come back, and instead of our attacking him we would be attacked. I suggested that I be given additional troops and be permitted to continue the advance on the existing axis. This move, I stressed, would have two advantages: firstly, it would keep the enemy at arm's length from Uri, and secondly, when the move to Poonch took place, which I suggested should be undertaken by an ad hoc column that could be formed, it would ensure that the ad hoc column's flank was protected when moving to an returning from Poonch. This suggestion, however, was not accepted, and I was informed by Major General Kulwant Singh that he was not interested in moving towards Domel, but was interested in reinforcing Poonch which was under enemy pressure.

I was then given further instructions. I was not to carry out any type of reconnaissance of the road from Uri to the Haji Pir Pass, since if I did so it would give the enemy an indication that I was changing my axis of advance from Uri–Domel to Uri–Poonch. An accurate road report would be sent to me and I could rest assured that all details relating to the route would be impeccable. An Operation Instruction was under preparation and would reach me in a few days. When I asked when this move to Poonch was to be launched, I was informed that the actual date could not be decided just then, as it was dependent on the progress made by 50 Para Brigade which was already on the move from Jammu to Poonch but was mot making fast progress. 161 Infantry Brigade's move, I was however told, would be about 18 November. This meant giving the enemy a four days' respite, and I was most unhappy about it. But a pincer movement on Poonch had been planned, and it was essential that the jaws snapped together simultaneously.

Before leaving the conference and returning to Uri, I again stressed a demand that I had made soon after being ordered to go to Poonch, that I could only carry out the role if I was allotted a minimum of one more infantry battalion. I was assured that I need have no worries on that score. I would have adequate troops not only to form the

The demolishing of the bridge at Uri presented the raiders with a yawning gap. It was to make a difference more momentous than the gallant Brigadier Rajinder Singh could have anticipated.

Seven months later, the Madras Engineers assisted by local labour took its repair in hand.

An aerial view of the bridge under reconstruction. The complete roadway had to be built anew as the abutments had been seriously affected by the explosion.

In May 1948, the new bridge was ready for use. Bakshi Ghulam Mohammed named it "The Bogey Sen Bridge".

Embussing his battalion, Lt. Col. Ranjit Rai moved forward to Baramula to check the tribal advance. He was killed not far from where this memorial tablet stands.

Had he been successful, Baramula would not have suffered this treatment at the hands of the tribals …

… or this.

Nor would this peace loving village have experienced rape, loot and arson.

column to Poonch but also to ensure the safety of Uri in my absence from the town.

The outline plan for the relief of Poonch was for 161 Infantry Brigade to move from Uri to Poonch over the Haji Pir Pass with two infantry battalions and attached troops. One infantry battalion was to be left behind in Poonch, and the remainder of the column was then to return to Uri. The battalion left behind in Poonch was to make contact with 50 Para Brigade the day after its arrival in Poonch, in the area of Kotli. 50 Para Brigade would then take this battalion under command, and moving to Poonch be responsible for the operations in that area.

On my way back to Uri, I stopped at Baramula and had a conference with Lt. Col. U. C. Dubey of 2 Dogra. I explained to him what was about to happen, and told him that his battalion would be the one to move to Poonch and return to Uri and thence back to Baramula, the other battalion, 1 Kumaon, being left behind in Poonch. I impressed on him the need for complete secrecy, and said that as he would be leaving his rear parties at Baramula and only taking the sub-units that would be necessary, should the column be involved in a battle, no warning order should be issued to the battalion. When the battalion did move out of Baramula, it should be stated that it was going to Uri for two or three days. The transport to lift the battalion to Poonch via Uri and back to Baramula would report to him on or about 17 November. On arrival at Uri, a further conference was held with the Commanding Officers of 1 Sikh and 1 Kumaon, and 1 Kumaon was ordered to start preparations for the move, and, as it would be left in Poonch, was ordered to bring forward from Srinagar any baggage or stores left in that place.

The period 14 to 17 November passed without the enemy engaging the defences at Uri. But there were definite indications that he had halted his rush to get away and was returning slowly but surely. The inactivity enforced upon 161 Brigade was causing me a great deal of concern, and as the Operation Instruction on the move to Poonch had still not materialised, I informed the Commander Jak Force on the morning of 17 November that any further delay might result in our meeting with opposition. He suggested that I was being unduly perturbed, and said the Operation Instruction was already on its way to me.

I received it at half past ten, and noticed that instead of giving me any troops, it required me to return to Srinagar immediately the Independent Rifle Company attached to 1 Sikh, this further depleting the strength in Uri. The courier who had arrived in a jeep from Srinagar was handed message to be delivered to the Jak Force Commander. In it I stated that I was quite prepared to return the Independent Company, and would do so after the arrival of the infantry battalion which I had stressed was necessary to hold Uri with 1 Sikh while I was away on the move to Poonch.

As the Signal's jeep was on its way back to Srinagar with my message, I received a signal message from Headquarters Jak Force informing me that as the advance of 50 Para Brigade was still behind schedule, the date of my departure for Poonch would be postponed by 24 hours to 19 November. This was bad enough, but worse was to follow. I received a message from Major General Kulwant Singh, about three hours later, informing me that no infantry battalion was being released to me.

As the situation was now developing into an argument between the Force Commander and his Brigade Commander, I decided not to use the wireless or telephone, but to write a personal letter and send it to him through a LO. I explained, as tactfully as was possible, that Uri could not be held effectively without two battalions, and especially so as there were distinct signs that the enemy was moving back towards Uri. Unless I was sent one battalion to assist 1 Sikh in holding Uri, a determined enemy attack could result in the loss of the town, in which case the column to Poonch would find itself marooned and would lose all its transport. If leaving Uri to be held by one battalion was a calculated risk I would take it, but in view of the enemy strength that was building up in the Uri area, I was firmly convinced that it would lead to serious trouble and I would therefore like the battalion from Srinagar to be established in Uri before I moved out.

My LO returned without an answer, but I received it at eleven o'clock the next day, 18 November. Major General Kulwant Singh stated in his letter that he had given my arguments careful consideration but disagreed with my views. From a study of the map he had convinced himself that Uri could be effectively held with one battalion and that the introduction of a second battalion was unnecessary. Consequently, he was not prepared to send me a battalion, and the task that he had set me should be carried out with the troops that I had with me. While I was composing a reply to Major General Kulwant Singh's letter, I received a signal stating that, in view of the continued slow advance by 50 Para Brigade, my advance to Poonch would now be postponed to 20 November.

In my letter to the Force Commander, I stated that I had taken many gambles with my truncated Brigade, but to move to Poonch leaving Uri to be held by one battalion was no gamble, it was asking to be hanged, drawn and quartered. As such, I regretted that I was not prepared to move to Poonch until one battalion was moved from Srinagar and located in Uri before I moved out. A study of the map would give him no idea of the problem involved, and I suggested that he come to Uri, get a view of the terrain, and permit me to explain the defensive system on the ground. I requested that as time was fast running out, I be sent an immediate answer to my letter.

I received a curt reply on the telephone—most welcome even if curt—that 4 Kumaon would be arriving in Uri, but was not to be committed on piquets but kept in the Uri bowl. The battalion would thus take over the positions now being held by 1 Kumaon.

Chapter 11

Diversion to Poonch

THE reconnaissance report of the road from Uri to Poonch over the Haji Pir Pass had been received on 16 November and was carefully studied. It stated that it was a one-way road, had a good surface, and that the bridges, although wooden, were strong enough to take the weight of an Armoured Car. Civilian buses had used the route in the past, and therefore the civilian buses being despatched to lift the troops and stores should experience no difficulties. The average speed that the column could attain was estimated to be ten miles in the hour; while it would be slower during the climb to the Haji Pir Pass, once the Pass had been surmounted the road permitted speeding. With this data to work on, it was calculated that the 35 miles to Poonch would take about six hours for the head and eight hours for the tail of the column to reach the destination. This allowed a two-hour margin for unforeseen contingencies and halts. With the start at seven o'clock, it was estimated that the complete column should be in Poonch by three o'clock in the afternoon, which would be ideal.

With 2 Dogra having arrived in Uri from Baramula, and 4 Kumaon from Srinagar having taken over from 1 Kumaon, the Poonch column—consisting of Tactical Headquarters 161 Infantry Brigade, one Armoured and one Rifle Troop of 7 Cavalry, 2 Dogra and 1 Kumaon, a medical detachment, a few engineers, and a detachment of Electrical and Mechanical Engineers—prepared for the move. The vehicles were loaded the previous evening, and by last light all preparations, it was reported, were complete. Provided that no further postponement order was received, the head of the column would pass the start line, which was the bridge site at the eastern exit of Uri, at seven o'clock the next morning, 20 November.

As the morning mist was lifting, the column of lorries moved out of Uri and headed for the Haji Pir Pass. With the exception of a few jeeps and 15 cwt trucks, two Armoured Cars and a heavy breakdown vehicle, the remaining vehicles in the fleet were those that had been captured from the raiders after the Shalateng battle and were being driven by civilian drivers provided by the Emergency Government.

The fatality of accepting a reconnaissance report at its face value, from sources uninitiated in military requirements, soon struck the column in the face like a sledge hammer. The so-called 'good road' was in a dreadful condition, its soft and muddy surface being akin to a skating rink. The gradients in places were steep and the numerous hairpin bends were negotiable at the first try only by the jeeps and 15 cwt trucks, the civilian buses having to be manoeuvred backwards and forwards several times before they could round them. The strict instructions that no type of reconnaissance was to be carried out in the vicinity of the road to Poonch, in order to maintain secrecy, meant that the column of lorries was soon strung out helplessly on a mountain road with no hope of extricating itself should it be subjected to even light enemy opposition. There was nothing to do but move forward at a rate of under two miles in the hour. Had a road reconnaissance been carried out, the vehicles accompanying the column would have been limited to jeeps and light load carriers. The sixty civilian buses would have been discarded for smaller vehicles.

As it happened, both 2 Dogra and1 Kumaon had to debus, 2 Dogra being ordered to make its way on foot and to secure the Haji Pir Pass, while 1 Kumaon was left to protect the vehicles and to hurry them along. With our timed arrival at Poonch by the afternoon completely out of the question, 2 Dogra took up defensive positions in the Haji Pir Pass area, 1 Kumaon and the major portion of the vehicles, which had arrived soon after last light, being harboured on the road. A stage of the journey which it was expected would take about four hours had consumed twelve, and we were still only one-third of the way to our destination. That the enemy had not engaged the column was extremely fortunate.

One of the vehicles allotted for the carriage of 1 Kumaon's stores had developed a mechanical defect prior to starting from Uri, and although it had eventually been started, it proceeded to stall continuously. This vehicle and five others, all carrying the rations and ammunition of 1 Kumaon, failed to make the Pass by last light and were ordered to harbour where they were, at milestone 7, for the night, and to join the column after first light the next morning. Two platoons of 1 Kumaon were left with them as protection.

Lt. Col. Dubey of 2 Dogra and I studied the route leading from the Haji Pir Pass towards Poonch, through our binoculars. It appeared to be a good stretch of road, zig-zagging its way down the Pir Panjal Range but with easy gradients and wide corners. On reaching the plain, it ran reasonably straight into the distance. Reference to the map showed that it crossed a stream named the Batar Nullah and then ran on to Poonch. The fourteen miles that had been completed had been hell, but now our troubles appeared to be over. The twenty-one miles to Poonch should be easily completed in three hours, which meant that a seven o'clock start should find the whole column in Poonch by ten o'clock. As we sat talking, Lt. Col. Pritam Singh of 1 Kumaon joined us. He reported the main column in, and explained the position regarding the small rear party in the vicinity of milestone 7. The whole area around us presented an atmosphere of peace and calm, with no sound of a rifle shot or the crash of a mortar bomb.

Suddenly the sky in the distance was lit up by sheets of flame. It was impossible to see what was burning, but it was assumed that it was probably a haystack. The flames were seen for some considerable time and then died down. Apart from this, there were no incidents that night.

At seven o'clock on the morning of 21 November, the column set off for Poonch with the Troops of Armoured Cars leading. The road was, as we had judged the previous evening, easy going, and the transport was experiencing no difficulty. At half past eight, however,

THE ROUTE FROM URI TO PUNCH

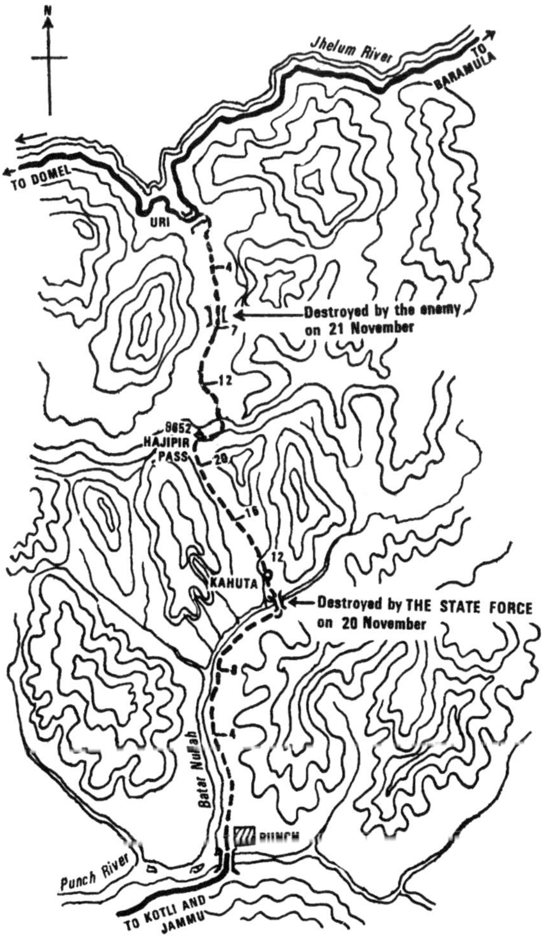

the Armour reported that it had been forced to halt because of a demolished bridge near the village of Kahuta, near the 11th milestone from Poonch. Detaching myself from the main body, I went forward to where the Armour lay halted, and was stunned by what I saw. A recently constructed wooden bridge, spanning the Batar Nullah, was a heap of charred ashes and was still smouldering in places.

The act of sabotage by an enemy agent or perhaps by the tribesmen themselves had a crippling effect. There was no way across the nullah bed for the heavier vehicles. It was strewn with large and small boulders, was ninety feet in width, and the banks were about twenty feet in height and perpendicular. The large column of civilian vehicles now began to pile up behind the Armoured Cars. The possibility of making a slope leading into the nullah bed was considered, but the idea was abandoned as it would have taken the whole day and perhaps even longer, and with both banks having to be treated simultaneously and massive boulders to be cleared in order to offer the vehicles a reasonable path, it was estimated that the time required would be not less than two days and could extend to three. There was only one solution to the problem: the baggage and stores of 1 Kumaon would have to be humped across the nullah bed and stacked on the far bank; that completed, the battalion would have to march the eleven miles to Poonch and obtain whatever transport was available to ferry its baggage forward. As the rations and ammunition lorries of 1 Kumaon had not yet arrived, the rations and ammunition of 2 Dogra were handed over to 1 Kumaon.

As the baggage of 1 Kumaon was being carried across the nullah by the men of 1 Kumaon and 2 Dogra, Lt. Col. Pritam Singh asked me whether it would be possible to leave him three jeeps. This request was agreed to, but the question was how to get them on to the nullah bed. If this could be done, the jeeps could thread their way between the boulders and run downstream until they found a sloping bank on the opposite side which would enable them to reach the road. The question of a party of men lifting a jeep and carrying it down was considered and discarded as being impossible. Then it was debated whether the vehicle would suffer serious damage if it was pushed over the side, but the 20 feet drop ruled out this course. The driver of a 15 cwt Dodge truck, with a winch attached, then came up with a brilliant idea. He suggested that if the winch hook of his vehicle was attached to the jeep, he would use his vehicle like a crane and lower the jeep gently into the nullah. This idea was immediately adopted, but two Dodge vehicles with winches were used instead of one, and to ensure that they were not dragged forward by the weight of the jeep, two Armoured Cars were lashed together and one was tied to a nearby tree with a strong rope. The two Dodge vehicles were then lashed to one of the Armoured Cars, and with the winch hooks of the Dodge trucks attached to the front and rear of each jeep, it was pushed to the edge of the bank and sent over the brink. It was then gently lowered to the nullah bed. Two further jeeps received the same treatment.

This operation completed, I walked across the nullah and on reaching the opposite bank saw a signal cable lying on the ground. I followed the cable for about thirty yards and came across a field telephone lying on the ground. I tried it, and my call was answered by a signaller of the State Force battalion in Poonch, whereupon I asked him to get me the Commanding Officer. In a few moments, a Lt. Col. Dubey announced that he was on the line. Introducing myself, I ordered him to come to the bridge near Kahuta immediately. He was hesitant to comply with the order, and I got the impression that he was very nervous. I informed him that if he did not report to me at the bridge within thirty minutes, I would be in Poonch within the next four hours and he would find himself in serious trouble.

Lt. Col. Dubey of the Jammu and Kashmir State Forces arrived at the bridge site in a jeep in about twenty-five minutes. He aporoached very slowly, and it was apparent that he was not in a very happy state of mind. When, however, he saw that we were not raiders but troops of the Indian Army, he quickly regained his composure. When he had done so, I asked him whether he knew who had burnt the bridge. His answer staggered me. He said that his platoon outpost at the bridge had seen first movement, and then lights, on the Haji Pir Pass the evening before. When he received this report, he had told it to remain in observation, but at about seven o'clock, the outpost had reported that shouts of "Pakistan Zindabad" were being raised on the Haji Pir

Pass. Convinced that the Pass was in enemy hands, he had ordered the platoon to fire the bridge and to withdraw immediately to Poonch.

He looked shamefaced and had nothing to say when I informed him that I and my troops had been on the Haji Pir Pass from the afternoon of the previous day, and I had seen the flames that had destroyed the bridge. There had been no shouts of "Pakistan Zindabad" either from the Haji Pir Pass or for that matter anywhere else, and what his outpost had reported was from their own imagination. I could only attribute their action to fright, as they had even left the telephone behind. I left him in no doubt that in giving the order to destroy the bridge, he had done exactly what the tribesmen would have prayed for but were not in a position to accomplish: the stranding of a motorised column racing to save Poonch from destruction.

Instructing him to leave his jeep at the bridge, so that Lt. Col. Pritam Singh could move forward quickly and join us on the road to Poonch when his unit and its baggage had been moved across the nullah, I set off with him, my Staff Captain, Captain Chadda, and a small escort to walk the eleven miles to Poonch. We were fortunate not to have to walk the entire distance, which would have wasted a great deal of time. The jeeps that had been lowered into the nullah bed had found a way up the bank about four miles downstream. Moving back to the bridge, they met us on the road. Taking two jeeps and sending one back to the bridge, we drove into Poonch. About three miles outside the town, on the road leading to the bridge, I found two Companies of the State Force deployed in the open space on either side. One of the Company Commanders informed me that the Companies had been rushed out to combat the tribesmen who had arrived at the bridge. The positions that they had adopted were incapable of offering more than a token resistance. I ordered Lt. Col. Dubey to instruct them to return to Poonch.

On arrival at Poonch town, Dubey took me to the palace of the Rajah of Poonch, where Brigadier Kishen Singh of the Poonch Brigade of the Jammu and Kashmir State Force met me. I asked for transport to be despatched to the bridge to lift the baggage and stores of 1 Kumaon, and the request was promptly complied with. I then went into conference with Brigadier Kishen Singh. The disastrous consequences of burning the bridge naturally formed the opening topic. I learnt that Poonch Brigade was ignorant of the fact that 161 Infantry Brigade was advancing on the town from the north and 50 Para Brigade from the south. No communication whatsoever had been sent to the Brigade by Headquarters Jak Force and a reference to the Operation Instructions issued to 161 Infantry Brigade and 50 Para Brigade substantiated Brigadier Kishen Singh's statement. Poonch Brigade did not appear on the Distribution List of either of them, while Jammu Brigade of the Jammu and Kashmir State Forces, which was operating in close co-operation with 50 Para Brigade, appeared on the Operation Instructions issued to Brigadier Y. S. Paranjpe, Commander 50 Para Brigade.

Poonch was admittedly isolated from Jammu, its road link having been cut by the enemy, and the only method of getting both the Operation Instructions to Poonch Brigade was by an air drop, or by wireless. Perhaps HQ J&K Force considered an air drop but vetoed it as they were likely to fall into enemy hands and endanger the entire operation. This was understandable. But the Tactical Headquarters of Jak Force was in Srinagar, and so was Headquarters Jammu and Kashmir State Forces, which had a direct wireless link with Poonch Brigade. A condensed message to Poonch Brigade, informing the Commander of what was about to happen was a very simple matter, yet this channel of communication was never utilised. One can only assume that the desire for strict secrecy had blurred the horizon. The fact remained that Poonch and Poonch Brigade, for whose benefit the operation was mounted, escaped attention as the Operation Instructions could not be delivered by hand. This lapse could have had far-reaching effects. Had the blown bridge been over a river instead of a dry nullah bed, 161 Infantry Brigade would not have been able to place 1 Kumaon in Poonch and would have had to return with the battalion to Uri.

Lt. Col. Pritam Singh arrived after an hour and joined in the conference. A survey of the hills overlooking the town showed many of them with sangars. Inquiries showed that these stone battlements had been constructed by the tribesmen who were in occupation of many of them. Asked whether any attempt had been made to dislodge them, Brigadier Kishen Singh replied in the negative. I immediately appointed Lt. Col. Pritam Singh as the Commander of Poonch, and had all the State Force Troops placed under his command, having first informed Brigadier Kishen Singh that I had no option but to take this step as it was essential that there was a coordinated plan for the defence of the area and I could not place Indian troops under his command. He agreed with the decision. I then ordered Lt. Col. Pritam Singh to liquidate the enemy holding the sangars on the hills as soon as he was in a position to do so, and to establish his own piquets in the area. Then the plan for the overall defence of Poonch area, and the town in particular, was discussed and an agreed solution arrived at. As matters turned out, it was the reinforcement of Poonch by 1 Kumaon that helped to save the town. 50 Para Brigade never reached Poonch. The State Force units and 1 Kumaon, with further troops that were flown in, held Poonch till a strong column was sent up from Jammu in November 1948.

We sat down to a quick lunch and, bidding good-bye to those present, I was about to get into my jeep to return to my command at the burnt bridge when I was handed an immediate signal: the small party which had been forced to harbour for the night in the area of milestone 7, on the Uri-Haji Pir Pass road, had been ambushed and mauled, and the wooden bridge at the site had been burnt. What the State Forces had done at the Batar Nullah had now been repeated by the tribesmen at milestone 7.

Speeding in a jeep to the burnt bridge over the Batar Nullah, I ordered 2 Dogra to make a dash for the Haji Pir Pass, impressing on the Commanding Officer that it was vital that the Pass be in our possession. The battalion was on its way in a matter of minutes. The drivers of the civilian vehicles, realising that an onward move to Poonch was no longer possible, had used their initiative and reversed their vehicles, parking them facing the Pir Panjal Range. Moving within a mile of the Pass, the battalion debussed and then proceeded on foot. Just before three o'clock, 2 Dogra reported that the Pass was in its possession and that no enemy had been encountered. This was good news since, had the enemy been in occupation of the Pass—and this was a live possibility—we would have faced an acute problem, particularly if he was holding it in strength. It would have called for a full-scale Brigade attack with three battalions, and all that was available was one battalion, and a raw one at that with no experience of battle.

Although it was now a Regular battalion of the Indian Army, 2 Dogra had attained that status after the termination of World War II. The original 2 Dogra, an extremely fine fighting unit with a long and distinguished record, had been lost as a result of the debacle in Malaya in 1942, and in order to resuscitate it, the Territorial Army battalion of the Dogra Regiment was given Regular status and designated the 2nd Battalion the Dogra Regiment. How this ex-Territorial Army battalion would perform, if faced by strong enemy opposition, was a matter of deep concern.

With the Haji Pir Pass firmly in our hands, the buses and load carriers which had been used to transport 1 Kumaon were now ordered to advance to the Haji Pir Pass, the Troop of Armoured Cars of 7 Cavalry acting as the Rear Guard. Just when it appeared that things were going our way, one of the Armoured Cars developed a mechanical defect and, after moving forward erratically for a few miles, petered out at the foot of the climb to the Pass. The fault lay in a defect in the electrical system, but just could not be traced. The services of the Electrical and Mechanical Engineers detachment, which had been detailed to accompany the column from Uri but which had been with the ambushed rear party, not being available, almost everyone had a shot at trying to locate the fault. After an hour had elapsed, and with the light failing fast, Major Rikhye and I were considering whether the armament and ammunition of the vehicle should be removed and the Armoured Car left in situ to be dealt with the next morning, when there was a shout from the Armoured Car driver. A jeep driver, who had stuck his head into the engine compartment of the vehicle, had started shaking various wires, and in doing so had inadvertently established contact. What he had touched he could not say, but in a few seconds the engine sprang to life, and with the

Armoured Car now leading, the tail of the column made the Pass soon after last light.

Remaining on the Pass for the night, the column continued its return to Uri the next morning, 22 November. The hills overlooking the road from the east were made the responsibility of 2 Dogra, while the Armoured Cars and the reserve Rifle Company of 2 Dogra were to protect the road itself and the transport.

Lt. Col. Man Mohan Khanna of 4 Kumaon, on hearing of the ambush at milestone 7, had on his own initiative rushed from Uri to the ambush area with two Rifle Companies of his battalion, with the intention of holding the area until the returning column linked up with him. He was, however, ordered to return to Uri by Headquarters J&K Force.

When the leading troops of our column reached the bridge at milestone 7, at a quarter past ten, they were presented with a scene of desolation. The wooden bridge, not unlike the one near Mahura but at a hairpin bend and over a re-entrant, was a mass of cinders. A few yards beyond the bridge and towards Uri was another hairpin bend, and on the far side of it, not visible to the advancing column lay the burnt-out vehicles, with ammunition scattered all over the road and against the sides of the hills. Six civilian vehicles had been burnt and three Army men and four civilians were lying dead nearby. The heavy breakdown vehicle was, however, undamaged. The mutilated corpses left no doubts that an element of Mahsuds had formed a part of the ambush party, their savagery towards the wounded and the dead following a well established and unmistakable pattern.

A subsequent inquiry into what had actually happened in the milestone 7 area showed quite clearly that it had resulted from carelessness. Having spent an undisturbed night on the hill slope overlooking the transport, the fighting element of the Rear Party, two platoons of 1 Kumaon, did not search the area after first light but, as the transport commenced to move forward, evacuated their defensive positions and moved down the hill towards the road. The leading vehicle had barely advanced thirty yards when the enemy appeared from around the bend, and shooting up the vehicles, advanced and attacked. One platoon, which was still moving down the hill, immediately took up a position and engaged the enemy, thus probably averting an even greater disaster. The platoon that had almost reached the road was able to scramble back up the hill. Had even a section been sent out to search the area before the order to move forward was issued, it could not have failed to detect the enemy on the road in the bridge area, and the ambushers would have been the ambushed. Withdrawing to Uri, the Rear Party reported the incident to the Commanding Officer of 4 Kumaon. A few days later, Pakistan Radio announced to the world that an Indian Army Brigade, with a column of over two hundred vehicles, had been annihilated by raiders on the road between Uri and the Haji Pir Pass on the Pir Panjal Range.

The task of constructing a crossing place at the bridge site was taken in hand immediately, the technique employed at Mahura of filling the gap with large rocks and boulders being resorted to. The manpower for the task was, however, about one quarter of that available at Mahura, and despite a great effort by the men, the progress was slow. It was therefore decided to cut slopes on both sides of the gap, so that the raising of the bed could be reduced by about half. At mid-day on 25 November, the crossing site, while not affording an easy passage for a heavy vehicle, was considered to be negotiable. The men had laboured for three days and three nights, and the strain had begun to tell. Two Dodge vehicles with winches made the initial crossing and, having been stationed on the far bank, with occasional assistance from the heavy breakdown vehicle, hauled out those vehicles which could not negotiate the crossing under their own power. About 60 per cent of the civilian vehicles required this treatment, but by four o'clock they were all across and the column moved to Uri, arriving an hour later.

The three days and nights spent in the vicinity of milestone 7 were fraught with danger. The enemy engaged us with long range fire, aiming it at the bridge site, presumably to stop or slow down the work. Fortunately, he kept his fire away from the sixty-eight vehicles lined up nose to tail on the road: had he set one of them alight, we would have been presented with a blazing inferno to extinguish which we had nothing. That he made only one attempt to close with the column was probably due to an ill-fated effort by about thirty tribesmen, who in the evening of 22 November made an encircling move to occupy a feature which overlooked the road. Spotted, they were permitted to advance as if undetected, and were then ambushed by a Company of 2 Dogra.

Chapter 12

Holding the Uri Bowl

The long respite from the pursuit they had feared enabled the panic-stricken tribesmen to recover their composure. From 13 November when Uri was captured they had, as a result of the "stay put" order from Jak Force, only been subjected to opposition from fighting patrols. Whether during the period 14 to 19 November they formulated the opinion that 161 Infantry Brigade was not going to continue its advance towards Domel, or assumed that the Brigade was halted in order to enable the logistical support to receive attention before any further advance was contemplated, is not known. What was clear was that when the information reached them that a very large motorised column had set out for the Haji Pir Pass from Uri, they realised that an immediate advance towards Domel was unlikely to take place, and that the Uri garrison had been weakened. They began therefore to move back towards Uri in strength.

The annihilation of the Uri garrison was almost certainly the main aim of their plan, and the party sent to the road leading to the Haji Pir Pass was probably given the task of destroying the road in order to arrest the progress of the motorised column should it decide to race back to assist in the defence of Uri. That it arrived at the wooden bridge at milestone 7 was probably due to its observing the small Rear Party on the road. As the burning of a wooden bridge is simple when compared to hacking up a road, they must have been very pleased with their effort. When the party returned to report the successful completion of their operation, the tribal leaders, now confident that the column moving towards the Haji Pir Pass would be stranded, focused their attention on the recapture of Uri.

The first objective chosen for assault was the hill feature point 4060, located to the north of Uri, code named Nalwar, and manned by a strong platoon of 1 Sikh. It held a commanding position, overlooking not only the Uri bowl but also the road leading from Uri to Baramula. While it was vital ground, it was by no means the only feature which came into that category, there being many others to the south, east and west of Uri. With 1 Sikh made responsible for piquetting the heights, the battalion had been completely deployed, with two platoons kept in the Uri bowl as the battalion reserve. To reach Nalwar piquet from Uri took over an hour, and involved crossing the River Jhelum by a steel rope bridge, wide enough to permit the passage of a loaded mule but with its wooden decking in urgent need of replacement, and thereafter was a steep climb to the top of the feature.

In the morning of 21 November, an old woman was seen approaching Uri along the road leading from the west. She was neither challenged nor stopped by the piquet located at the western exit of Uri, which had been instructed not to bar her passage. When she entered the camp, Lt. Col. Sampuran Bachan Singh, of 1 Sikh, met her and having asked her to rest awhile, offered her a cup of tea which she accepted after a certain amount of persuasion. Although she was quite a harmless old lady, she had come from the direction of the enemy, and Sampuran, a bit puzzled, asked her what she was doing wandering about by herself in a dangerous area. She said that she came from a village a few miles down the road, which was occupied by the raiders, and as she did not like their behaviour she was going to her daughter in Srinagar. She soon became talkative and stated that the enemy, present in their thousands, were mainly Pathans, and had all types of arms. When asked what the tribesmen felt about the fighting to-date, she stated that she had heard them say that they had suffered severe casualties. They were very sore about it, but they had impressed on the villagers that they intended taking their revenge in the very near future. One Pathan, who was said to be a famous tribal chief had, in fact, boasted that he would score great victories on 22 and 24

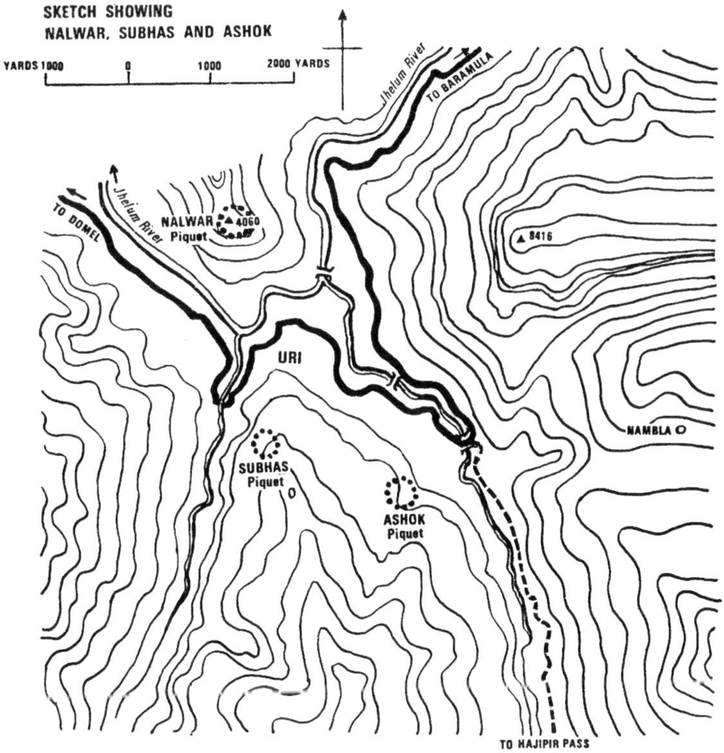

November. He had called for porters to carry the rations and beddings of his men, and in order to assure the porters that they did not have far to go, had pointed out the two features that would be attacked. She then pointed towards Nalwar and in the direction of a piquet to the south of Uri which had been given the code word “Subhas”. When she said that she would like to continue her journey, Sampuran sent for a jeep and instructed the driver to take her to Srinagar, and although she stated that she would prefer to walk, she was persuaded to accept the ride. As one could not be too careful, Srinagar was contacted as soon as the jeep had moved off and a request made that the jeep be met at the Rifle Range and guided to Bakshi Ghulam Mohammed’s residence, and Bakshi be requested to ensure that she did not move back towards Uri.

Just about this time, the information relating to the ambush at milestone 7 was received in Uri, and all the piquets were alerted. Nothing untoward happened, however, and the night of 21 November passed by quietly. Soon after ten o’clock on the night of 22 November, however, Nalwar piquet reported that a large body of the enemy was approaching. They were shouting and screaming, presumably un-nerve the piquet or perhaps to bolster up their own courage, and soon grenades began bursting all around the piquet position. It was apparent that the enemy had encircled the piquet, and it was now merely a question of time before they closed in upon it.

The 1 Sikh reserve of two platoons and the 4 Kumaon reserve of one Company were ordered to reinforce the piquet immediately. Although strange to the terrain, and it was dark, the reinforcements set off at great speed and by an almost superhuman effort reached the piquet in just under half an hour. On their way forward they encountered and dispersed the enemy who had formed up behind the piquet in the hope that it would withdraw and run into the ambush. The now heavily reinforced piquet engaged the enemy and forced him to withdraw, leaving behind two medium machine guns, one three-inch mortar base plate, five light machine guns and rifles and ammunition. From the enemy dead lying at the site, the casualties inflicted were estimated to be about one hundred killed and wounded.

Nalwar had had a narrow escape, and was immediately built up to one full Rifle Company, since it was not improbable that the enemy might have another go at it in even greater strength. The old woman's words were now taken at their face value and a plot was hatched to give the enemy a right royal reception if he came to Subhas. A rapid deployment was made in the defences and one more Rifle Company was kept ready for use at Subhas. To reinforce this piquet would have taken a great deal of time so it was decided to move a Company into a position in the close vicinity of Subhas on 24 November, so as to have it readily available in the area should its services be required. In order to conceal from the enemy, the knowledge that it was known that Subhas was the next target of attack, no abnormal activity was permitted in the piquet area. The company, platoon and section commanders of the reinforcement Company visited the piquet on 23 November, in the guise of the daily maintenance parties, and having seen the position, returned to brief the Company in the Uri bowl. The Mountain Battery registered targets all around Uri, without giving any indication that the Subhas area was the main target. With trip wire tied between the trees and booby traps laid, everything was ready by the afternoon of 24 November.

The reinforcement Company infiltrated forward during the day, and was concentrated just below the piquet line well before last light. As a result of the reconnaissances carried out the previous day, it had been decided to locate it in the already existing bunkers, which would be doubled in strength, and to get the sub-units in position so that the men could view the position and be given their tasks before darkness set in. This was successfully achieved, and the Mountain Battery laid its guns so as to answer the call for fire from Subhas without any delay whatsoever. At half past nine, although the enemy had not appeared, all the troops were ordered to "stand to". He arrived soon after ten o'clock and found himself ambushed. With Verey lights lighting up the area, the piquet was presented with a perfect target. The withering fire from the two Rifle Companies and the rain of shells that descended on him shattered the enemy so completely that he withdrew hurriedly. Reports from agents placed the enemy casualties at about two hundred killed and wounded, while intelligence from other sources stated that the Pathans were furious at having been asked to launch these attacks, which they had been assured were easy and unlikely to meet with serious resistance. Many decided to go back home.

Uri had survived two determined attacks on it, success to the enemy in either of which would have been disastrous. Had just one battalion been left in Uri when the Poonch column set out, two of the most important piquets at Uri would probably have fallen, and the Poonch column left high and dry on the Haji Pir Pass road. That the personnel with the stranded Poonch column could have found their way to Mahura, over the hills, is true, but all the vehicles, stores and baggage would have had to be be abandoned. With the enemy occupying two commanding heights at Uri, and a big boost given to his morale, to have recaptured the features would have been an extremely difficult task, necessitating the move forward from Srinagar of all the troops located in the Valley.

The advance of 161 Infantry Brigade down the road towards Domel was now out of the question. The task of reorganising the Uri defence system was therefore taken in hand. It was a disappointment for the Brigade, which had been riding on the crest of a wave, and its only consolation was that it had assisted in saving Poonch.

A comprehensive report was sent to the Commander Jak Force in Jammu, relating the experiences of the column from Uri to Poonch and back to Uri, and an assessment of the situation that faced the Poonch garrison. It was recommended that Poonch should be immediately established as an Independent Brigade directly under Headquarters Jak Force, and that Lt. Col. Pritam Singh, the Officer Commanding 1 Kumaon, should be given the rank of Brigadier. This, it was stressed, was necessary as Brigadier Kishen Singh of the State Forces was also in Poonch, and although he had agreed to place the State Force troops under Pritam Singh, his prestige, in the eyes of the officers and men of the units located in Poonch, would be undermined. This could be avoided if Pritam Singh's promotion was announced immediately.

In support of the formation of an Independent Brigade, it was emphasised that there was neither a secure motorable road nor an animal-cum-porter land route from Uri to Poonch. The administration of the Poonch garrison, unless 50 Para Brigade opened the land route from Jammu to that town, would have to be by air-drops, and by airlifts when a landing ground, which Pritam Singh had been instructed to lay out, had been prepared. The administration and possible reinforcing of Poonch could, therefore, be best effected from Jammu, where the facilities existed, and not from Srinagar which, once the snows came, would be bereft of aircraft. Finally, it was made clear that 161 Infantry Brigade could not effectively control the operations that would take place in the area of Poonch, it being impossible to influence any situation that might arise, other than by offering advice over the wireless link.

Headquarters Jak Force's reactions to these recommendations were contained in a signal making Headquarters 161 Infantry Brigade directly responsible for the administration and conduct of operations in the Poonch area. A telephonic communication with the Force Commander, explaining the difficulties of implementing the order, met with a sharp rejection. A further suggestion that as 50 Para Brigade was to link up with the Poonch garrison, an action that was now beyond the scope of 161 Infantry Brigade, he might consider placing Poonch under 50 Para Brigade was also rejected. At the time that the suggestion was made, 50 Para Brigade was still trying to make its way to Kotli, and it was the most obvious thing to do to place Poonch under its command, thereby making the link-up between 50 Para Brigade and 1 Kumaon from Poonch an operation conducted by one commander. That 50 Para Brigade did not eventually reach Kotli and the link-up with Poonch never materialised had no bearing on the insistence of Headquarters Jak Force that 161 Infantry Brigade must be wholly responsible for Poonch. The enemy and the massive Pir Panjal Range had made physical contact with Poonch impossible, and all that 161 Infantry Brigade could offer was lip service.

It did not take long for the incongruity of 161 Infantry Brigade being made responsible for Poonch to become apparent. All the demands from the Poonch garrison were forwarded to Headquarters Jak Force for implementation, and the introduction of the extra link was placing an undue load on 161 Infantry Brigade Signal Section which had to decode and then encode all the signal message before passing them on to Headquarters Jak Force. The freedom of action of the Commander Poonch garrison was also being curbed, as before he undertook any operations he was required to submit his plans for approval. He was invariably given a free hand, since to attempt to suggest a change in the commander's plans, in a battle being fought at platoon or company level, with no knowledge of the terrain other than that depicted on a small-scale map, would have been ridiculous and might have led him into a tactically unsound manoeuvre.

Meanwhile, Lt. Col. Pritam Singh had asked for the personnel of the Rear Party, who were from his battalion and who had been ambushed on the road to the Haji Pir Pass, to be sent forward to rejoin the battalion. Composed of his unit Quartermaster Staff and two rifle platoons, the battalion was unbalanced without them. These personnel were despatched from Uri to Jammu by road, with orders to report at Headquarters Jak Force, who had been requested to induct them into Poonch without delay. Headquarters Jak Force now began to see the light, and in a few days the Poonch garrison was made into a Brigade, and Lt. Col. Pritam Singh given the rank of Brigadier. He was a tough, rugged soldier, eminently suited for the role that he was charged with. That he held Poonch, which was isolated for nearly one year, speaks volumes for his fighting qualities and ability.

With Poonch off its hands, 161 Infantry Brigade took stock of the situation facing it in Kashmir. 1 Punjab having moved to Jammu after the capture of Baramula, and now 1 Kumaon placed in Poonch, the Brigade was back to four infantry battalions. The terrain that it was responsible for, and the task that faced it, were both formidable. After careful consideration, it was assessed that one more infantry battalion was the minimum requirement, and in view of the fact that the Brigade had surrendered one battalion, 1 Kumaon, for the defence of Poonch, it was considered automatic for Headquarters Jak Force to replace it. A request for the extra battalion, together with the deployment of the Brigade on the arrival of the new unit in the Valley, was sent to Headquarters Jak Force. It was specifically stated in the request that the deployment of the Brigade, including the infantry battalion asked for, was based on holding the territory recaptured from the tribesmen. Two battalions were required to hold Uri, one to protect the thirty-two miles of road in-between Uri and Baramula, one battalion to hold Baramula and its environs, and one battalion to be held in reserve in Baramula.

The signal from Headquarters Jak Force was a flat refusal to send in another battalion, with a rider included which informed me that my responsibility was not only the area captured from the tribesmen, but the whole of Kashmir and Ladakh.

For the first time since I had taken over command of 161 Infantry Brigade, I began to wonder whether Jak Force, and perhaps even Army Headquarters, were really serious about the operations in the Valley. First the security of Jammu had been given pride of place when 1 Punjab was whisked away from the Brigade soon after it had advanced from Baramula and no replacement was agreed to, then Poonch was given preference rather than an advance towards Domel, and, once again, no replacement for the battalion placed in Poonch. Although I did not mention it to my Staff Officers, I had a feeling they shared the impression that was gaining strength in me that 161 Infantry Brigade was the orphan child of Jak Force, and that the Kashmir Valley was regarded as a secondary theatre of operations compared with Jammu and Poonch.

With the fifth infantry battalion denied to 161 Infantry Brigade, there was no option but to deploy the troops available in such a manner that the Brigade could honour its commitments without last-minute adjustments. The following dispositions were, therefore, adopted:

URI

Main Headquarters 161 Infantry Brigade
One Mountain Battery
One Troop Field Artillery
One Field Company, Madras Engineers
1 Sikh
4 Kumaon
3 Light Field Ambulance.

BARAMULA

One Battery Field Artillery less one troop
One Squadron Armoured Cars 7 Cavalry less one troop
2 Dogra.

SRINAGAR

Rear Headquarters 161 Infantry Brigade
Headquarters Sri Garrison
One Troop 7 Cavalry
6 Rajrif
Motor Transport Company, ASC
Composite Platoon, ASC
Ordnance and EME detachments.

This deployment left the vital line of communication between Baramula and Uri completely without troops, except for the daily move down the road by a Troop of Armoured Cars from Baramula. To leave it unprotected by night was not a justifiable risk, but it was dictated by the paucity of troops. With the troops committed to piquets and living in bunkers, it was essential that they should be relieved after a reasonable spell of time, and the infantry battalion located in Srinagar was, therefore, not only the relief battalion but also the Brigade reserve. The system of relief decided upon was for the battalion in Srinagar to move to Baramula, the battalion in Baramula to Uri, and one of the Uri battalions to Srinagar. This ensured that Uri was always garrisoned by a battalion that had spent some time in the area and knew it well.

The remainder of Brigade Headquarters had arrived from Ranchi on 26 November, and after certain elements moved forward to join Main Headquarters in Uri, the Rear Headquarters settled down in Srinagar.

The enemy had meanwhile become very active on the Uri front and engagements by night became a regular feature. The writing was on the wall: he was going to make another determined attempt to recapture Uri.

Between the period 22 November, when Nalwar piquet was first attacked, and 9 December, the piquets protecting Uri were assaulted sixteen times in varying strength. The attacks were invariably mounted after dark, and on some nights two, and even three, attempts would be made on the same piquet. The enemy, however, had no success, as the piquets stood firm and struck back hard. After each attack on a position, the piquet location was studied and adjustments made to strengthen it even further. In certain cases, it necessitated the re-siting of the piquet, some being subjected to such treatment on as many as six occasions. Meanwhile, every effort was being directed towards not giving the enemy a free hand to dictate the shape of the operations. Our patrols continued to be very active, the long range ones penetrating deep and harassing the enemy. He did not appear to be anxious to close with them, preferring to discourage them from advancing too close with fire from extreme ranges. Patrolling alone, however, was no adequate answer to combating the enemy's designs. The area was extensive, mountainous and in places thickly forested. While enemy movements could be watched and neutralised by day, there were many hours of darkness which gave him ample scope.

161 Infantry Brigade had, from the date of arrival of its first unit in the Valley, been faced by an enemy many times its number. This had necessitated the surrendering of the initiative to him on occasion, but it had always been wrested back at the first opportune moment. With the Brigade now tied down to a defensive role, the initiative had passed back to the enemy, and it would be months before it could be regained. This involved the dictation to us of the place, date and time of his attacks by the enemy, who had the ability to achieve surprise. In order to combat this dangerous factor, it was essential that the Brigade was forewarned of possible enemy actions, and this could only result from a very efficient Intelligence system. Utmost attention was therefore given to building up such a system, the standard aimed at being that the Brigade should always be a clear jump ahead of the enemy. Only then would it be possible to redeploy the troops in sufficient time to counter a threat on a lightly held piquet, or to move them to an enemy target that was not being manned.

Vigorous patrolling, round-the-clock interceptions of all the enemy's wireless traffic, strict security precautions to be observed by all ranks in conversation with strangers, or in their hearing, and in all communications on telephone or wireless links were intensified, and constant reminders issued. But these measures were not nearly sufficient; they had to be supplemented by the use of reliable agents. I therefore decided to visit the Emergency Government and to request it to make available to me a number of individuals with an intimate knowledge of the area between Baramula and Domel. These individuals, I intended stressing, should be those whose occupation in the past made it necessary for them to wander about the area. This would ensure not only that they knew the area well, but that their presence in it would not arouse suspicion. The personnel whom I had in mind for the role were the Forest Rangers.

It was my intention to approach Bakshi Ghulam Mohammed, who had been a pillar of strength, and, apart from the personal bravery that he had displayed more than once, had impressed me as being a man of action. The idea of approaching Bakshi was not uninfluenced by a marked change that I had noticed in Sheikh Abdullah over the short period that I had known him. The change was not in his attitude to me—he was always very courteous and friendly—but to the over-all situation in Kashmir. From an individual who had initially evinced keen anxiety regarding the safety of Kashmir and its people, as the military situation improved he had become obsessed with his own importance. His interest had veered from the tackling of the many pressing problems which demanded his undivided attention and time, to the building up of his popularity with the masses. On second thoughts, however, I decided to pose my problem and request to Sheikh Abdullah, since he was after all the leader of the Emergency Government.

As it had become a routine matter for me to call on Sheikh Abdullah every time I visited Srinagar, in order to brief him on the situation, on arrival I was led straight into his drawing room. As Bakshi Ghulam Mohammed, D. P. Dhar and Ghulam Mohammed Sadiq, who were normally present during my visits were away at the time, they were summoned to come over to Sheikh's house, and I sat down with Sheikh Abdullah to have a cup of tea. Every time that I visited Sheikh Abdullah, he would sooner or later resurrect the unfortunate case of the two National Conference Volunteers who had been killed on the night of 5 November and tell me what a tragic loss it had been. The first few times I reiterated my sympathy and said that it had been an unfortunate accident. But when I found the matter being brought up again and again, I felt it was time for me to put a few basic facts before him.

I asked him how many times he had demanded an apology from the tribals who had killed thousands of people of Kashmir in their advance to the Valley. Those killings had been deliberate murder, without any semblance of an accident. I could see that he was taken aback and was searching for an answer. Without waiting for his reply, I pointed out that in defending the Valley, 161 Infantry Brigade had never at any time either asked for, or used, a single man from the National Conference volunteers to take up arms and assist it in battling against the tribals. It had not done so at the time of the battle of Badgam, when the situation was precarious, nor when the tribesmen were four miles from Srinagar, at Shalateng. The request had not been made because, even had I produced the weapons of the sick and wounded in the hospital and at Badami Bagh Barracks and handed them over to the National Conference volunteers, they would have been untrained and unskilled in their use. To have moved them into the battle area would probably have resulted in their suffering casualties because of their inability to operate tactically, and I could rightly have been labelled a murderer. The battle had, therefore, been fought entirely by my weak Brigade. The Brigade had suffered casualties in both officers and men in the various engagements that it had fought, but had accepted them willingly in order to save the Valley from the bloody massacres that had drenched Muzaffarabad and Baramula. The despatch of parties of National Conference volunteers on information-obtaining missions, I reminded him, had been ordered without the request or the knowledge of 161 Infantry Brigade. That they had done good work was undeniable, and I had greatly appreciated the reports that I had received from him. He had dwelt at length at my first meeting with him on the fate that had befallen Maqbool Sherwani, one of his most loyal and competent

Volunteers, at the hands of the tribal raiders. Sherwani had first been virtually crucified and then shot by the tribesmen: in short, he had been murdered. Yet, after the first meeting, he had never mentioned Sherwani's name to me again.

At this point Sheikh Abdullah tried to halt me, but I was in no frame of mind to be stopped and sought his indulgence for just a few more minutes. I then related to him the incident in which a Company Commander had been shot in the leg by a sentry of his own Company, for failing to answer a challenge made after dark, and explained to him that incidents such as this had happened in the past and would happen again in future wars. Then turning to Badgam, I reminded him of my report in which I had stated that the 4 Kumaon Company had been shot at from the rear by individuals located in the houses in Badgam. While expressing sympathy, he had dismissed the incident with the remark that Badgam had always been a troublesome village. Major Somnath Sharma and many of his men had been killed in the battle, and I had stated at the time that while he might consider Badgam a bad village, I was of the opinion that the armed men in the village were probably tribals who had infiltrated into it and held the people to ransom. The point I wished to stress, however, was that Major Sharma had shown deep concern for the village and had not fired back at those who were harassing him, lest innocent people were killed or wounded. It was well within his right to have done so, as his command was being endangered, but he stayed his hand and spared the lives of the villagers. This incident alone should be a clear indication that my troops were not trigger happy, and kept their heads in deciding whom to shoot at and whom to avoid.

Finally I asked Sheikh Abdullah a pointed question: If Maqbool Sherwani's torture and murder at Baramula was any indicator of the tribesmen's attitude, and had my Brigade been defeated at the battle of Shalateng,what did he visualise would have happened to him as the head of the National Conference volunteers? "If Sherwani on capture was murdered, what is the treatment that would have been meted out to the people of Srinagar, and yourself in particular?"

Sheikh Abdullah did not answer my question. He suggested that my tea had gone cold, and ordered that it be taken away and replaced by a fresh cup.

Bakshi Ghulam Mohammed, Ghulam Mohammed Sadiq and D. P. Dhar arrived soon after and within minutes of one another. When they had settled down, I gave a resume of the latest situation, and having completed it, suggested to Sheikh Abdullah that as he was busy with other pressing problems and I had a few points for discussions, I might take them up with Bakshi and any others that he might care to bring along to my Rear Headquarters. Sheikh agreed, and Bakshi, Sadiq and D. P. Dhar came to my Rear Headquarters.

I suggested this since it would have been in the nature of an anti-climax if, having impressed on Sheikh Abdullah the fact that 161 Infantry Brigade had never committed a single inhabitant of Kashmir in battle or on a dangerous mission, I now made a request for some to risk their lives in a dangerous role. Bakshi, Sadiq and D. P. Dhar, I knew, would take a more objective view and if it was possible to meet my request, they would immediately provide me with the right material.

I explained to Bakshi, Sadiq and D. P. Dhar the situation that faced 161 Infantry Brigade, and stressed that only an efficient Intelligence coverage of the area would neutralise the advantage held by the enemy, and, having described the type of individual who would best fit the bill, suggested the Forest Rangers. There was immediate agreement, and D. P. Dhar was given the responsibility for selecting and sending me the personnel. The Forest Rangers arrived the next day and were detailed for duty with Brigade Headquarters and certain selected units. Fully conversant with every trail, marked or unmarked on the maps, they moved across the mountains and through the forests with incredible speed, and produced the most accurate information regarding the enemy strengths, location and movements. In addition, as the maps of the area were quite inaccurate in certain areas, they were most useful in removing points of doubt and enabling corrections to be made.

This contribution to 161 Infantry Brigade's effort was quite outstanding, but Bakshi perhaps did the Brigade an even greater service. In the course of our conference, I had mentioned to him that I had often met an individual named Pir Maqbool near Mahura. He had told me that he lived in a village in the area, and had asked me more than once if he could be of any service. He appeared to be a good type, and as he had a certain amount of influence in the area, I suggested that he might be able to assist. Bakshi Ghulam Mohammed cautioned me to be very careful in my dealings with Pir Maqbool, and advised me not to display any suspicion but not to let him come anywhere near my troops. I made a note of this advice, passed it on to my unit commanders, and politely resisted all Pir Maqbool's suggestions that he come to Uri whenever he had shot any wild game to present it to me. I would go out and meet him on the road near Mahura. Bakshi's warning was timely, as Pir Maqbool defected to Pakistan some time later and is presumably still there.

The existence of the 1,854 officers and men of the Jammu and Kashmir State Forces in Badami Bagh Barracks, in Srinagar, came to light about this time. It was suggested to me by Headquarters Jak Force that some of them might be usefully employed in the collection of Intelligence, but it was rejected for obvious reasons. Intelligence, battlefield intelligence in particular, is not a subject that can be treated light-heartedly. Those engaged in obtaining it must have unbounded courage, and be prepared to sacrifice their lives. Fictitious reports are more dangerous than no reports at all, and can jeopardise the safety of a whole command. The attitude that had been adopted by the State Force personnel in Badami Bagh Barracks had shown a marked disinclination to face the enemy, and it was hardly likely that it had undergone any change. The Forest Rangers, on the other hand, were brave to the marrow, and no matter how perilous the mission allotted to them, never failed to carry it out with both speed and efficiency.

During the first week of December, the tactics employed by the enemy underwent a radical change. The battle formations adopted made it obvious that the enemy was composed not solely of tribesmen, but included a percentage of either regular or irregular troops. Patrols also reported having seen sub-units of various sizes dressed in uniforms and equipped with modern weapons and wireless sets, while the

Uri used to be a flourishing little town until the tribal raiders razed it to the ground.

Piquets, heavily bunkered, were located on the lofty heights overlooking Uri to keep the enemy at bay ...

… whilst the swift flowing Jhelum River roared by.

Reconnaissance patrols were also active, studying every inch of the country, in order to keep 161 Brigade one jump ahead of the enemy at all times.

The initial part of the route from Uri to the Haji Pir Pass was easy going, but soon after commencing the climb it became tortuous.

The Haji Pir Pass, bleak and desolate, but commanding a wonderful view of both sides of the Pir Panjal Range. The sheets of flame from the bridge across the Batar Nullah, destroyed by the State forces, were clearly visible from here.

This bridge constructed in the dark at the western exit of Uri by the Madras Engineers heralded the Spring offensive of 1948

The tribals were meanwhile moving to the site of this bridge at M. S. 7 and their successful ambush. The damage is being surveyed by Maj. Gen. Kulwant Singh and Brigadier L. P. Sen

Maintaining a piquet in winter was hard work and called for extreme fitness of both men and animals …

… when the snows melted it was no relief as the sun's rays were hot and equally trying.

What the mules were unable to negotiate earned them a well earned rest …

… but men had to take over the heavy loads and scale the steep mountain sides.

standard of the enemy's wireless communications showed a marked improvement, indicating that they were in the hands of well trained signallers. The almost regular nightly assaults on the piquets, however, decreased in the weight of the attacks, and there were reliable reports that the enemy was moving to the feature running from the Haji Pir Pass to Uri with the intention of occupying a defensive position. Whether the weather had dictated this change in tactics, or whether there was some deeper plan could not be fathomed. Light snowfalls had commenced on 6 December, but the snow had melted on striking the ground. On the night of 8 December, however, the fall had been heavy, and the mountains surrounding Uri were eight inches deep in snow.

On 9 December, one platoon of 4 Kumaon was ordered to carry out a reconnaissance along the feature leading to the Haji Pir Pass, as far as the village of Bhatgiran, and to confirm or deny a strong report that the enemy was in that area. The going, because of the snow, was heavy and difficult, but the platoon made good progress and at mid-day reached a point from where it could see the village, which consisted of a few huts. As the platoon commander took up his binoculars to search the area, the platoon came under very heavy fire from what was a well entrenched enemy. Realising that he was faced by a minimum of two Rifle Companies, the platoon commander decided to withdraw, having successfully completed his mission. The enemy followed the withdrawing platoon, which fought a skilful rearguard action and passed through its own piquet line unscathed. Engaged by the piquets, the enemy withdrew.

The next day, 10 December, a Company of 1 Sikh, under the command of Major Ajaib Singh, was sent out to engage the enemy and to force him to withdraw. The enemy was engaged, but was far too well entrenched. The Company of 1 Sikh then withdrew in good order, the enemy following up once again but being repulsed by the firm base piquets. Although it had not suffered any casualties, the Company felt that it had delivered quite a knock to the enemy. It was thought possible that he might decide that things were becoming unpleasant and withdraw. On 11 December, therefore, one section was sent forward to ascertain the position, but on return it reported that there were very definitely two enemy Companies in position with a possible third in depth.

The enemy had meanwhile proclaimed his presence in the area. At about ten o'clock, while the section was moving forward, he brought the road leading into Uri from the east under fire from light machine guns, enforcing the halting of all traffic, and in fact placing Uri in a state of partial siege. The Brigade was now left with no option. The enemy just had to be forced to withdraw. Given the paucity of troops, however, forming a striking force of reasonable strength was a problem. Two Rifle Companies of 4 Kumaon were collected by thinning down the piquets held by that battalion. Sent forward to engage the enemy, the Companies got to within one hundred yards of the enemy, the Companies got to within one hundred yards of the enemy defences and came under very heavy fire. It was soon discovered that the enemy was a battalion in strength, well dug in and well led, and identified as Frontier Scouts. Just when the situation facing the two Companies, which had been pinned to the ground, was getting very serious, one of our fighter aircraft happened to fly over Uri, arriving purely by chance. The pilot was contacted by ground control and directed over Bhatgiran, and briefed that the position would be indicated to him by a "T" laid out with ground panels. Simultaneously the Commander of the two Companies of 4 Kumaon was ordered to display a "T" with his ground panels. A "T" laid out with ground panels indicates to the aircraft very close contact with the enemy, the enemy being at the other end of the head of the "T". How the pilot managed to detect in the snow the ground panel signal, which is white in colour, is a mystery but see it he did, and diving into the attack he caught the enemy with two bombs and then straffed the position. Under the cover of this support from the air, the two 4 Kumaon Companies were able to break contact and withdraw.

With the reinforcements despatched from the Kumaon Regimental Centre, to bring 4 Kumaon up to war establishment, had arrived a platoon of boys. These lads were from the Boys Company which was customary to have in each Regimental Centre. The sons of ex-soldiers and serving personnel of the Regiment, they were recruited and trained from a very young age in the Centre until such time as they reached the age laid down for enlistment. With their education and careful training, they were regarded as potential non-commissioned officers and specialists. In its anxiety to reinforce 4 Kumaon, the Regimental Centre had sent to the battalion almost everyone it held who was from 4 Kumaon, and the boys earmarked for 4 Kumaon had been included in the party. Lt. Col. Man Mohan Khanna, commanding 4 Kumaon, was not a little annoyed when he discovered this, and gave orders that these youngsters were not to be drafted into the Rifle Companies but were to be formed into a special platoon which he placed in the charge of a specially selected platoon commander. He issued instructions that under no circumstances was the Boys Platoon to be placed in a situation which might result in its being involved in a battle. The boys, however, were not happy at being kept in cotton wool, and as a result of their persistent pleas to be allowed to see some fighting, when his two Companies moved out to engage the enemy on the morning of 11 December, Lt. Col. Khanna agreed that they could move as far as the piquet line and take up a position there. He, however, instructed the platoon commander to locate them on a safe flank, and to give them the impression that they were holding an important position, but which would in fact be well out of harm's way.

As the two withdrawing Companies of 4 Kumaon were nearing the piquet line, the enemy, who was following, decided to outflank them and sent a platoon on a wide flanking movement to get into position and attack them from the rear. This enemy platoon apparently saw what appeared to be an unoccupied knoll in a very suitable position from which it could achieve its task, and moved towards it. This knoll was the one position considered safe and was occupied by the Boys Platoon. Seeing the enemy heading towards his position, the platoon commander alerted his command, but ordered the boys not to fire except on his order. He found himself in a peculiar position. He had been instructed not to involve the boys in a battle, but a situation had arisen in which the boys were going to be involved in battle whether he liked it or not. When the enemy platoon had come to within fifty yards of the knoll, he realised that his platoon had to open fire and he gave the order to do so. The aim of the boys was straight and true, and a completely surprised enemy halted in his stride and then hastily withdrew, leaving behind his dead and a few wounded. The chest of every boy in that platoon expanded two inches. They had had a stunning success in their baptism of fire, had routed the enemy platoon that had tried to challenge them, and had inflicted casualties on it without receiving a scratch. It was no longer possible for anyone to tell them that they were too young to be soldiers.

With the road leading into Uri was still unusable owing to enemy fire, it was decided that only a full-scale attack by a battalion could remove the thorn in our side. Apart from making the road unusable, located as he was, the enemy could mount a heavy attack on the piquet line which, if successful, could almost make Uri untenable for us. It was not an attack that could be delayed. With heavy snowfalls almost every day, the area between the piquet line and the enemy was already about two feet deep in snow. To move forward to the attack would be hard enough, but then the attacking unit would also have to return. The enemy, on the other hand, would move downhill towards Uri, and if successful in his attack, would stay put. The only way in which it was possible to assemble one battalion for the attack was to relieve 1 Sikh of its defence commitments, and to hold the piquet line with a reduced strength by deploying the Brigade reserve of two Companies of 4 Kumaon.

The orders given to Lt. Col. Sampuran Bachan Singh, commanding 1 Sikh, were that his unit would move out of Uri in the early hours of the morning of 13 December, would pick up his sub-units in the piquet area, which would have been taken over by 4 Kumaon, and advance along the ridge towards Bhatgiran. His firm base would be the 4 Kumaon held piquet line. When contact with the enemy had been made the battalion was to attack and force the enemy to withdraw. This having been achieved, the battalion was to withdraw to Uri by the same route taken when advancing to Bhatgiran, and having passed through the firm base of piquets was to come into the Uri bowl. Those sub-units of the battalion which would join it on its reaching the piquet line, would return to their respective piquets, but the 4 Kumaon personnel holding them in their absence would not be withdrawn until the next morning. As the Company commanded by Major Ajaib Singh had carried out the patrol on 10 December and knew the area, it was suggested to, and agreed with, the Commanding Officer that Major Ajaib Singh's Company should lead the advance. Regarding air support, Headquarters Jak Force had been approached and had stated that it would be provided, weather permitting. As the weather was still murky, it was doubtful whether it would materialise.

In the early hours of the morning of 13 December, 1 Sikh moved out of Uri, and having reached the piquet line was joined by its sub-units from the piquets. Then, led by Major Ajaib Singh's Company, the battalion advanced along the ridge towards Bhatgiran. With further snowfalls, the going was heavy and difficult, but satisfactory progress was made, and by mid-day, the battalion reported that it was in the area of the previous contacts made with the enemy. During the advance, the leading Company had observed and reported small parties of the enemy, probably those manning outposts or observation posts, abandoning their positions and rushing back. They made no effort either to slow down or halt the advance of 1 Sikh. This was, however, no reason to conclude that the main strength of the enemy had been withdrawn from the area. Unfortunately, that was the conclusion arrived at by the Commanding Officer.

Two factors had contributed towards Sampuran Bachan Singh finding himself the Commanding Officer of 1 Sikh. The first was the removal of all British Officers from the battalion prior to its move into the Valley, and the second, the death of Lt. Col. Ranjit Rai on 27 October on the outskirts of Baramula. A Territorial Army Officer posted with the Sikh Regiment, he was neither professionally qualified nor competent to command a Regular battalion. Lt. Col. Rai had, in fact, at his initial briefing at Army Headquarters, requested that he should be sent a capable Second in Command, as Sampuran, by virtue of his service in the Territorial Army, was now his senior Major and as such his Second in Command, but was incapable of holding down that appointment. With this background, but, owing to some previous friction between himself and his most capable Company Commander,

Major Ajaib Singh, he placed his confidence in and leaned heavily on his Subedar Major.

Subedar Majors, as a whole, are excellent soldiers with years of service and experience behind them. Rising from the ranks to the position of the senior Junior Commissioned Officer of a unit is no mean feat, but they understandably have their limitations in so far as tactics and strategy are concerned. Their main experience as leaders is generally limited to the command of a platoon, and on occasions to that of a company. In training during peace, the Junior Commissioned Officer is never exercised in command of a unit of the size of a battalion; it is confined to the company level. There have been cases during a war when a Subedar Major has taken command of a battalion which has suffered a total loss of all its officers, but this is for a limited time until the arrival of reinforcement officers, and is exceptional. The appointment, peculiar to the Indian Army, was created during the period when the officering of the Indian Army was confined exclusively to the British, the main function of the Subedar Major being to advise the Commanding Officer on matters pertaining to the customs, peculiarities, welfare and morale of the men enlisted in the unit. Never at any time has a battalion commander shed his responsibility for the tactical handling of his unit and made it the prerogative of the Subedar Major.

Having reached the point of his previous contact with the enemy, on 10 December, Major Ajaib Singh halted his Company, placed it in position and walked back to consult his battalion commander. He informed him that although he had not been fired upon, the enemy was in the area, and a battalion plan of attack should now be formulated. To his amazement, Sampuran Bachan Singh stated that he did not accept the report that the enemy was in the area, and despite Major Ajaib Singh's protests that his reading of the situation was the correct one, Sampuran turned to the Subedar Major for his opinion. The Subedar Major immediately agreed with his Commanding Officer. He too was of the opinion that there was no enemy in the area. Now convinced that he was correct, Sampuran, ignoring his senior Company Commander, decided after a consultation with the Subedar Major that it was time to return to Uri. Moreover, instead of ordering the battalion to retrace its steps in accordance with the orders that had been given to him, he decided that it would be quicker and easier to descend from the heights to the road leading from the Haji Pir Pass to Uri.

When given this order, Major Ajaib Singh protested most vehemently. He informed the Commanding Officer that it violated all

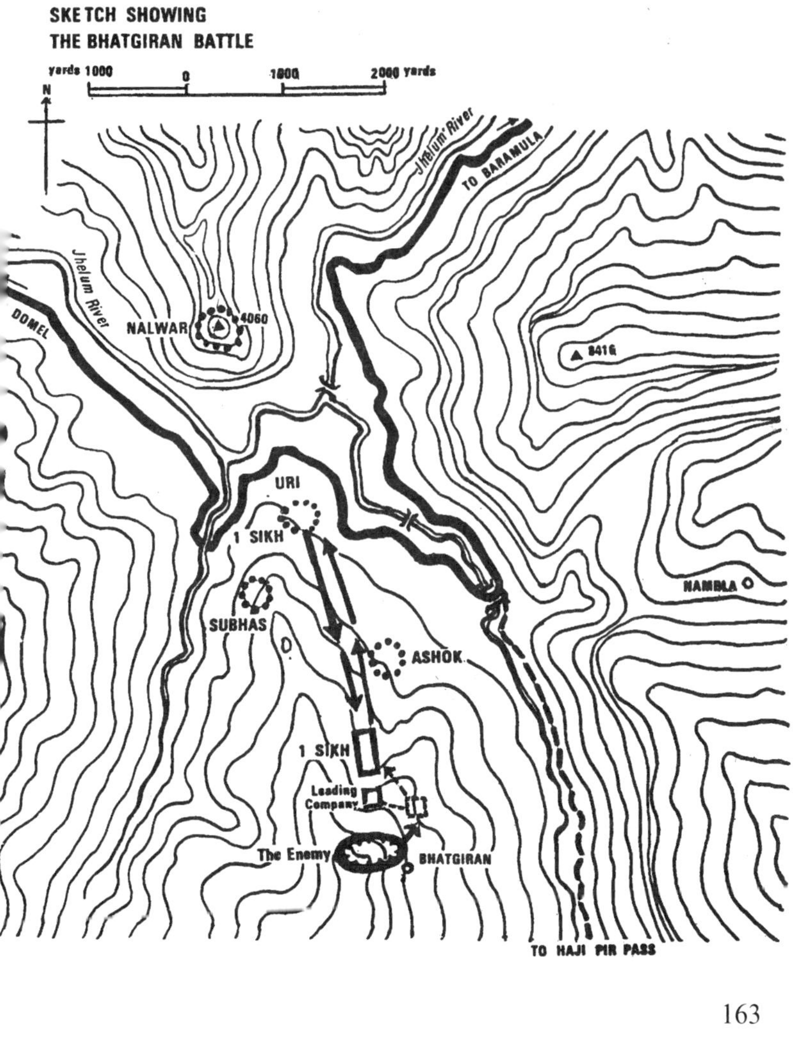

the tenets of mountain warfare, and to order the battalion to move from the heights, down a re-entrant, and on to the road was asking for serious trouble and could even be suicidal. Once again Sampuran Bachan Singh consulted the Subedar Major, who agreed with the Commanding Officer's plan—he could hardly do otherwise as he had helped to formulate it—and Sampuran, turning to Major Ajaib Singh, repeated his order. Ajaib Singh continued to protest but was cut short by his Commanding Officer who told him not to argue and to do what he was told. As he walked back to his Company to pass on the battalion commander's intention and plan, undetected by 1 Sikh was a strong enemy battalion of Frontier Scouts a bare one hundred yards away, watching every movement and awaiting an opportunity to strike.

Returning to his Company, Major Ajaib Singh gave the necessary orders to move to the road via the re-entrant. The leading platoon rose, and followed by the rest of the Company, commenced the move. No sooner had the whole Company entered the re-entrant than it was trapped by murderous fire that poured into it from the well-concealed enemy overlooking the re-entrant. Here was a situation that the enemy had prayed for but had never thought possible. It was a colossal blunder that could not go unpunished, and it did not. Lt. Col. Sampuran Bachan Singh immediately realised the extent of his error, and in an effort to extricate the trapped Company, ordered the nearest platoon to attack the enemy. This platoon was led by Jamedar Nand Singh, VC who ordering it to fix its bayonets, charged headlong into the enemy. The full fury of the enemy fire was then turned on this platoon. It was decimated, but it permitted Major Ajaib Singh's Company to scramble back to the top of the ridge. Then started a fierce fire battle between the two battalions.

Taken completely by surprise and caught out in the open, 1 Sikh found itself at a serious disadvantage, and Sampuran Bachan Singh having been shot in the leg, 1 Sikh was ordered to withdraw. The withdrawal of 1 Sikh was hotly pursued by the enemy, and the pursuit was only arrested by the excellent work of the firm base piquets, including the one manned by the Boys Platoon of 4 Kumaon, who, seeing action for the second time in a matter of days performed like seasoned warriors. 1 Sikh descended from the Bhatgiran feature into the Uri bowl.

1 Sikh suffered 61 killed and 59 wounded, a high percentage of the casualties being the officers and non-commissioned officers. As a battalion, it was operationally unfit for any further action until such time as it could make good its losses in leaders. It was ordered to prepare to move back to Srinagar and was replaced in Uri by the 6th Battalion The Rajputana Rifles (6 Rajrif). With Sampuran Bachan Singh wounded, Lt. Col. Harbakhsh Singh, who was Sri Garrison Commander, was relieved of that appointment and appointed the Commanding Officer. That many who were wounded in the Bhatgiran battle survived is to the credit of 3 Light Field Ambulance, located in Uri. Thirty-six seriously wounded were operated upon in 27 hours, the medical personnel resting only when the last patient was off the operation table.

With 1 Sikh now operationally unfit for battle, a request was sent to Headquarters Jak Force for two more battalions. One was required in replacement of 1 Sikh, and, in view of the fact that in a week or so the Banihal Pass would be snow-bound and would remain in the state until the following spring, another to meet unforeseen eventualities. It was stressed that with 1 Sikh non-operational, 161 Infantry Brigade consisted of two Regular Battalions, 4 Kumaon and 6 Rajrif, and one Territorial Battalion (now turned Regular), 2 Dogra. With the advent of snow within the next few days, the Brigade would be marooned in the Valley for four to five months, with no hope of being reinforced should this be necessary. It was impressed on the Commander Jak Force that the demand had not been pitched high, nor was it unreasonable in view of the very large stretch of territory that had been made the responsibility of the Brigade.

Headquarters Jak Force agreed to moving in only one more battalion, asserting that the request for a second battalion was lavish and unnecessary. The 3rd Battalion The Garhwal Rifles (3 Garhwal), commanded by Lt. Col. L. S. Negi was moved to the Valley, and none too soon, as on 20 December, forty-eight hours after 3 Garhwal arrived, a heavy snowfall blocked all road communications over the Banihal Pass.

161 Infantry Brigade found itself segregated from the rest of Jak Force, by road and by air, until the first week of April. The Brigade consisted of:

Headquarters 161 Infantry Brigade
One Mountain Battery
One Battery Field Artillery
One Field Company Madras Engineers
A Squandron 7 Cavalry
1st Bn. The Sikh Regiment
6th Bn. The Rajputana Rifles
2nd Bn. The Dogra Regiment
4th Bn. The Kumaon Regiment
3rd Bn. The Garhwal Rifles
3 Light Field Ambulance
One Motor Transport Company, ASC
Composite Platoon, ASC
Ordnance Detachment
EME Detachment.

Chapter 13

Hazards of Snow

THE night following the Bhatgiran battle was fraught with dangerous possibilities. In order to enable 3 Light Field Ambulance to attend to the relatively large number of casualties, many of whom were in a serious condition and required immediate surgery, all restrictions relating to lighting were relaxed in the Field Ambulance area. The limited lighting produced by the generating sets were supplemented by Petromax lamps, the bright glare from which made the low watt electric bulbs appear dim. That the lit-up area would present to the enemy a wonderful target was fully realised and accepted. It was taking a grave risk, especially as the enemy was known to be equipped with mortars, but as he had not trained his fire on Uri in the past, it was hoped that he would stay his hand for just that night.

The perimeter defences caused greater worry. Against the barest minimum requirement of one and a half battalions to man them, they were now being held by just one battalion, 4 Kumaon. In order to take over the 1 Sikh piquets, 4 Kumaon had had to prune down its own piquet strengths, and all piquets were now held with reduced garrisons. This had been accepted as being a purely temporary measure, as on its return from Bhatgiran, the 1 Sikh sub-units, totalling half a battalion, were expected to resume responsibility for their own piquets, the 4 Kumaon 'stand-ins' rejoining their own charges. With the Bhatgiran battle taking an unforeseen turn, and 1 Sikh unable to re-assume its piquet responsibility, the calculated risk had boomeranged fiercely and had placed Uri in a vulnerable position.

What was even worse was the fact that there was now no reserve that could be drawn on, the only troops available in the Uri bowl being an extremely tired and dispirited battalion in a semi-disorganised state. Although all piquets were warned to expect an attack, and they would doubtless have hit back hard, yet an attack delivered in strength and with determination had every chance of creating a serious breach in the defence which could not have been easily repaired. Strangely enough, the expected attack did not materialise.

6 Rajrif, commanded by Lt. Col. S. S. Kalam MC had already been ordered to move from Srinagar to Uri, and was expected to arrive soon after first light the next morning, 14 December. It would have done so, but for enemy action. It reached the outskirts of Uri at seven o'clock, but enemy light machine guns raked the road with fire, halting the progress of the motorised convoy. They were immediately engaged by a troop of Armoured Cars which had accompanied the column and were silenced. Entering Uri without damage, 6 Rajrif was immediately allotted the 1 Sikh commitments and assumed them with remarkable speed. With the perimeter once again held in reasonable strength, and with a readily available reserve, 1 Sikh was struck off all duties in order to enable it to finalise its preparations for its return to Srinagar. This was effected two days later, when the position in Uri was considered to be fully stabilised.

Reconnaissance and fighting patrols towards Bhatgiran were immediately intensified, the enemy being kept under constant observation and harassment. The intelligence reports trickling in indicated that he had suffered severe casualties over the period 10 to 13 December, particularly on 12 December when engaged by the two 4 Kumaon Companies and the fighter aircraft that had arrived over the battle area at such an opportune moment. Moreover, the increasing weight of the snowfalls was stated to be placing a great strain on the enemy in terms of administrative problems. This latter assessment was, however, not given much credence. 161 Infantry Brigade's piquets were located in areas with equally heavy snowfall, and although the administrative problem was difficult it was certainly not an insurmountable one, and not even a passing thought was given to the withdrawing of the piquets. What was interesting in the reports received was the constant repetition of a visible lowering in the enemy's morale. There were strong rumours that a withdrawal was imminent. Patrol reports also pointed in the same direction, and it was no surprise when in the morning of 20 December, a platoon patrol from 4 Kumaon entered Bhatgiran and reported it clear of the enemy. The same evening, Rear Headquarters 161 Infantry Brigade in Srinagar reported that a heavy snowfall had blocked the Banihal Pass and made it impassable for any kind of traffic.

The steady increase in the weight of the snowfalls and the ever-darkening clouds had left little doubt that the days before the Pass would be closed to traffic were numbered. A hasty review had, therefore, been made of the stockpiling of supplies and ordnance stores which would be required to see the Brigade through the next four months. Shortages were telephoned to Headquarters Jak Force and were promptly despatched to the Valley by road convoy. There was, however, a complete void where welfare and amenity stores for the troops were concerned. It was essential that these were available in sufficient quantities in order to provide the men with some form of relaxation. During the next few months they would be unable to receive or despatch any mail to their families, and when not out on operations would be cooped up in bunkers on the heights or at the base of the mountains. An immediate signal, requesting these stores, was therefore despatched.

Two days later, Major Derek Bobb, the DAA & QMG at Rear Headquarters 161 Infantry Brigade, informed Main Headquarters that three crates of amenity and welfare stores had arrived, and was instructed to forward them to Uri. There was a distinct sense of jubilation when the truck bearing the crates arrived. Now, it was felt, the troops who had gone through the most trying times would have something to keep them cheerfully occupied. The three crates were ripped open almost simultaneously, but their contents were greeted with horrified stares and the stifling of gasps. Neatly packed in them were nothing other than hockey sticks and hockey balls! Immediate remedial treatment was indicated, and took the form of a flash call to Headquarters Jak Force in Jammu. It was answered by a keen young Staff Officer who, not without justification, as most telephone conversations were carried out in veiled language, assumed that the words Ludo, Draughts and Snakes and Ladders were code names for either units, places or warlike stores. Gentle persuasion, however, convinced him that they had no operational significance. The stores, very fortunately, arrived twenty-four hours before the Banihal Pass closed.

The last convoy, of just under one hundred load-carrying vehicles, with rations and ammunition, was less fortunate. Its abandonment, to lie buried in snow until dug out and retrieved in April, resulted from the rash act of a young officer. Battle areas have a strange fascination for rubber-necks. These individuals, who do nothing but get in the way of busy men working against the clock, are a plague to any Commander or Staff Officer. One such rubber-neck was the Assistant Provost Marshal of Headquarters Jak Force. Although 161 Infantry Brigade had no provost personnel on its strength, the APM arrived in Srinagar on 18 December by road, and spent the next day wandering round Srinagar and Uri, the visit being more a social than a business one. He was jokingly informed by a Staff Officer that if he did not get back to Jammu immediately, he would probably find himself spending the next few months in the Valley.

With patches of snow and a wet surface slowing down the rate of advance of the motor convoy winding its way to the Banihal Pass, orders were issued on the morning of 20 December that no vehicle, civilian or military, was to proceed beyond Veranag, which lies on the Kashmir side of the Banihal Pass, until the last vehicle of the incoming convoy had reached that point. The APM must have been well aware of the order, as his request to be given exemption from the restriction was firmly refused. Apparently, with the clouds darkening and the snowfall thickening, he exercised his appointment and persuaded the Civil Police at Veranag to permit him to move forward. The Military Police Pilot jeep, in its enthusiasm to give the APM a clear run, halted the convoy, very unfortunately at a point where the climb to the Pass was at its steepest. It was a disastrous gesture, from the point of view of the convoy and 161 Infantry Brigade, as the enforced halt caused many vehicles to stall, while others found it difficult to move forward. By the time that these difficulties had been overcome and the convoy had once again begun to move forward, a blinding snowstorm descended making further progress impossible, and it was trapped. One hour's delay had done irreparable damage.

To those troops who came from areas subjected to snow, the conditions were not strange or abnormal, but there were many, the Rajputs and the Madras Engineers, for example, to whom snow was a novel experience. Although puzzled at first, they very quickly acclimatised themselves to it, and weathered the storms as well as their more habituated comrades. The heavy snowfalls of the next few months played amazing tricks with the landscape. What had been folds in the ground or deep re-entrants now appeared as flat fields of snow. The heavily bunkered piquets, which had been sited with meticulous care in order to ensure a field of fire of from 75 to 100 yards, were now found, in some cases, to be under snow or the vision of the garrison limited to a distance of 5 to 10 yards. Strenuous efforts were made to clear the snow, but it soon became apparent that it was a vain effort. There was no option other than to re-site a number of them, but this was not as simple as it would appear, owing to the difficulty in ascertaining what was solid ground and what was thin air. The barbed wire entanglements and the anti-personnel mines and booby traps that had been laid to protect the piquet were also undetectable, and to retrieve them from under the snow was hazardous. They were therefore charted, and the new bunkers that were constructed had to be protected afresh.

There were cases of twisted ankles and barked shins caused by taking a step without realising what was in front, but the most remarkable experience fell to the lot of the Brigade Education Officer. Why Rear Headquarters had brought him to the Valley from Ranchi no one quite knew, as there was neither time nor scope for educational training; further he was about fifty years of age. In order to protect him from the rigours of the long winter, the Engineers had built for him a wooden shack. His absence at breakfast and lunch the next day also went by without comment, but when he failed to put in an appearance at dinner for the second night in succession, inquiries were made to ascertain whether he was sick. When his batman announced that he had not seen him for twenty-four hours, telephone calls were made to all units in Uri, Baramula and Srinagar. No unit reported knowledge either of him or of his whereabouts. An immediate search was, therefore, laid on and very naturally started at his shack.

There were no notings on the papers lying on his makeshift writing table to indicate what his plans had been or what his intentions were. His batman, who was then questioned, was quite definite that the Education Officer had been in the shack at six o'clock the previous evening, as he had left him five minutes earlier to have his food. When he had come in the next morning with a cup of tea, he did not find him in the shack and had presumed that he had gone out somewhere. It was agreed by everyone that were he inside the Uri perimeter, someone would have seen him, and the conclusion drawn was that he might have strayed out of the perimeter as a blinding snowstorm was raging at the time. This was possible, as the eastern sector of Uri was bare, with no piquets guarding it.

We were wondering what to do, as darkness had set in and to conduct a search outside the perimeter in the dark was asking for trouble, when someone, pointing to a large pile of snow which lay to the left of the door of the shack, suggested rather facetiously that he might be buried under it. It was well worth exploring, and two officers assisted by the batman using their hands as shovels commenced to remove the snow. When about four feet of it had been shovelled away, we found the Education Officer fast asleep. He was picked up and rushed to the Mess and a Doctor sent for from the Field Ambulance. A hot drink revived him, and when he had almost fully recovered, he told us what had happened. He had left his shack to come to the Mess when something struck him on the head: what had happened after that he just did not know.

In trying to reconstruct what must have happened, there was agreement on all hands that after he had stepped out of his shack, the strong breeze which was blowing at the time must have resulted in the shack door slamming, and the five feet of snow that was on the roof must have come hurling down. One thing was quite evident, he had suffered no ill-effects from his prolonged confinement under the snow. In fact, he told us that he had slept very soundly and that it had been wonderfully warm! This the Doctor confirmed would be correct as the snow being porous would present no breathing difficulties, and it would also provide warmth. He did, however, emphasise that survival would have been dependent on the weight of further snowfalls, and how quickly the individual was recovered. His advice to us not to carry out the experiment was superfluous.

Patrolling problems also came sharply to the surface. The snow, varying in depths from four feet upwards, limited speed in movement from about one mile in every hour to as little as one mile in every two hours. It taxed the energy of the men to an extreme degree. It was much too dangerous to go floundering through the snow, as there was always the possibility of being caught in an embarrassing state of unreadiness by the enemy. Lt. Col. Lachmann Singh Negi, the Commanding Officer of 3 Garhwal, was most indignant when ordered to send out a patrol to an area under heavy snow. He informed the Brigade Major that what Brigade Headquarters apparently did not realise was that his men were five feet in height and the snow was six feet deep in the area. This outburst did not impress either me or my staff. The Brigade Major was told to tell Lt. Col. Negi that it was not the intention that his men should go under the snow, we would like them to go over it, in the same manner as the Kumaonis, who were about the same height as his Garhwalis, had done two days earlier. The Garhwalis carried out the patrol and did it extremely well, and Lt. Col. Negi was never permitted to forget his fabulous statement.

As the winter progressed, patrols, especially those despatched on long range missions, faced many hazards, avalanches being the most feared. It was made a standard drill for them to report their exact location every half an hour, if on the move. A Rifle Company of 2 Dogra, on a patrol to Gagarhil, about ten miles to the south of Rampur, was fortunate in escaping what could have been a disaster. An avalanche, composed of snow and large loose boulders, about two hundred yards in width, came roaring down the mountain side and piled up to a height of about forty feet in the Valley below. The leading platoon had passed that way exactly three minutes previously, and for ten dreadful minutes the Company Commander did not know whether his leading platoon had been trapped and destroyed. Nor did the platoon know what fate had befallen the Company, as the signaller with the platoon tripped and fell when trying to scurry out of the way and damaged his wireless set.

Frost bite, that dreaded incapacitator of the careless, unwary or unfortunate, claimed a few victims in the early days. Immediate action was taken to educate all ranks in the do's and don'ts of combating it. The root cause in the initial cases was ascribed to men who had walked in the snow, not necessarily those who had been on patrol, placing their booted feet against a stove or a brazier in order to warm them. That the number of frost bite cases became insignificant after the instructions had been issued, and amputations a rarity, speaks volumes for the very careful attention paid to this subject by leaders of all ranks down to the most recently promoted Lance Naik.

Keeping the troops warm, and at the same time ensuring that their mobility remained unaffected, presented a major problem in those areas which were subject to sub-zero temperatures, pitchforked into Kashmir at short notice, and initially in cotton uniforms and bedding adequate only for the plains, the equipping of the Brigade with winter uniforms was inadequate, thanks to the shortage of time and the transport difficulties. Woollen clothing in the form of Battle Dress blouses and trousers, Balaclava caps, woollen gloves and extra blankets were received, but in many cases they were used stock and being almost threadbare provided little warmth. Warm underclothing was sent up in short supply, as were greatcoats. The troops were, however, infused with a remarkable spirit, and accepted the shortcomings without a murmur. By day they kept themselves warm by sitting in the sun, if it was shining, or moving about, and, by pooling their blankets, provided themselves with reasonably warm beds at night.

The sentries, especially those manning the heights, which on occasion were swept by gale-force icy winds, required special attention. The Battle Dress provides little protection to the small of the back, and with some hospital cases arising form ailments to this part of the anatomy, Poshteins were purchased from the trade in Srinagar. These knee-length leather coats with an inner lining of fur, while providing the necessary protection, denied the sentry freedom of action in operating his weapon, a difficulty which was aggravated by the double pair of gloves which were also essential. The Kangrie, an earthen pot filled with glowing embers and suspended in front of the body by a string which runs around the back of the neck, is commonly used by the Kashmiris. These were purchased, and by discarding their gloves and clasping the Kangrie, the sentries kept their trigger fingers warm and ready for instant action.

With no further advance contemplated until the spring, a close survey was made of the territory which had been made the responsibility of 161 Infantry Brigade. It was broadly the whole of Kashmir, Gilgit and Ladakh, covering about 35,000 square miles. For obvious reasons, the control of this vast area was neither within the compass of one Infantry Brigade nor was it seriously expected. What was expected, however, was that the Brigade should hold the area up to Uri and the Valley which was nearly 6,000 square miles. In order to carry out this task, it was of vital importance that information of both operational and non-operational significance was collected and made known to all unit commanders. Meetings were, therefore, held with the civilian officials and the Forest Rangers in order to extract from them all information that might prove useful.

The meetings, conducted with a critical study of the map, produced invaluable data relating to every road and track running into the Valley, with a special emphasis on the ability of vehicles, men and animals to use them during the winter months; the bridge classifications and possible crossing places over the unbridged streams; the depth of snow that could be expected in the various areas, based on past experience, and any villages that might be termed hostile and likely to harbour the enemy. In compiling this information, D. P. Dhar of the Emergency Government, who remained in the Valley throughout the winter—Sheikh Abdullah and Bakshi Ghulam Mohammed having gone to Jammu—was most helpful in the suggestions that he offered and the information that he obtained for us.

It was, perhaps, unfortunate that Sheikh Abdullah and Bakshi Ghulam Mohammed were both away from the Valley during the winter of 1947–48. This was a crucial period. Bakshi was definitely unhappy at the thought of being away from the Valley for what would be a lengthy period, but Sheikh Abdullah gave me the impression that he was not going to be boxed up in the Valley, and he more or less insisted on Bakshi accompanying him. Jammu and Kashmir is admittedly one State, but Kashmir had suffered a severe blow from the raiders and Sheikh Abdullah would have been wiser not to leave the Valley and its people at a time when they required all the help, guidance and alleviation.

The extensive area of responsibility and the paucity of troops made impossible the garrisoning of many points and precluded the drawing up of an operational plan that would cater for every contingency. Many had to be faced and dealt with as and when they arose, and the only way to cope with them was to withdraw troops from the defences which did not appear to be likely to be subjected to an immediate attack, deploy them in the threatened area, and then rush them back to their original defences when the situation had been stabilised. It was, infact, a constant manoeuvre of robbing Peter to pay Paul. With the intelligence data constantly being checked and re-checked, and the Situation Map meticulously maintained and kept up to the minute, the chances of being surprised were reduced to a negligible degree, and the Brigade, instead of aiming at being one jump ahead of the enemy, now set its target at being two jumps ahead.

Snow and the hostiles were not the only problems that faced us. Water and salt also entered the lists to make matters more difficult. The mountain streams came into spate on occasion and threatened our hastily constructed wooden bridges. The one constructed in the vicinity of the diversion around the demolished bridge at the eastern exit of Uri was saved by the Engineers who tied ropes to it and hung on for grim death. Then the Flume Line either had a natural break or was sabotaged, and put the road between Rampur and Mahura out of commission for five days. This artificial channel, built of wood, conveys the water from the Jhelum River at Rampur to the Power House at Mahura. It is visible for almost its complete length, running along the side of the hills to the south of the main road and at a height of about sixty to seventy feet. A break results in the water pouring out and carrying mud and stones on to the main road. Fortunately, we knew the answer to this hazard, the headworks at Rampur being ordered to cut off the water. But salt confronted us with a real problem.

Kashmir had always been reliant on the import of salt into the State. With the formation of Pakistan, and that Dominion cutting off supplies in an effort to exert pressure, the shortage of salt had become acute by December 1947. So valuable was this commodity that porters employed by units requested salt in lieu of cash for their services, and units, without realising the consequences of their action, became very generous in their distribution of this item of their rations. The act, though humane, was indiscreet, as in early February 1948 the Brigade Supply Officer announced that there was no more salt in his Depot and that there was none to be purchased locally. This was a very serious state of affairs, as without salt the health of the troops would be endangered.

There was an immediate exchange of signals with Headquarters Jak Force, who correctly pointed out that it was a very difficult task to despatch salt to the Valley, the weather having turned for the worse and making flying conditions dangerous. It was, however, suggested by Headquarters 161 Infantry Brigade that if there was a break in the weather and the Air Force could free-drop bags of salt to the east of Baramula, a lookout posted on the roof of a house would direct retrieval squads to wherever he saw a hole in the snow. There was four feet of snow in the area of Baramula when the Indian Air Force flew in three Dakotas, a week later, and carried out a free-drop. All the bags were retrieved. It was not found necessary to issue any orders regarding the conserving of salt: the troops had learnt a lesson the hard way.

Chapter 14

Psychological Warfare

FOLLOWING the withdrawal of the enemy from the Bhatgiran Ridge, an uneasy lull developed along the front line, but it was soon disturbed. Early in Jammu 1948, a body of hostiles, better organised than the tribesmen, made their appearance on the heights in the vicinity of Uri. Clad in uniform identical to those worn by the troops of 161 Infantry Brigade, they were reasonably well equipped with arms and wireless communications and employed tactics which, although not of a high standard, clearly indicated that they were not just a bunch of recruits but trained soldiers. At first sight it was assumed that a Regular Pakistan Infantry Brigade had moved into the line, since there had been constant and dependable reports from intelligence sources to the effect that Pakistan Regular troops were milling about in the area between Chakothi and Muzaffarabad. It was essential that the true picture was obtained, and fighting patrols and wireless intercepts very quickly cleared the air. The new arrivals were identified as Azad Kashmir Poonch battalions, or AKP for short.

These AKP battalions, raised mainly from released Poonchie Mussalmans of the Pakistan Army, with a percentage of Punjabi Mussalmans, and defectors from the Jammu and Kashmir State Forces, had been grouped under AKP Brigades, three battalions to each Brigade. The battalions were commanded and administered by ex-Jammu and Kashmir State Force officers, and officers on deputation from the Pakistan Army, while the companies and platoons were led by ex-junior and non-commissioned officers who had been elevated to the ranks of Major, Captain and Lieutenant. The Brigade Commanders and their Staffs were Regular officers of the Pakistan Army, which also produced a large percentage of the personnel required to man the specialist platoons, such as the Signals and Mortars, and was also entirely responsible for the planning and administration of the AKP Force.

With the raising of the AKP formations and units, the services of the tribals from the NWFP were not dispensed with. They continued to serve in the area, arriving under their own tribal leaders, and from knowledge gained over the next few months it was found that their tenure of duty was for one month, after which they would be relieved by fresh batches of equivalent strength. The date of the relief was between the third and fifth of each month and followed a set pattern. The outgoing tribals would be very active during their last week, in which they would blaze off all their ammunition, and the relief after showing great activity on arrival would then drift into a state of lethargy only to brighten up again in the last week before the relief date. These tribal lashkars or bands, each numbering between one thousand and twelve hundred in strength, were attached to and operated with each AKP battalion. The reason for this strange grouping is difficult to understand, and it can only be presumed that it was considered that the newly raised AKP battalions were in need of moral support and a hard core which could play the role of "shock troops". If this was the object, and both intelligence reports and captured AKP personnel seemed to confirm that it was so, it backfired badly from the point of view of harmony and maintenance of discipline. It was not long before the Pathans treated the Poonchies with scorn and openly told them that they were useless, while the Poonchies reciprocated the compliment by referring to the Pathans as rogues.

An agent, despatched to Muzaffarabad from Uri in order to obtain further information of the AKP set-up, was apprehended near Chakothi by an AKP patrol but managed to escape, and confirmed this reading of the situation. Taken to the battalion Headquarters, he had been placed under arrest in the guard tent. There he met a companion in distress, a senior NCO of the AKP battalion who had been de-striped and awarded twenty-eight days' rigorous imprisonment. Extremely embittered, the ex-NCO informed the agent that prior to issuing the Pathans with their rations, he had placed his rifle on the ground, and on completing his task his weapon was untraceable. All his pleas for its return had fallen on deaf ears, and his appeal to the tribal leader had earned him a rebuke for having had the audacity to suggest that one of the Pathans had stolen it. He went on to say that the Pathans adopted a most patronising attitude towards the Poonchies, and refused their share in manning the piquets and heights by night, asserting that they had not come to Kashmir for that purpose. They were only interested in having a good time in the villages. In the early hours of the morning, as the guard and the dejected ex-NCO lay asleep and the sentry sat huddled up in a blanket which covered his head, the agent rolled under the tent flap, and creeping into the darkness made good his escape.

Assessments made after the initial clashes with the AKP units showed that they were brave but very badly led. They would move forward with determination, but would falter when faced with strong resistance or when in danger of being outmanoeuvred. Under such circumstances, their leaders would waver and either lose command and control or resort to tactics which were suicidal. Most of the casualties suffered by the AKP can safely be attributed to indecision at a critical juncture, or foolhardiness. After a spell of costly and abortive attacks, the AKP units adopted the practice of advancing to a position well out of range of our small arm fire, and commencing to fire for hours on end without any chances of inflicting damage. In order to encourage this practice, patrols would set out in their direction, and having moved into the bed of a dry stream, would return to Uri undetected by the enemy. This resulted in every enemy weapon opening up, and in cases continuing to fire at a rapid rate, with intervals, for hours after the patrol had returned to its base.

The Pathans, on the other hand, confined their activities to sniping at the road and launched the major night attacks. The sniping had more nuisance value than danger attached to it. Immediately a sniper disclosed his position with a shot, he was stalked, or jittered with the threat of a stalk, whereupon he invariably took up a position behind a rock, fired about ten rounds in rapid succession and slipped away. The ineffectiveness of the sniping can be gauged from the fact that in four months of sniping at the road, which was very heavily used, the net result was eleven wounded.

Towards the end of January, Psychological Warfare was introduced. This took the form of a Medium Wave Radio Station designating itself Azad Kashmir Radio. It broadcast items of news of astounding successes on the Uri front, vitriolic attacks on Sheikh Abdullah, Bakshi Ghulam Mohammed and the National Conference, and biographies of the senior commanders of the Indian troops operating in Kashmir and Jammu. The author of the biographies was handicapped by not having access to facts but overcame the deficiency by utilising a very fertile imagination. His vocabulary, unfortunately, was acutely limited and that essential ingredient of this type of warfare, subtlety, was completely absent. What was lacking in this sphere, was compensated for by a number of sentences, obscene and vulgar to a degree, which garnished the end of each revelation. What these tirades were in aid of was difficult to understand, as whether a senior officer was unaware of his parentage—and apparently every one was, this assertion being the mildest—was unlikely to materially alter the course of the operations. Nor was there any frightful urgency to accede to the biographer's impassioned pleas to ascertain the truth of his statements.

Perhaps realising that these efforts to discredit the senior officers in the eyes of the men were not having the desired effect, they were supplemented with "live" broadcasts along the front line. This necessitated an enemy company or platoon taking up a position in the vicinity of one of the piquets of 161 Infantry Brigade and engaging it in conversation. Commencing with the asking of questions of a harmless nature, it would soon develop into a wordy battle in which the troops of 161 Infantry Brigade gave an excellent rendering of unprintable phraseology. It was, in fact, of such a high order that the enemy, apparently unable to stomach it, decided on occasion to vindicate his honour by abandoning his positions and rushing forward in attack. No worse mistake could have been committed and he paid heavily for it, with nineteen counted killed in the first incident and twenty-three in the second. Although it was unnecessary, the troops of the Brigade were warned not to permit themselves to be provoked into such rash actions.

The battlefield area was not the only place where talking out of turn was dangerous. That the enemy had sympathisers who were acting in the role of agents was well known, and accepted as being quite normal. Their main spheres of operation were Srinagar and Baramula. Though 161 Brigade's intelligence set-up had reached a very high level of efficiency, there was no room for complacency or grounds for assuming that the enemy was not equally well equipped. That every move to and from Uri was made known to the enemy was confirmed by our counter-intelligence, but to hide them from prying eyes was virtually impossible. This caused quite a lot of concern, as it was vital that the enemy was kept ignorant of the fact that Uri was lightly held with only two battalions, that the thirty miles between Uri and Baramula were completely devoid of troops, and that Baramula and Srinagar had between them three battalions, one of which was being built up to operational efficiency and was not immediately ready for action. With this information in his possession, it would not have been difficult to place 161 Infantry Brigade in many awkward and dangerous situations. As there was no possibility of the Brigade being reinforced until the Spring, it was decided that it would be reinforced, in the minds of the enemy, by fictitious methods.

This was urgently necessary, as the enemy had stepped up the tempo of his attacks against Uri. These had once again become almost a nightly affair. The lower piquets, which were more easily accessible because of the lighter snowfall in their vicinity, now became the main targets. 'Jitter' and 'Fort', located on the western perimeter of Uri, and manned by 6 Rajrif, received more than their fair share of attention. Lightly held initially, as each attack was met and repulsed, the piquets were strengthened both with troops and barbed wire entanglements, reinforced with anti-personnel mines and booby traps. At first the attacks were launched exclusively by units of the AKP, and then the Pathan tribals took over, presumably to show them how it should be done. With the Brigade reserve committed to strengthening the piquets, it was found necessary to move forward 3 Garhwal from Srinagar to Uri. The move forward of this battalion, which was virtually the only potential reserve in the Valley, had been delayed until it had become essential. It amounted to placing a major portion of the eggs in one basket, but if that basket was not held by strong hands, an unfortunate slip could result in many a shell cracking.

An intercepted wireless message engendered the idea of reinforcing Uri by fictitious methods. On arrival in Uri, 3 Garhwal despatched a two-Company patrol towards Salamabad. Instead of wearing steel helmets, the Companies sported what are commonly referred to as Gorkha hats and which constitute the head-dress both of Garhwalis and of the Gorkha Rifles. The intercepted message, from an AKP battalion to its Brigade Headquarters, made reference to a Gorkha battalion operating on its front. This was too good to be missed, and 1 Gorkha Rifles was immediately included in the Order of Battle of 161 Infantry Brigade. In order to establish the existence of the battalion in the minds of the enemy, wireless sets were netted in to the wave lengths being utilised by the enemy, and messages were transmitted to and from 1 Gorkha during the next ten days. The strictest security measures were employed but quite a number of indiscretions were permitted to creep in. That the presence in Uri of 3 Garhwal would also be known to the enemy was fully expected. It was too much to hope that its move from Srinagar through Baramula had passed by undetected. An intercepted message confirmed our expectation. In the enemy's estimation, however, Uri was now held by four battalions, 6 Rajrif, 4 Kumaon, 3 Garhwal and the fictitious 1 Gorkha.

In order to build up the strength by yet another battalion, half the strength of the Sikh Mountain Battery in Uri was slipped into Srinagar in the returning ration lorries. They were then moved back again in a large convoy of three-ton vehicles, three men in each vehicle standing up and revealing themselves to prying eyes in Baramula as the convoy sped through. Indiscreet statements dropped in Baramula referred to them as the 1st Batalion Patiala Infantry. The day after its arrival in Uri, "1 Patiala Infantry" was sent out on a patrol to a spot where it could not escape the attention of the enemy. It was not long before the enemy wireless was reporting the presence of a Sikh battalion in Uri, referring to it three days later as the 1st Patiala Infantry.

These "extra reinforcements" did not, however, deter the enemy from continuing to mount assaults against the piquets. To impose caution on him and, if possible, to dampen his ardour, every stratagem was resorted to. An ancient and functionless electric generator, which must have weathered many storms in the ditch in which it lay near Heman Buniyar, was retrieved with great care and transported to Uri, where it found a similar grave. It was explained to interested bystanders, who were watching its retrieval at Heman Buniyar, that it was required to enable us to electrify the protective wire at Uri. Patrols which visited the villages adjacent to Uri, during the next few days, were instructed to advise the villagers to take especial care of their cattle and not to permit them to approach the wire lest they be electrocuted. It was not strange that the villagers accepted what was told to them as they were totally ignorant of modern warfare. A village to the north of Uri had been hastily evacuated a few days previously by the headman, who had despatched a delegation to Uri to report that a large bomb lay unexploded in a field. An Engineer detachment was rushed to the village, and returned with the auxiliary tank jettisoned by a fighter aircraft.

The story of the electrification of Uri's defensive wire entanglements was soon confirmed in the enemy's mind as three buffaloes, quite clearly driven forward by the enemy, sauntered down the road towards Fort piquet after dark and were killed. They had not been engaged by the garrison, the damage being done by a hail of rocks that flew through space as the gun cotton slabs and primers, placed in the midst of a tar barrel filled with large stones, were ignited by a fuse attached to a trip wire. The sound of the explosion, which was accentuated by the stillness of the night, and the blinding flash that preceded it, made an immediate impression on the enemy, the tribals in particular. A wireless intercept informed the Headquarters at Muzaffarabad that there was unassailable proof that the protective wire at Uri was electrified and no further attacks would be launched until a supply of wire cutters with rubber handles was received.

Captain Kumar of the Madras Engineers, who had produced the infernal machine which had created such a deep impression on the enemy, had been nick-named "Snags" by his brother officers. This was because he invariably cited at least three "snags" in any engineer task allotted to him. Whether they existed or not, these drawbacks were automatically over-ruled and Kumar never failed to complete his task on schedule and in a most efficient manner. When asked whether there were any "snags" connected with the device that he had produced, Kumar assured everyone that there were none whatsoever and quipped that the Engineers would show the Infantry how to destroy an enemy section or perhaps even a platoon with one shot. As soon as the eagerly awaited report from the piquet was received the next morning, Kumar was summoned to Brigade Headquarters but his Second in Command sent back a message that he had already left Uri to inspect the bridges on the main road and would not return before the evening. His prolonged absence merely whetted the appetite of those awaiting him. Kumar more than held his own, maintaining that had the three buffaloes been an enemy section, the result would have been equally spectacular.

Whether it was due to the phoney electrification of the Uri wire entanglements or the fictitious number of battalions in the area, intelligence reports pointed to the enemy deciding to halt his attempts to reduce Uri by direct assaults against the piquets. There were frequent reports that the plan was to bypass it, cut the road at some suitable point between Uri and Baramula, and having isolated the garrison to force it into surrender when its means of subsistence ran out. This was wishful thinking on the part of the enemy. The possibility of Uri being isolated had received serious consideration and the garrison was stocked to withstand a siege of two months at full scale, and four months at half scale. By that time the Banihal Pass would have opened and further reinforcements could have been moved into the Valley to relieve the siege. The danger that Uri faced, if an encirclement materialised, was not related to the garrison being starved into surrender, but the bald fact that the eastern sector of Uri was unmanned because of the paucity of troops. The enemy, if he gained a foothold on the road leading from Uri to Baramula, would most certainly probe towards Uri, and the weakness of the eastern perimeter would be discovered. In order to counter that threat, the existing defences of Uri would have to be weakened somewhere, and this could be ill-afforded. An attempt would certainly be made to break the siege by moving forward the battalion from Baramula and making 1 Sikh responsible for that town in addition to the rest of the Valley, but the chances of a single battalion raising the siege were very limited. It was, in fact, the one plan that it was hoped the enemy would never consider and execute.

The intelligence cover was immediately increased, and a special section concentrated on the task of watching all signs relating to any attempt at encirclement. During the first week of January, information was received at about eight o'clock at night that a band of three hundred tribesmen were on the move to occupy the heights to the south of the main road in the vicinity of Mahura. The route of advance was said to be via the Haji Pir Pass. There was no time to check the accuracy of the report. It could have been a rumour designed towards a removal of troops from Uri, or it could have been factual. Whichever it was, immediate action was necessary to checkmate the move whether it materialised or not.

The Commanding Officer of 2 Dogra was telephoned and ordered to despatch two Rifle Companies from Baramula to Mahura to be in position on the heights by midnight. It was snowing heavily as the two Rifle Companies moved to Mahura in lorries, and although the drive was difficult, they reached their destination, scaled the snow-covered hills and were in hastily prepared defences by mid-night. Whether the tribals came, and having seen that the area was occupied by troops decided to withdraw, or whether it was just a rumour, is not known; in any case the threat did not materialise. After a two days' stay at Mahura, the two Rifle Companies of 2 Dogra were returned to Baramula, and the line of communication was once again bereft of troops.

The enemy continued to be very talkative and reports of an encirclement persisted from many sources. While they could not be disregarded, at the same time it would have been tactically unsound to react to every one of them. The best one could do was to watch for any definite indication and then to act fast. Such an indication was received from a most unorthodox source. Arriving in Srinagar to visit Rear Headquarters 161 Infantry Brigade, on 15 January 1948, I went to visit a friend and was told that he had gone to Nedous' Hotel and I would find him in the bar. On entering the bar, he greeted me like a long lost friend and invited me to join his table at which were seated a young Irish couple, the McDermotts, both of whom I had met previously.

McDermott was in the Kashmir State Education Service and a Master in a school at Baramula which had not reopened since the sacking of the town by the tribesmen. He and his wife were, therefore, living in a houseboat in Srinagar. In the course of the conversation, Ms McDermott suddenly asked me whether I had any troops at Mahura. Although stunned by this sudden question, I reacted quickly and telling a white lie assured her that Mahura was garrisoned. From the look on her face, I realised that she was doubtful of the veracity of my statement, and so I asked her. "Why, what's worrying you about Mahura?"

"My bearer told me there was a rumour in the bazaar that the raiders were going to attack Mahura and blow up the Power House," she said. "He also said that a friend of his who works in the Power House was worried because there were no soldiers anywhere near Mahura."

My host then chipped in. "Yes, I've also heard that rumour, and I'm sure you must have too, Brigadier."

"Yes, I've heard it," I replied. "but if and when the enemy threatens the Power House he will be suitably dealt with."

"But how are you going to do that?" asked Ms McDermott, "you'll be unable to get at them with the Jhelum River in-between, and no bridge to cross it."

"We'll deal with them effectively enough," I replied, and, as if to make light of the conversation, added: "Don't you start a scare by buying up all the candles in the city."

I was anxious to race back to my Rear Headquarters to issue orders for moving troops to Mahura. However, lest my hasty departure be interpreted as my having been alarmed, I stayed with the party for half an hour more and then left on the plea that I had another call to make. Reaching my Rear Headquarters, I took a hurried look at the map.

To meet the previous threat to Mahura, which did not materialise, two Rifle Companies of 2 Dogra had been rushed to the area from Baramula. It had by no means been the best method of dealing with the situation as it had seriously weakened the Baramula defences which required a minimum strength of one battalion. A risk was taken as speed was the dominant factor. The time available to man the heights overlooking Mahura was limited. Motor transport to lift the troops was readily available at Baramula while there was none at Uri. The 2 Dogra Companies were, however, returned to Baramula after a period of 48 hours, as soon after it was felt that the danger was past.

The impending threat was of a different caliber and posed a far more serious problem. It was being delivered, for the first time, from the north bank of the River Jhelum, which for many miles of its stretch was bridgeless, making it extremely difficult to come to grips with the enemy. From positions along the north bank of the river, the enemy could command many miles of the main road, and if not kept at arm's length he could do extensive damage to the Power House. Further, if he continued his advance eastwards, he would threaten Baramula. The hitherto adopted policy of plugging gaps as and when they arose could no longer be pursued, nor could Baramula be weakened. A permanent garrison at Mahura had now become a vital necessity, and it would have to be held in strength, a battalion being the minimum.

There was, therefore, no option other than to reduce the strength at Uri from three to two battalions, undesirable though it may have been. 4 Kumaon, the reserve battalion, was in consequence given orders to undertake the role.

The Bausian Ridge on the north bank of the River was the obvious position to hold, as it not only overlooked the Power House but also commanded the main road. There were two ways to get to it, by crossing the bridge over the river at Uri and advancing to it along the north bank, or to come to Mahura by the main road and to find a crossing place over the Jhelum in the area of the Power House. Having rapidly considered the pros and cons of the two routes, I selected the advance along the main road, firstly because it would be quicker and easier to get to Mahura, and secondly because there was a possibility that 4 Kumaon advancing along the north bank of the river in the dark might quite easily clash with the enemy who were also heading, I presumed, for Bausian.

Having arrived at a decision, I telephoned Lt. Col. Man Mohan Khanna of 4 Kumaon in Uri and ordered him to move with four Rifle Companies to Mahura as quickly as he could. The remainder of the battalion could remain in Uri and move forward the next morning. Man Mohan Khanna told me that there was a blinding snowstorm raging and progress would be very slow, but he would collect his Companies and get to Mahura as quickly as he could, and estimated his time of arrival at about eight o'clock the next morning. I told him that I would get to Mahura by seven o'clock and would meet him on his arrival.

4 Kumaon moved out of Uri soon after midnight, and considering the appalling weather conditions, did extremely well to reach Mahura a few minutes after seven o'clock in the morning of 16 January. After I had quickly told the officers why it was essential that Bausian Ridge be occupied by us, reconnaissances were carried out, and to our horror we realised that there was no ready means of crossing the Jhelum river, about 60 yards wide and in a raging torrent. The bridge that had once stood there had been dismantled. Although the pillars were still intact on both banks, reconstruction of the bridge would require

trained Engineers and could not be completed in under three days. To attempt to swim across would have been suicidal.

Bausian Ridge towered above us, and was presumably still unoccupied by the enemy as we were not fired upon. If the enemy occupied it, not only would he make the road unusable for us, but he would rake the Power House with fire. With the personnel unable to operate the generators, Srinagar would once again be in darkness.

To have ordered 4 Kumaon to retrace its steps to Uri and to cross the bridge and advance to Bausian along the north bank of the river was possible, but was rejected. The battalion had had a grueling march of seven hours in order to get to Mahura, and it would have taken at least another twelve hours to get to Bausian via Uri, in the dreadful weather and ground conditions that prevailed. The move along the north bank would also have to be conducted tactically as the enemy was quite obviously in the area. This would curtail speed which was so vital. I was on the verge of contacting Lt. Col. Kalaan of 6 Rajrif, and telling him to collect the Madras Engineers and any other spare personnel in the Uri bowl, form them into three *ad hoc* Rifle Companies and move them to Bausian via the north bank of the Jhelum River, when Dame Fortune smiled on us.

A Company Commander of 4 Kumaon, still searching the area to find a possible crossing place, noticed a steel wire hawser with a traversing pulley spanning the river. The mist hanging over the area had obscured it. The Power House staff was immediately contacted but could not offer any advice as to its strength, as it had been out of commission for a number of years. The receptacle which was once attached to the pulley was also not available, but fortunately the rotating drum and the wire used to ferry the receptacle to and fro across the river was found in a store shed, though in a very rusty condition. All that was now required was any type of box or large basket, large enough to accommodate one man, and an attempt to ferry the troops across would commence.

A suitable container was found. It was a large dealwood box which had once served the purpose for which it had been manufactured, the carriage of tins of Lipton's tea. Now it was to serve another purpose.

Lashed with steel wires, the box was attached to the pulley and the Platoon Commander of the leading platoon stepped into it and was slowly and gently let down to the north bank over the roaring torrent. It was a frightening moment. Had the wire hawser snapped, it was certain death. On reaching the north bank, the Platoon Commander jumped out and the box was hauled back by the rotating drum to the Power House bank, and the remainder of the platoon ferried across. It was a slow and labourious task, but at the end of three hours the first platoon was across the river. It was instructed to occupy Bausian Ridge as quickly as was possible, and while it climbed the feature, the ferrying of the second platoon commenced. Fortune had smiled on us in the nick of time by giving us the means to cross the river and save the Power House, as on reaching the summit of Bausian, the leading platoon saw the enemy approaching the ridge from the north.

The enemy was in strength, but apparently surprised to see troop movement on the feature, and unaware of how strongly Bausian was

SKETCH SHOWING
THE CROSSING OF THE JHELUM RIVER
AT MAHURA

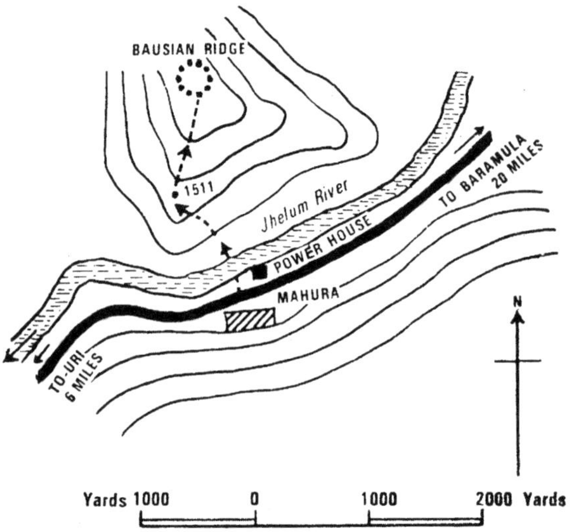

held, he halted, stared, and then withdrew very fast. The occupation of Bausian had saved the Mahura Power House and ensured the protection of our vital road line of communication, perhaps by one hour. Lt. Col. Man Mohan Khanna and his gallant men had achieved what had seemed impossible a short while earlier. 4 Kumaon reinforced the platoon on Bausian with the remainder of the company by the same hazardous ferry and the Engineers reconstructed the dismantled bridge in a matter of three days, thereby ensuring that the Bausian feature could be speedily reinforced should it ever be necessary to do so. The battalion was permanently located in the area, and for the first time since capturing Uri the line of communication from Baramula to Uri could be said to have been afforded protection.

While we were still congratulating ourselves on having stymied the enemy's attempt to occupy Bausian and thus to deprive the Valley of its electric power and deny to us the use of the road from Baramula to Uri, we received a severe jolt. A threat developed in a totally unexpected quarter, and our informant was none other than D. P. Dhar.

"DP" as he was affectionately known, was regarded by 161 Infantry Brigade as a pillar of strength. Energetic to a marked degree, he spent a great deal of his time visiting the major towns and villages in the Valley, encouraging and assisting the local administration, and doing all that lay within his power and slender resources to overcome difficulties. One such visit took him and a colleague to Handwara. This major town, about forty-five miles to the north-west of Srinagar and about twenty-five miles to the north of Baramula, the route being via Sopur, was not garrisoned by troops of 161 Infantry Brigade. This was not because its importance had not been realised: it was simply because of the lack of troops to protect every nook and corner. In arriving at the deployment of the troops in the Valley, it was thought that Handwara was unlikely to be threatened, and even if it was, the threat would be minor in nature, limited perhaps to a party of twenty or thirty. In consequence, it was decided that the needs of Handwara could be served by the occasional visit of a motorised patrol. A troop of Armoured Cars drove to Handwara

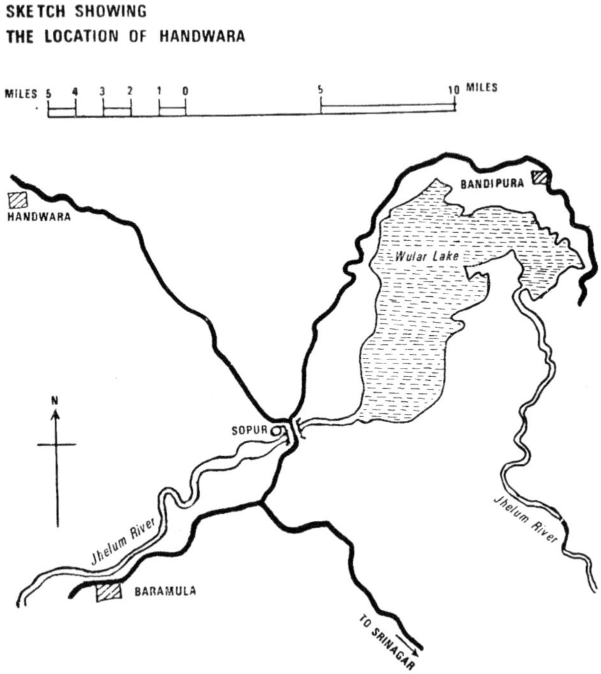

at varying intervals, when it was not required for any other task. All reports had indicated that the area was clear of the enemy, and there was no indication or rumour that there was likely to be any change in the situation.

On his arrival in Handwara, "DP" was prostrated with a severe attack of malaria and was confined to the house. It was while he was in bed with a high temperature that a local resident rushed in to tell him that a party of the enemy had reached the town and that a quisling had informed them that he was present. The enemy, the informant said, must be already on their way to apprehend him. "DP" required no second warning: he rushed to the bedroom window, which luckily was at the rear of the house, and climbed out into the snow. It was an escape by a hair's breadth, as the enemy entered by the front door a few moments later. Lying low until darkness, "DP" and his colleague managed to get a motor vehicle and returned to Srinagar.

It was about eleven o'clock that might when a messenger arrived with this information. I happened fortunately to be in Srinagar. A troop of Armoured Cars and two Rifle Companies of 1 Sikh, placed under the command of the Second in Command of the battalion, were ordered to move to Handwara, the advance to commence at first light. The road to Handwara, the stretch from Sopur to Handwara in particular, was difficult, the surface being treacherous on account of frozen snow. Despite the fact that all vehicle tyres were fitted with skid chains, the speed of the column had to be kept low in order to avoid any accident. The journey to Handwara took four hours, and soon after ten o'clock, the Rifle Companies of 1 Sikh debussed on the outskirts of the town and, with the Armoured Cars in support, moved forward to search out and engage the enemy. This presented no problem. When the enemy learnt of the arrival of the troops they took to their heels, but were pursued and engaged. After a sharp skirmish they surrendered. It was a platoon in strength, and having been disarmed it was embussed in lorries and despatched under escort to Baramula.

From information extracted from the enemy, 1 Sikh learnt that the platoon was the advance element of a force of about three hundred in strength, the rest following a day or two behind it, and heading Handwara. The two Rifle Companies of 1 Sikh were, therefore, deployed astride the route leading into Handwara from the west, and awaited the arrival of the main body of the enemy. It was observed the next afternoon moving steadily forward into the trap that had been laid for it. It would have resulted in a perfect ambush, had an enemy sympathiser not rushed forward at the eleventh hour and screamed to the enemy to withdraw. The main body came to sharp halt and, turning round very quickly disappeared into the distance. It was a great disappointment to the troops: had the enemy not been warned, not one of them would have had an earthly chance of escaping. It can only be presumed that the enemy column made its way back to Muzaffarabad, whence it had come, as Handwara and the area around it were not subjected to any further hostile activity.

The captured enemy personnel were well equipped. They were clothed in Khaki Serge Battle Dress, wore woollen gloves, mufflers and

Service Greatcoats, and their equipment consisted of light machine guns, sten guns, rifles and grenades. The platoon commander had a pair of binoculars, a compass and maps of the area. On being questioned, he became quite talkative. He had been a Havildar Clerk in the Quarter Master's Office of Pakistan's 14th Punjab Regiment, and had accepted the offer of a commission as a Lieutenant in the Azad Kashmir Forces. He had been put through courses in minor tactics and weapon training, and on reporting at Muzaffarabad had been appointed a platoon commander. His platoon was composed entirely of Punjabi Mussalmans all of whom had been recently released or were ex-soldiers. This had been his first assignment. The platoon had advanced from Muzaffarabad at the rate of about ten miles per day, moving from one major village to another, the remainder of the column being a day or two behind him. His orders were to go to Handwara and there await the arrival of the main body. He had no idea what the plans were thereafter. The platoon commander and his platoon were sent to Srinagar and accommodated in a Prisoner of War Camp until despatched to Delhi by air in late April.

The successful outcome of Operation Handwara, it was assumed, would earn the Brigade some sort of congratulatory message from Headquarters Jak Force. The reply to the signal message reporting the incident in detail was totally unexpected. It was a short and terse signal which read: "The Force Commander wishes to be informed immediately how the enemy came to Handwara." It was obvious that the intention of the message was: "Explain at once why you permitted the enemy to come to Handwara." As it would have served no useful purpose to reiterate that the paucity of troops precluded the Brigade sealing every approach to the Valley and that the enemy could, if he chose to, appear anywhere and at any time, the query from Headquarters Jak Force was treated literally and the following answer sent: "Captured enemy platoon commander confirms that he and his men came on foot." There were no further exchanges on the subject.

Chapter 15

Foiling Encirclement

THE failure of the diversionary threat must have reached the enemy Headquarters at Muzaffarabad very quickly, probably through a wireless set with the main body of the enemy, as there were signs of intensified activity in the Uri-Mahura area. Fresh reinforcements were both observed by the troops and reported by agents to be moving forward. 161 Infantry Brigade's patrol programme was accordingly stepped up, and attempts at encirclement were thwarted by fighting patrols. The main burden fell on 4 Kumaon in the Mahura area. With strikes at every possible opportunity both by day and by night, the enemy was given no respite. Sultan Dacchi was raided and the enemy put to flight, and shortly after that another strong fighting patrol of 4 Kumaon surprised and scattered a large enemy concentration at Bijhama.

Similar surprise assaults were launched in other areas, and in due course the area north of Uri and Mahura was cleared of the enemy. The senior enemy commanders did not appear to take kindly to the reverses being suffered by their tribals and troops, and decided to sack the commander of the enemy operating in the Mahura area. This information was handed to us by one of our agents who added: "The enemy commander is being removed by his superiors on a charge that his failure to achieve any type of success creates a strong suspicion that he is actively collaborating with 161 Brigade."

There was a lull in enemy activity for about a week, and then came the information that the new incumbent had arrived and had taken over command. His first action was to give his men a pep talk. He said his orders were to capture Mahura and he was going to do so. He had been told that offensive spirit was lacking but from that moment onwards things would be different. While his command was reducing Mahura, others would capture Uri. With the strong reinforcements that were being sent forward, and would be arriving very shortly, he had no doubt that he would successfully implement the orders that had been issued to him. His name, according to our informant, was Khalil, and he wore the badges of rank of a Brigadier.

Concurrently, with the arrival of the new commander in the Mahura area, Azad Kashmir Radio stepped up its tirades and issued ominous daily warnings of what was about to befall both Uri and Mahura. Those serving with 161 Infantry Brigade were advised to accept the friendly warning and to depart when the going was good. To be stubborn and shortsighted and to treat a friendly gesture with contempt, the broadcast said, would be foolish in the extreme. As time sped by, the cajoling made way for sarcasm and threats, and finally a reversion to the initial tone of obscenity and abuse.

In the hope that word would get back to us and result in a splintering of the hard core defences, the enemy took to openly boasting in the hearing of the local villagers of their projected plans, and nominated actual dates. These plans varied from full-scale attacks on Uri or Mahura, to strong attacks against particular piquets. Although none of them materialised, they definitely had a nuisance value, as piquets had to be alerted on the off-chance that the threat might be carried out. The only plan that the enemy rank and file and the tribals neither bragged about nor discussed was the one aimed at crossing the Jhelum River between Mahura and Baramula, and, having cut the road, to attack from an easterly direction first Mahura and then Uri. It was something that had to be kept a closely guarded secret. It was known only to the senior enemy commanders, a very few trusted lieutenants, and—quite unknown to them—to the target of attack, 161 Infantry Brigade.

It was not that the enemy sent a copy of the plan to 161 Infantry Brigade in error. His very movements in the area of Mahura had made the intention crystal clear. The point at which the river would be crossed and the date were, however, questions the answers to which 161 Infantry Brigade would have to obtain by every means at its disposal. Each little bit of information regarding the enemy was, therefore, assembled in order to solve these two riddles.

SKETCH SHOWING THE AREA
NORTH OF MAHURA AND RAMPUR

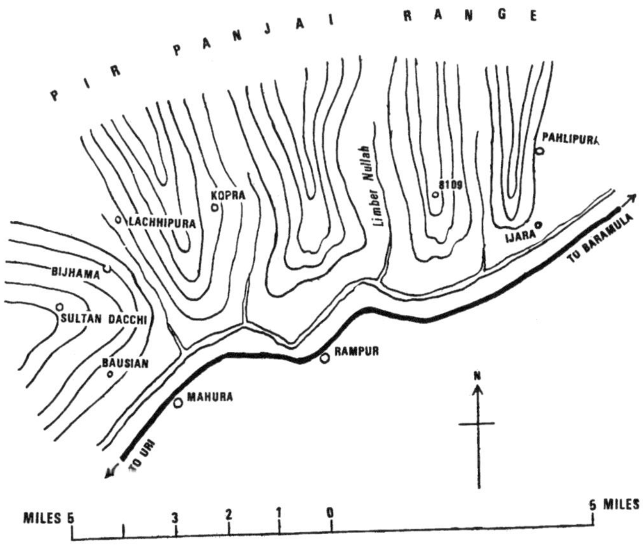

The enemy build-up in the Mahura area gained momentum with the arrival of the new commander. He was certainly far more methodical and capable than his predecessor. Efforts to obtain his identification were not successful; all that was established was that which was already known, that he was named Khalil and was a Brigadier. This meant nothing as it was, in all probability, a pseudonym. What was intriguing was his assertion that he knew the commander of 161 Infantry Brigade very well.

A few days after his arrival, "Khalil" sent an emissary to make contact with me. This individual, a relation of the headman of Lachhipura village, came to the bridge over the River Jhelum at Mahura and surrendered himself to the 4 Kumaon platoon guarding the bridge. He asked to be escorted to the Commanding Officer, for whom he had a message. Lt. Col. Man Mohan Khanna interviewed the messenger and then telephoned me in Uri, whereupon I informed him that I would come to Mahura immediately. On arrival, the emissary was produced before me. He stated that his whole family was being held as hostages and would only be freed when he returned. He was extremely nervous and pleaded that he should not be subjected to any form of interrogation regarding the enemy, as he had taken an oath that he would not reveal anything. He was assured that he would not be detained and that his request would be respected, whereupon, relief from the mental strain from which he was obviously suffering evinced itself in a flood of tears. He was given a cup of tea and told to rest for a few minutes.

Having recovered his composure, he produced a slip of paper which he stated had been handed to him by the enemy commander. It was unsigned, but the emissary was categorical that the message had been written in his presence by an officer wearing the same badges of rank as myself. The message requested that I agree to a seven-day cease fire, commencing at midnight, and stated that, as the writer knew my signature well, as a guarantee that his message had actually been delivered to me, I should hand the messenger a packet of ten Gold Flake cigarettes, endorsing the packet with my signature in ink.

A packet of ten Gold Flake cigarettes was produced, signed in ink in the presence of the courier, and handed to him with the instructions that he should hand it over to the author of the note and inform him that his message had been received and that the answer would be delivered at ten minutes before midnight. The handkerchief that had been used to blindfold him when he had been led to the HQ of 4 Kumaon was then replaced. Led back to the point where he had surrendered himself initially, it was removed and he was permitted to return to Lachhipura village.

Man Mohan Khanna and I sat on a patch of green grass and discussed the strange request. We agreed that it was much too rich to stomach. Over the past few weeks every possible means had been utilised to harass the enemy and to break up his concentrations, and here was a suggestion that was tantamount to saying to 161 Brigade, "Please stop harassing us and let us gain a position of advantage from where we can cut your throats." 161 Infantry Brigade was playing for time, the time when the Banihal Pass would reopen and make possible the induction of further units into the Valley. The enemy was simultaneously forcing the pace, bent on launching his attack and reducing the relatively weak garrisons holding Uri, Mahura and the Valley to a state where reinforcements would be desperately needed to face a situation identical to that which existed when the troops were first flown into the Valley. 161 Infantry Brigade was not prepared to cooperate in hammering a nail into its own coffin. There was only one possible answer to the request, and it was delivered at ten minutes before midnight: the field guns located in Uri blazed the rejection.

Enemy activity in the area north of Mahura now increased to quite an alarming extent. It was evident that the area was being heavily reinforced. To ensure that the Bausian feature was reasonably strongly held, and capable of withstanding a determined assault against it, it was strengthened with additional sub-units of 4 Kumaon, wired and mined. A battery of mountain guns in support of the position would have been a valuable asset, but unfortunately there was only one battery of four guns, and they were required to provide the defensive fire for the Uri piquets. The field artillery in Uri, while it could engage certain targets in the area to the north of Bausian, could not, because of intervening features, afford close support fire to the Bausian garrison.

There was also no possibility of making use of the field artillery in Baramula as there were no suitable positions for its deployment. The Bausian garrison had therefore to rely upon the 4 Kumaon three-inch mortar platoon which, despite suffering from severe range limitations, had been allotted the task.

Constant verbal threats notwithstanding, the enemy avoided Bausian like the plague and it remained a sharp thorn in his side. It soon became clear that his intention was not to stir up a hornet's nest, but to lull the defenders into a state of security, and by surreptitious means to work his way past Bausian to a position from which the value of holding Bausian would be nullified. In order to reach this position, and in order to ensure that the movement of his troops from west to east was not subjected to a sudden strike from Mahura, he began occupying piquet positions on the features to the north of Bausian from which he could get good observation and give early warning.

While by-passing Bausian and proceeding to his selected concentration area in the east, the enemy, in order not to attract undue attention, limited the number of personnel who moved each day to about one hundred armed men and fifty porters. These personnel moved in groups of about fifteen to twenty, at varying intervals, commencing each day soon after nine o'clock. During the afternoon and evening, the porters were observed returning, sauntering back in twos or threes as if they were harmless villagers. All armed bodies of men were immediately engaged by the field artillery firing from Uri. Each subsequent enemy advance was made a bit further to the north, until eventually the route followed was out of the range of the guns even when firing with super charge. It was then only possible to keep a count of the armed personnel who passed by each day, so that there would be some idea of the strength that would have to be combated when the time to strike arrived.

From our intelligence sources it was known that the enemy was concentrating in the Limber Nullah area, and it was decided to permit him to do so completely undisturbed, in the hope that he would be lulled into believing that we were quite oblivious of the fact. When, however, a report was received that he had moved further east and had reached Pahlipura village, immediate steps were taken to verify this but, as was expected, it was false. Had he advanced as far as Pahlipura, an attack with the battalion located in Baramula, 3 Garhwal, would have had to be mounted, as he would have been much too close to Baramula and the Valley.

The enemy's discipline during this period of March, when he was concentrating his force, was very good. All villages were avoided and there was no sign of movement in the concentration area by day nor the flicker of a light by night. In order to educate him, and make movement by 3 Garhwal from east to west along the north bank of the Jhelum river appear a matter of routine patrolling, both to him and any agents in Baramula, 3 Garhwal was ordered to send out patrols of varying strengths both by day and by night along the north bank of the Jhelum river as far as Ijara. This, it was hoped, would also give the impression that the river between Ijara and Rampur was being neglected. From the enemy's point of view it was perfect. This stretch of the river has many easy crossing sites where the banks slope gently and the current is relatively slow. The hills on the south bank were easily accessible, and sufficiently distant from both Baramula and Mahura to ensure that, when occupied eventually, neither garrison would know until it was a fait accompli.

The stretch of river from Ijara to Rampur was, however, far from being neglected. On the contrary, it was receiving specialised treatment. Located in well-concealed observation posts along the whole length were small groups of men equipped with binoculars, and in communication with Uri by wireless. These groups critically studied the movements of all individuals approaching either the north or south banks of the Jhelum river, and reported everything in the nature of strange or suspicious behaviour. Soon after darkness set in, the day observers would be withdrawn and replaced by similar groups who positioned themselves at various points close to the river. The enemy, however, was extremely cautious and gave away nothing. Our observers possibly considered it a waste of effort since, in order to eliminate idle chatter and possible speculation which might have reached the enemy's ears, the enemy's intended plan of action had not been divulged to the men, nor the plan to counter it. This remained a closely guarded secret, known only to Lt. Col. Man Mohan Khanna and myself.

The plan, in brief, was to permit the enemy encirclement party, which was reported to be the 4th AKP battalion and a hard core of two thousand five hundred tribesmen, to concentrate undisturbed in the Limber Nullah. When the concentration was completed and before they could attempt the river crossing, they would be first sealed off in the Limber Nullah and then annihilated. The sealing off of the enemy in the Limber Nullah would be effected by 3 Garhwal who would advance from Baramula and capture the feature point 8109, and by 4 Kumaon who would advance from Mahura and occupy the Kopra feature. 1 Sikh would move forward from Srinagar to Baramula, and be responsible for manning the defences evacuated by 3 Garhwal, two Rifle Companies being held in readiness to move to the Heman Buniyar Nullah area when ordered.

The timings in the plan could not be firmly laid down, as the advance by 4 Kumaon to Kopra was dependent on the success attained by 3 Garhwal, and the move to the Heman Buniyar Nullah area by two Companies of 1 Sikh, on the success gained by 4 Kumaon. If everything went according to plan, the enemy would be presented with four options: to fight the Garhwalis, or fight the Kumaonis, or attempt to cross the river in which case he would meet opposition from 1 Sikh, or to beat a retreat which would entail climbing the 13,000 feet Pir Panjal Range which was covered by deep snow. In order to present him with this situation, knowledge of the date of completion of his concentration and the date of his attack were absolutely vital requirements, as on them hinged the D day and H hour for the launching of 161 Infantry Brigade's strike, which had to be swift and sure.

Daily reports of the enemy strengths that had by-passed Mahura and moved eastwards did not, initially, appear to cause any undue alarm at Headquarters Jak Force in Jammu, but as the running total mounted to a sizeable proportion, there were signs of uneasiness. Headquarters 161 Infantry Brigade was asked to report what it was doing about it. The simple reply that the situation was well in hand, while accepted at first with a certain amount of relief, began to be

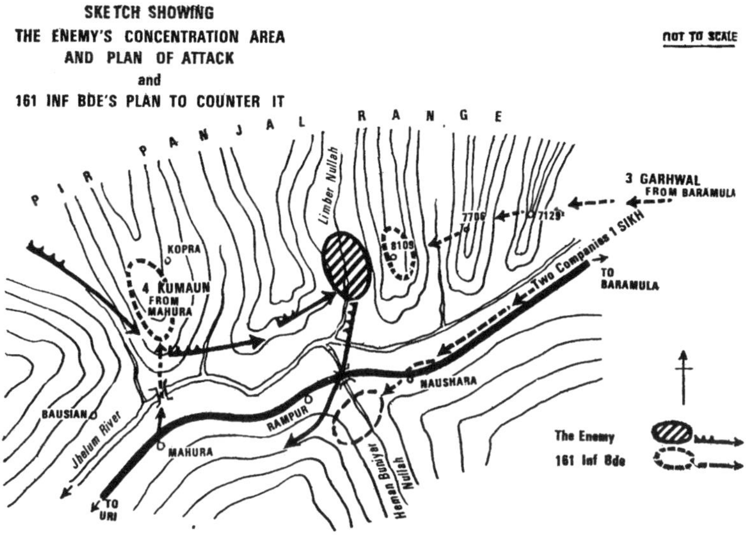

sarcastically referred to as masterly inactivity. Perhaps it appeared that way as Headquarters Jak Force had not been informed of the enemy's intention or of the plan to combat it. To have passed this information would have necessitated using the wireless link, which was considered unwise as there was a possibility of leakage or the cracking of the cipher by the enemy. Further, with the Banihal Pass under heavy snow and impassable, there was nothing that Headquarters Jak Force could do to assist, other than providing air support which could be called for at the last moment.

To have been stampeded into action would only have resulted in an engagement with an indecisive result, probably favourable to the enemy. A trap had been baited. It was hoped that, with luck favouring us, the stalker would experience that dread of the hunter—the sudden realisation that he was the one who was being stalked. He would not be given the chance to sit down and consider why and how it happened. He would be struck a well-directed blow from which recovery would be impossible.

Chapter 16

The Move to Leh

MEANWHILE the Brigade intercept sets, which had from time to time picked up messages being passed in the Gilgit area, reported increased activity concerning what the enemy had code-named "Operation Sledge". It was evident that the operation had either been launched or would be within a few days.

Operation Sledge was planned in Army Headquarters, Pakistan, and launched from Gilgit in mid-February 1948. The target was Leh, the capital of Ladakh. The enemy force employed to implement the plan was composed of a strong element from the Gilgit Scouts, defectors from the Jammu and Kashmir State Forces, and tribals. In concept it was ambitious, involving a movement on foot of over three hundred miles over most inhospitable terrain, but, apart from the distance to be covered, it was by no means a pioneer effort. Fur dealers and other traders had used the route for many decades, and there was no possibility of the force becoming involved in a major engagement. All that might have been encountered were minor skirmishes against weak opposition. The route followed the banks of the Indus river. The first point at which opposition might be encountered was Skardu, garrisoned by a weak State Force battalion. After neutralising this garrison, the enemy force would proceed unimpeded along the road, attack Kargil on its right flank, held by a very weak State Force detachment, and move thence to Leh.

Pakistan's assertion was that the invasion of Kashmir in October 1947 by tribesmen from the NWFP had come as a complete surprise to her. Gullible individuals were led to believe that the tribal action was motivated by a burning desire in the hearts of the tribesmen to "liberate" their Muslim brothers from the tyranny of a Hindu regime. No such reason could be advanced for the invasion of Ladakh. The Ladakhis are Buddhists whereas the "liberators" were not of that faith, nor had the Ladakhis asked for assistance. They had been living a life of peace and contentment for decades, with little, if any, external interference with their way of life. Yet, even to the homeland of these peace-loving people Pakistan brought war.

The blatant act of aggression was the more odious for the fact that the people of Ladakh were unarmed and in consequence were incapable of offering anything more than verbal resistance. Nor were there any troops, Regular or Irregular, readily available to come to their aid in the defence of their homeland. Was it a burning desire to acquire territory as bleak and desolate as the NWFP that prompted Pakistan to engage in this escapade? Or was there some other reason, and was she encouraged and persuaded by others to undertake it? This only history will answer. The fact, however, remains that the episode was engineered by Pakistan, and an Irregular Force, now under her command and control, played the major part in the attempt to subdue Ladakh.

The success of the operation, as envisaged by the planners, was dependent on three factors: the ability of the men to walk the distance, the logistics, and the annihilation of the opposition that might be encountered at Kargil. Segregating the Kashmir Valley from Ladakh was the massive Great Himalayan Range, with the 16,427 feet Zoji La Pass the only route across it. This Pass, usable during the summer months, was universally accepted as being an impregnable barrier during winter, the exceedingly heavy snowfalls making its crossing during the months of October to May unthinkable. There was no airstrip at Leh. Its reinforcement with troops, even had an airstrip existed, would have been extremely difficult because of the adverse flying conditions during winter. The door to Leh was wide open. Success was assured, even if the rate of advance was maintained at short stages of about ten miles per day.

The threat to Leh might never have materialised had Maharajah Hari Singh taken the action that should normally have followed the events of July 1947 and dispensed with the services of Major Brown and his British colleagues of the Gilgit Scouts. When he received the report of his Chief of Staff, Major General Scott, that the British officers of the Gilgit Scouts had told him they had all opted for Pakistan, he must surely have realised that his territory was being protected by personnel whose loyalty lay elsewhere. As it was 30 July 1947 when they made their announcement, and the Dominions of India and Pakistan did not come into being until 15 August, there was ample time for the ruler to refer the matter to Lord Louis Mountbatten, in his capacity as Viceroy of undivided India. If the Maharajah so desired, he could have asked for the services of British volunteers who would be willing to serve the State regardless of his final decision on which Dominion he would accede to.

Major General Scott would certainly also have gauged the feelings of the rank and file of the Gilgit Scouts, and it is presumed that he informed the ruler that they were unlikely to swear allegiance to him. These men, after all, had never formed a part of the Jammu and Kashmir State Forces. They had been enlisted by and served the British exclusively. It is, therefore, natural that they would be influenced by the action of their British officers, whom they knew and under whom they had served, in preference to taking an oath of allegiance to someone with whom they had had little connection over a period of about twelve years.

Considering the position of Major Brown and his British colleagues, their opting to serve Pakistan was not extraordinary. All British officers serving in the undivided Indian Army had been called upon to decide whether they wished to serve India or Pakistan, should their services by required, or to take their release, the terms of the release benefits being extremely generous. Pakistan's requirements of British officers far exceeded those of India, the ratio of non-British officers serving in the undivided Indian Army, being ten Indians to one future Pakistani. It was, therefore, natural that the majority of those British officers who wished to serve on opted for Pakistan, where their chances of being absorbed were much brighter.

What is very difficult to understand, however, is Major Brown's subsequent conduct which culminated in his hoisting the Pakistan flag in the lines of his command, the Gilgit Scouts, on 4 November 1947.

On 3 June 1947, with the retrocession of Gilgit to the Maharajah of Jammu and Kashmir by the Government of Great Britain, and with it the Gilgit Scouts, Major Brown and the other British officers of the Gilgit Scouts automatically came into the service of the Government of Jammu and Kashmir. As such, if they served on, which they all did, they owed loyalty not to Britain or to undivided India but to the Maharajah. Their position was identical to that of officers of the British Army loaned to and seconded for service with the Timbuctoo Rifles. Even on 15 August 1947, when the Dominions of India and Pakistan came into being, the position remained unaltered, as the State of Jammu and Kashmir was not part of either India or Pakistan. When the Maharajah signed the Instrument of Accession with India on 26 October 1947, honour and loyalty, qualities which would have been expected of these individuals as British officers, dictated that they make an immediate request for release from their appointments. Gilgit was now a part of India, and they had opted to serve Pakistan. It would have been the right and honourable thing for them to do. Their subsequent actions, however, betrayed a complete lack of these qualities. They stabbed the Maharajah of Jammu and Kashmir in the back, and joined hands with his enemies. This led to the butchering of men, women and children in the massacre that took place a few months later at Skardu, for which they must be held indirectly responsible.

Skardu came under pressure from enemy forces that moved down from Gilgit in February 1948. The Gorkha Commanding Officer, of the weak 6th Battalion, the Jammu and Kashmir State Forces, soon found that his best chance of survival, if he remained in the Skardu area, lay in evacuating his lightly held outpost positions and concentrating his unit in the Fort. Within the precincts of the Fort, he also accommodated a number of women and children, and in order to conserve the available foodstuff, placed everyone on a minimum ration scale. Attacks against the Fort were delivered at periodic intervals, but a steady and firm defence repulsed them, the casualties inflicted imposing caution on the enemy. However, the overall situation in Kashmir was such that no aid could be expected by the garrison at Skardu. The enemy's next step would be to lay siege to Skardu. It was in these circumstances that the Commanding Officer at Skardu Fort signalled Headquarters 161 Infantry Brigade for permission to slip away from Skardu and to head for Kargil.

His stock of food, he stated, was dwindling slowly but surely, and there was no possibility of replenishing it locally. The ammunition situation, though not precarious, was not in a healthy state. The reduced ration scale was already having a noticeably adverse effect on the physical condition of his men, which would further deteriorate as the days passed. If given permission to withdraw from Skardu, his rate of movement, and the distance to be covered each day, would be limited to that which the sick and wounded, and the women and children, could cope with. Forced marches were not possible in their case. He planned, therefore, to slip them away each night, in small batches so as to avoid detection, with a small protective party. When these batches were sufficiently far away from Skardu, he would evacuate the Fort with his main body and fight a rear-guard action back to Kargil. Here he would link up with the State Force detachment, and together they would present the enemy with a much stronger front.

There was no alternative to the proposed withdrawal plan, and although it carried some hazards it promised hope of success. It was not the request of a coward, but of a gallant soldier who realised that Skardu Fort, if encircled, was incapable of being relieved, and his men, and the women and children who had entrusted him with their safety, would receive no mercy from the enemy. Skardu, moreover, taking into consideration the situation as it existed at the time, was of neither strategical nor tactical value. Its relatively small garrison was quite incapable of either seriously harassing the enemy or denying him access to the east should he desire to proceed in that direction. It was in fact nothing other than a Flag Flying Outpost, which would one day be forced into surrender through starvation and the inability of the garrison to strike back in self-defence.

A signal message, stressing the position and the difficulties that were facing the Skardu garrison, and emphasising that they would increase as each day went by, was despatched to Headquarters Jak Force. It was very strongly recommended that the Commanding Officer's request should be acceded to immediately. As time was of vital importance in ensuring that the disabled, and the women and children, were well clear before the Fort was evacuated, an answer within the next few hours was requested. A feeling of despair descended over Headquarters 161 Infantry Brigade when Headquarters Jak Force's reply was received. It stated that the withdrawal from Skardu was not agreed to, and that the commander would be ordered to stay put.

This refusal was not passed on to the Commander of the Skardu garrison. A second signal was despatched to Headquarters Jak Force, emphasising again that Skardu had neither strategical nor tactical value, that it would be subjected to a siege in a few days, and that as the siege could never be relieved, it was throwing away human lives without obtaining any benefit whatsoever. Operation Sledge, it was stated, was about to be launched by the enemy at any moment, and because of the logistical problems involved, the number of troops or tribal or a mixture of both would have to be limited. The presence of the Skardu garrison would not prevent that number being mustered, nor could it interfere with their progress towards the east. If, however, the Skardu garrison was permitted to withdraw to Kargil, together with the detachment already at Kargil, it could present a much bolder front, and with the enemy line of communication stretched, it would not only survive but also be a thorn in the enemy flank.

Headquarters Jak Force evidently did not appreciate the arguments advanced. It made no reference to them, and issued a cold sharp order that Headquarters 161 Infantry Brigade would immediately order the commander of the Skardu garrison to fight to the last man and the last round, and that a confirmation that this order had been passed to Skardu and understood would be signalled back as quickly as was possible. The Jak Force instructions were carried out, and an acknowledgement received from Skardu. Headquarters Jak Force was informed that the message had been passed and had been understood.

Fifteen days later, Skardu sent a signal to the effect that the enemy had occupied every vantage point around the Fort, and that as any movement out of it drew fire, which was resulting in casualties, patrolling outside the Fort was no longer possible. The inevitable had happened—Skardu was besieged. An attempt was made to relieve the siege of Skardu in late May 1948, but the State Force troops that moved out made very little progress against determined enemy opposition and withdrew. An air effort was then mounted to drop ammunition and supplies but this proved too costly in casualties sustained by the defenders, who had to battle with the enemy to recover the stores that landed in the area outside the Fort. In early September, their last round of ammunition fired and their ration store empty, the Skadu garrison, too weak physically to offer any further resistance, was forced to surrender, and, with the women and children that it had striven so desperately hard to safeguard, met a fate equalled only by the rape and massacre of Baramula.

On 3 March, a few days after it had been encircled by the enemy, Skardu Fort reported by signal that about five hundred armed men and about two hundred porters had arrived from the direction of Gilgit. They had camped the night in the vicinity of Skardu town, and had set off the next morning in an easterly direction, presumably heading for Kargil. This information was also confirmed by a wireless intercept, and left no shadow of doubt that Operation Sledge was now under way. This information was passed to D. P. Dhar, who immediately requested that a conference be held to find ways and means to combat it. During the discussion that followed, "DP" evinced deep anxiety at the prospect of Leh being attacked. The Ladakhis, he stressed, were completely unarmed and at the mercy of the raiders. The monastery at Leh would be ransacked, and unless we did something about it, there would be serious repercussions in the Buddhist world. It was unanimously agreed that we must do something about it, but do what was the question. There was only a small State Force detachment at Kargil, and from reports received its morale was low. It could not be expected to arrest the move of the raiders towards Leh. To get to Ladakh from the Kashmir Valley was also said to be an impossibility at that time of the year, as dividing the two was the Great Himalayan Range, thickly covered with snow—an insurmountable barrier.

On occasions such as this, when facing a problem that appears to have no solution, helplessness generates many solutions prefixed with an "if". The most frequent "if" concerned the Skardu garrison, which was the only major force located on the Ladakh side of the Great Himalayan Range: "if only we could find a way of getting the Skardu garrison back to Kargil". Various suggestions were made, such as getting it to slip out in the dark through the cordon that had been thrown around it, and to carry out a forced march to Kargil, bypassing the enemy column that was already on its way. This was neither militarily sound, nor for that matter practicable. The enemy surrounding Skardu would have got the information very quickly to the advancing force by wireless signal, and the Skardu garrison would have had little chance of survival. The opportunity of reinforcing Kargil had been irretrievably lost, and the Skardu garrison was now akin to the paste in a sandwich. The gloom in which the conference terminated was relieved by but one ray of hope: everyone agreed to give the matter further thought.

The ray of hope was transformed into a rainbow the next evening. In a casual conversation, Lt. Col. G. G. Bewoor, who had taken over as the Commanding Officer of 2 Dogra from Lt. Col. U. C. Dubey, mentioned that 2 Dogra, during its service as a Territorial Battalion, had enlisted, among other classes, a number of Lahulis. Many of them were still serving in the battalion, including two officers, Captain Prithi Chand and his cousin Captain Khushal Chand. Lahul, situated in the north of what is now the State of Himachal Pradesh, has a contiguous border with Ladakh, and over the centuries there has been close affinity between the Lahulis and the Ladakhis. "Perhaps," Bewoor suggested, "it might be worthwhile asking Prithi Chand and Khushal whether they and a few Lahuli other ranks would volunteer to go to Leh and organise its defence." It certainly was worth trying, and Gopal Bewoor was asked to sound Prithi Chand and Khushal.

In his talk with them, Lt. Col. Bewoor did not use persuasion nor did he in any way minimise the dangers that would have to be faced. Having explained the situation, he told the two young officers that the only available route was via the Zoji La Pass, over the Great Himalayan Range, which was covered in snow to a depth of about thirty feet. Local experts, he said, were emphatic that no one had attempted to negotiate it under such conditions and to do so would be courting disaster. He asked them to consider the matter very carefully, assuring them that no adverse opinion would be held against them if they decided not to undertake the task.

Leaving the two officers to deliberate over the proposition, Bewoor returned to the conference room and had barely seated himself, when Prithi Chand and Khushal Chand appeared. Without hesitating for a second Prithi Chand said: "We'll go to Leh." It was immediately decided that volunteers should be called for from the battalion, the target being set at about forty. This would form a strong platoon with a signal detachment. The number of forty was arrived at so as not to unbalance 2 Dogra, which had an operational role in Kashmir, and also because of the logistical problem involved. The call for volunteers produced a remarkable response, every Lahuli volunteering and a large number of Dogras in addition. A very strict medical examination was conducted, and eventually fifty were selected, forty to form the party to go to Leh and ten to be held in reserve to replace any casualties that may be suffered in the selected forty prior to the date of their departure.

The formulating of an Administrative Plan, to cover every possible requirement of the volunteers to Leh, was taken in hand. It was realised that once the party had set out, there was no earthly chance of making good any deficiency. It would have to suffer the consequences of an oversight until such time as the weather improved and air drop was possible, and that would probably not be earlier than two months. Lists were prepared, checked, re-checked and added to as omissions came to light. Extra winter clothing, Gilgit boots, gloves, snow goggles and other such items necessary to combat what would be sub-zero temperatures and possible blizzards were purchased from the shops in Srinagar. Then, besides the normal rations, an assortment of tinned products was included. Most important of all, medical panniers had to be equipped with medicines and drugs to cater for ailments that would normally be attended to in a hospital by a trained doctor, and a certain number of men had to be educated in their use.

In addition to the weapons with which the platoon would be armed, one hundred rifles were collected from the State Force Armoury and included in the load that would be carried to Leh. The rifles, and the ammunition that accompanied them, were to equip the Ladakhis so that they could take an active part in defending their homeland. With the selection of a suitable wireless set with which to ensure communication, and the men practised daily in tying the various loads and placing them on pack ponies, the column was equipped and ready to move by the middle of March.

D. P. Dhar had, in the meantime, been busy collecting the pack ponies for the column. As these animals were used exclusively during the summer months by the tourists who camped and trekked in the Valley, and were let out to graze during the "off-season", it was no easy job to obtain them and even harder to get their owners to undertake any task in the winter. Moreover, in order to maintain secrecy, he could not tell the pony owners where they were expected to go. The ponies were, however, an operational necessity and "DP" succeeded in obtaining them, and had them concentrated at Sonemarg. In order to economise in the number of personnel to be fed, it was decided that there would be one man to ten pack ponies.

As Headquarters Jak Force permission was necessary before launching the Leh volunteers on their way, and it was not considered prudent to send a signal, even in cipher, a comprehensive letter enumerating every detail was prepared and carried to Jammu by two volunteers who agreed to tackle the snow-bound Banihal Pass. This, in itself, was a commendable effort as it presented danger at every step. Three days after their departure from the Valley, Headquarters Jak Force acknowledged receipt of the letter and stated that it was being examined. Days sped by, and when no reply was received by mid-March, an urgent reminder was signalled to Headquarters Jak Force. The answer stated that the matter was still under consideration. Further reminders, stressing that each day's delay would bring the enemy closer to Kargil and possibly arrest the advance of the volunteers to Leh, had no effect. It was always the same answer: "still under consideration". With the enemy presumably making good progress, the Leh volunteers champing at the bit to take off, and D. P. Dhar and his colleagues of the Emergency Government in the Valley showing signs of increased anxiety, a final request was made to Headquarters Jak Force for an answer. When the same reply, "still under consideration", was received, Captain Prithi Chand was told to take off.

The Leh party was transported to Sonemarg, together with their baggage, in motor transport that had been assembled in Baramula, and on arrival married up with their pack ponies. Loading the animals, the column moved forward to Baltal. Here many of the pony leaders, having been made aware of the further moves, refused to continue with the column, and were returned to Sonemarg for return to their homes. One can hardly blame them for their attitude. This was madness and suicidal, they said. The Zoji La had never been crossed other than in the summer months, and they were not going to risk it.

Basing his column at Baltal, Prithi Chand moved forward with a few men to prepare the Zoji La Pass for the assault. It was necessary to create avalanches, and this was done by beating drums in the stillness of the night. This procedure continued over three nights and then Prithi Chand signalled that he was ready to make the attempt to cross the Pass. There was no contact with the column for the next forty-eight hours, and then came a signal that the crossing had been successfully accomplished without a casualty, and that the column was setting out for Kargil on its way to Leh.

No amount of praise will suffice to laud this great effort. Many hardened mountaineers, who knew the Zoji La Pass well, had shaken their heads and said it could result in a disaster to tackle it at that time of the year. There is no denying, that it could have resulted in the loss of the complete column, and no one suffered more from anxiety than myself and 2 Dogra. The wireless link at Brigade Headquarters was kept working from the moment Prithi Chand announced that he was ready for the assault on the Pass, and there were almost hourly inquiries whenever contact was made. When the success signal eventually came through, everyone in 161 Infantry Brigade felt ten years younger. Fortune had truly favoured the brave.

A signal was despatched to Headquarters Jak Force stating that the Zoji La had been crossed and the column under Prithi Chand was on

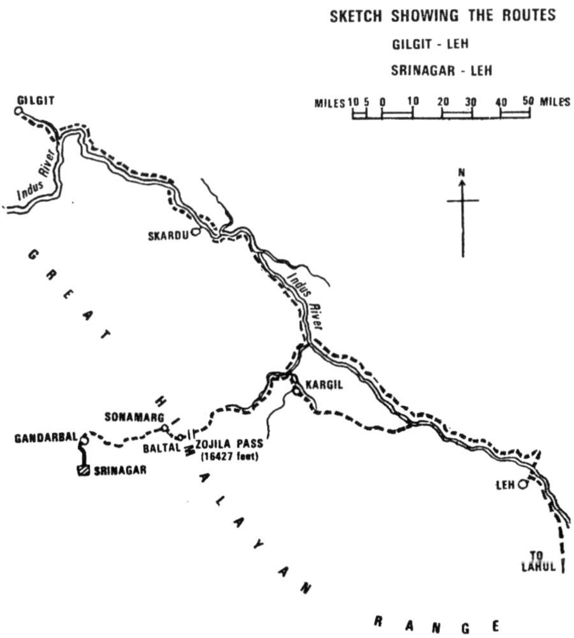

its way to Kargil. There was an immediate reaction. A signal message was received stating that a letter was being despatched by hand of the couriers who had arrived with Headquarters 161 Infantry Brigade's letter. When the couriers arrived, having once again braved the Banihal Pass, the letter did not contain the necessary sanction to despatch the column, this incidentally being necessary to support the expenses incurred in equipping the column. It called for an immediate explanation. The source of the trouble was that Prithi Chand's party had been designated by me as "Leh Force". HQ Jak Force demanded on whose authority this nomenclature had been given. The military definition of the word "Force" was explained in detail, and garnished with examples such as "Paiforce" (Persia and Iraq Force) which was in being during World War II. The letter stressed that there was and would only be one "Force" in Jammu and Kashmir State, and that was Jak Force. A signal stating that "Leh Force" had been instructed to change its designation to "Lehdet" (Leh Detachment) closed the issue, and sanction, ex post facto, was duly received.

Prithi Chand and his men reached Leh without encountering the enemy. The rifles and ammunition were distributed among suitable young men and they were given hasty training in their use. Defensive positions, based on a bridge, were taken up and the arrival of the enemy awaited. He arrived in due course and was surprised to meet stubborn opposition. Every attempt to overrun the defences met with a serious reverse, until eventually, finding that his attacks were proving to be too costly, the enemy abstained from attempting to proceed to Leh.

Prithi Chand and his gallant band of men were later joined by two Companies of the 2nd Battalion 4th Gorkha Rifles, who had been despatched by the recently revived Headquarters Western Command from Manali in the Kulu Valley, and carried out an equally prodigious march over heights extending to 15,000 feet, through Lahul on to Leh. That Leh was held, and the enemy deprived of the pleasure of sacking and looting it, was the outcome of a great deed which will find few equals in military history. It called for unbounded courage, determination and stamina, and these qualities and more were amply demonstrated by the defenders who took the first shock of the attack, the two officers and their gallant men from 2 Dogra of 161 Infantry Brigade.

Chapter 17

Brickbats for Bouquets

THE planning and preparations to combat Operation Sledge, though they were time-consuming and involved a great deal of effort, were not permitted to distract from the serious threat at our doorstep on the Uri Front, or to hamper the measures necessary for the slowing down of the enemy build-up in the Limber Nullah area. The threat on both these fronts was increasing with each day. What 161 Infantry Brigade had done everything possible to avert, the facing of major engagements simultaneously on two fronts, was on the way to becoming a stark reality. Playing for time was very necessary, but it would be hoping too much to expect the enemy to stay put in the Limber Nullah until such time as the Banihal Pass was open and strong reinforcements could move into the Kashmir Valley. Every advantage rested with the enemy, the most disconcerting of all being that he held the initiative.

With an open motorable road at hs command, he could move forward anything that he chose to, and could blitz 161 Infantry Brigade at Uri on a date and at a time which suited him.

Serious though the situation was, 161 Infantry Brigade was by no means depressed. Its morale was much too high for that. Being outnumbered by the enemy—at the worst the odds had been about ten to one against us, and were now estimated to be in the region of six to one—was accepted as normal. What was causing a certain degree of frustration was the fact that all efforts directed at obtaining the probable date of strike by the enemy concentrating in the Limber Nullah had not borne fruit. If we could get some inkling of it, we could strike first, and the numerical advantage held by the enemy, the possibility of being presented with attacks on two fronts, and the initiative that he held would all be erased at one fell swoop. The enemy choice of the Limber Nullah as his concentration area suited us admirably, and would eventually be to his disadvantage if it was struck at the correct moment. As far as 161 Infantry Brigade was concerned, there was no latitude for launching a "hit or miss" operation. When battle was joined, the enemy force in the Limber Nullah would have to be so completely routed that it would never present another threat.

Our intelligence sources continued to report that strong enemy reinforcement had arrived, and were earmarked to arrive, on both fronts. In the Mahura area, an Azad Kashmir Brigade composed of the 3rd, 4th and 5th AKP battalions, together with three thousand Pathan tribesmen from the NWFP, were reported to have arrived by 1 March. The task of effecting the river crossing in an area between Baramula and Rampur, it was stated, had been assigned to the 4th AKP battalion and two thousand five hundred tribesmen. The 3rd and 5th AKP battalions and five hundred tribals were to remain concentrated in the area of Lachhipura, but whether they were to be held in reverse or had been allotted some other role could not be gleaned. What was known, however, was that certain elements of both these battalions were being utilised in a porter role, carrying forward ammunition and stores for the concentration in the Limber Nullah. The locals, who had been press-ganged into porter duties, had not reacted kindly to the possibility of being shelled and shot at by our patrols when accompanying armed men, and more often than not had jettisoned their loads and returned home.

This information about the behaviour of the locals was comforting, not that we wished them any harm, but purely from the point of view of its effect on the enemy's build-up programme, which would be retarded. The enemy, then, suddenly changed his methods. All moves to and from the Limber Nullah by daylight ceased, and infiltration by night was substituted. It was no longer possible for us to keep any sort of a reasonably accurate running total of what numbers had moved through, and our assessment had to be based on past averages and intelligent guessing. With the enemy's security measures also being tightened up, the use of agents to confirm or correct our assessment was no longer possible.

Meanwhile, the melting snows had changed the situation confronting Uri. What had been difficult or inaccessible areas, now became fit for occupation and movement. In early March, a patrol of 2 Dogra, this battalion having moved to Uri from Baramula and relieved 3 Garhwal, which had returned to Baramula, reported that the enemy had returned to the Bhatgiran area and was digging in. This news was disturbing. Quite apart from the fact that it constituted a definite threat to Uri from the south, it also indicated that the enemy had visions of encircling Uri from that area or of isolating it by bringing the road from Mahura to Uri under fire.

His previous attempts in December 1947 had resulted in 161 Infantry Brigade reacting violently. It would have done so again, but unfortunately there were now less troops available to remove the hornet's nest. There were just two units manning the Uri defences, 5 Rajrif and 2 Dogra, and one Rifle Company of 3 Garhwal, which had been retained in Uri as the Brigade reserve when the battalion returned to Baramula. To attack Bhatgiran, previous experience had shown, required one full strength battalion, and it was not available. In view of the Limber Nullah build-up, neither 4 Kumaon, from Mahura, nor 3 Garhwal could be touched. At Srinagar was 1 Sikh, its role the protection of the Valley and Handwara, and earmarked to move to Baramula and on to Heman Buniyar when the Limber Nullah battle erupted. There was no option other than to live with the threat, and to deal with it if, and when, the enemy decided to sting us.

The enemy in the Bhatgiran area fortunately adopted a most passive attitude. He made no attempt to interfere with Uri or its defences. This was very strange, as it was the most obvious thing to do. His patrol activities were also inclined to be slack, but there was a live danger that in a fit of enthusiasm a patrol might venture as far as Uri's eastern perimeter, in which case it would have discovered that it was completely devoid of troops. This might have encouraged the enemy to move round and occupy a feature in the area, and had he done so, it would have made matters extremely difficult. It was now no longer possible to take the risk which had, in the past, been accepted. 2 Dogra was ordered to thin out some of its piquets and to form an ad hoc Rifle Company, and to establish a piquet on the Nambla feature. Other than one minor patrol clash in the area to the south of Nambla, the enemy made no attempt to engage or dislodge Nambla piquet.

It would be incorrect to give the impression that the enemy on the Uri front was completely inactive. He was extremely active in some areas, but showed a distinct partiality towards certain piquets which he attacked with almost monotonous regularity, despite his being repulsed on each occasion. His tactical ability, fortunately, lacked a sense of adventure. At no time did he attempt to infiltrate in-between the piquets and attack the Uri bowl which, especially on a dark night, was easy. A report was received one day that he intended doing so, the gun areas and Brigade Headquarters being the selected targets. This called for emergency measures. The Commanding Officer of the Field Ambulance was, however, most indignant when he found a platoon of infantry digging trenches in the hospital area. He was emphatic that the protection of the patients was the responsibility of the Field Ambulance, and insisted that he would undertake the task with his own men. All he required was the loan of three Bren guns. It was found impossible to persuade him to let those more accustomed to operating Bren guns assist him, and eventually three light automatics, withdrawn from units, were handed over to his command. The expected attack did not materialise, and it was providential that it did not, as there would have been a number of casualties, the majority of them in the Mountain Battery and Brigade Headquarters. In the eagerness to ensure an all-round defence, two of the Bren Guns allotted to the Field Ambulance were so aligned that they would have made matters most uncomfortable for the Mountain Battery, and the wooden building of Brigade Headquarters would have had more perforations in it than a sheet of postage stamps.

Along the road between Rampur and Uri, however, the enemy had a far greater measure of success. In terms of casualties inflicted it was very light, but the enemy action had nuisance value and imposed delays on the road convoys. Snipers, initially equipped only with rifles, took up positions on the hills on the north bank of the Jhelum river, to the east and west of Bausian, and fired at men and vehicles moving along the main road. Then, realising that the rifle fire was not arresting movement along the road, light machine guns were brought into action. With the river intervening and the snipers constantly changing positions, it was not possible to stalk them, but every counter-measure was taken to deal with this situation, the most effective being the stationing of an Armoured Car in a particularly troublesome area, the sniper fire being answered with bursts of automatic fire while men and vehicles continued to run the gauntlet.

Enthusiasm coupled with foolhardiness, however, resulted in an avoidable loss. A young Company Commander, ordered to carry out a reconnaissance, tried to run the gauntlet in a truck, in the back of which were sitting his three platoon commanders. A burst from an enemy automatic wounded all four of them, the driver of the vehicle, who escaped being hit, driving the vehicle out of range and into a safe area. With the firing at the road increasing in intensity each day, although it was by sheer good fortune that it met with no further success, it was decided not to tempt Fate too far, and orders were issued that the movement of vehicles and personnel would be confined to the hours of darkness. This succeeded in keeping the convoys moving, and although the enemy continued to fire when he heard the sound of a vehicle, the firing by night was erratic and did no damage.

Denial of the use of the road during the hours of daylight was, however, something that could not be accepted for a protracted period.

Strong counter-measures were taken to remove the sniper menace, but the odds were definitely in favour of the enemy. While our sniper had to locate and engage a pinpoint target, the enemy sniper had a relatively large target to aim at in the shape of a vehicle. The whole Squadron of Armoured Cars was, therefore, brought into action, and taking up positions opposite known and favoured positions of the enemy snipers, they sprayed the area with automatic fire whenever a sniper came into action. It certainly assisted in large stretches of the road being declared "Green", and the restriction on movement along the road by daylight was lifted, although one or two areas remained "Red" until well into April. Over these "Red" stretches one had to take a chance by making a quick dash.

Despite the steady enemy activity on the Mahura front, intercepted signal messages from Brigadier Khalil to Jamil, who was evidently his superior commander with his Headquarters at Muzaffarabad, gave indications that the target date for the implementation of the plan to cross the river would not be earlier than some time during the first fortnight of April. This was a wide range, and what was important was the actual date. Khalil's signals were therefore given very careful study. It was he, after all, who would nominate the date and it was hoped that while doing so he would make a slip. Khalil's signals made one thing very clear, he was not going to attack before he had received all his requirements.

Whether it was impatience over the delay in launching the encirclement attack on the Mahura front, or perhaps a spur from superior Headquarters to do something, the linked piquets, Fort and Jitter at Uri, once again began to receive attention. Still manned by 6 Rajrif, they appeared to have been singled out, probably because they were almost at ground level and easily accessible. After a few half-hearted attacks, probing in nature, an attack fiercer and more determined than Uri had ever experienced previously was mounted against them.

The attack was delivered soon after midnight under a very bright moon. The Pathan tribals, having crept forward stealthily, rushed the barbed wire fence protecting the two piquets, filling the air with blood curdling screams, whistles and shouts. Before their wire cutters could create a gap, withering fire from both piquets took its toll and the attackers withdrew. Assault after assault, each one of greater weight and intensity followed. The Brigade reserve, the company of 3 Garhwal, was immediately moved forward and located in depth in-between the two piquets in the event of a breakthrough. The garrisons of Fort and Jitter were, however, taking a heavy toll of the enemy, hurling back every attack and inviting the enemy to have yet another try. This behaviour of the tribals, in mounting attack after attack, was a distinct departure from their previous practice. It was immediately realised that something unusual had constrained them into this course of action.

It was not until just before first light that they finally broke action and withdrew, and then the reason became apparent. While clearing the area of the killed, one victim, who was lying against the barbed wire, was identified as a very important tribal leader. In his pocket was a letter, in which the writer expressed supreme confidence in his ability

SKETCH SHOWING THE ATTACK ON FORT and JITTER PIQUETS

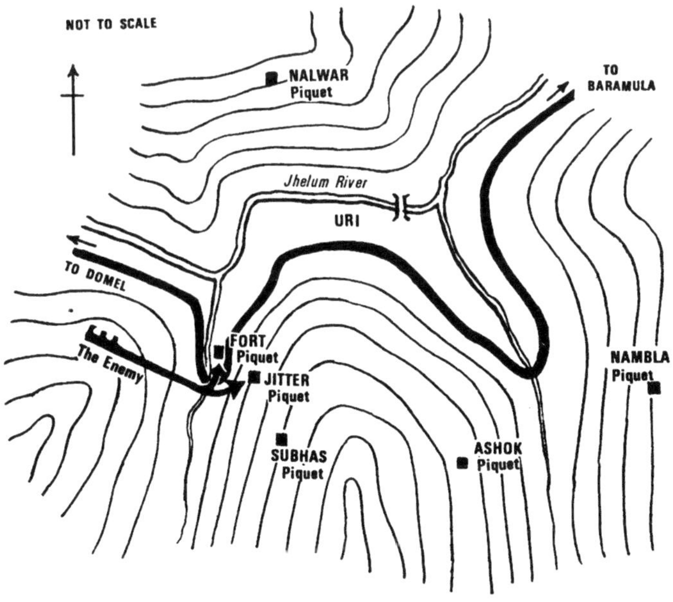

as a leader of men in battle, and stressed that he had been especially selected to proceed to Kashmir to prove to others, less capable, that the Uri defences were by no means impregnable.

That the tribal leader was a brave and fearless man is unquestionable. The very position where his body lay was a clear indication that he had been in the forefront of the battle. It was probably he who attempted to cut a gap through the wire, as cutting pliers lay close to him. He was given a burial with all the honours due to a brave man. The fanaticism displayed by his followers, in launching attack after attack, was clearly with the object of recovering his body. In trying to do so, they had suffered very heavy casualties, and presumably arriving at the conclusion that Fort and Jitter were much too strongly held to be subdued, and with the light approaching, withdrew. No further attacks were delivered at these two redoubts.

The concentration in the Limber Nullah continued to build up, but incredibly sluggishly. The last week of March arrived, and there was still no indication as to when Khalil intended striking. The melting snows must have caused Jamil a great deal of concern, as, during the first week of April, almost every intercepted message sent by him to Khalil urged the latter to get a move on and stressed that every day's delay would benefit 161 Infantry Brigade and make his task harder. Jamil was perfectly correct, but Khalil did not appear to share his apprehensions. He invariably replied to the effect that he intended making a very thorough job of his role, but could only do so when he was fully prepared and in possession of all the equipment necessary. In order to set Jamil's mind at rest, he stated in a message: "The enemy is fast asleep. He has no idea of what is about to happen. His days are numbered. When I strike, victory is assured." Even this message did not appear to impress Jamil, who continued to stress that time was fast running out. Unfortunately for both Jamil and Khalil, it actually had.

Contrary to expectations, the Banihal Pass opened to wheeled traffic three weeks in advance of the estimated date. In the first week of April, 161 Infantry Brigade received a surprise bonus when the 1st Battalion The Madras Regiment (1 Madras) reported for duty in the Valley. With the weather over the Pass clearing, air traffic to the Valley was also resumed. 1 Madras was immediately allotted the role of protecting the line of communication from Baramula to Rampur. One Rifle Company took over the piquets in Baramula, thereby permitting 3 Garhwal, less its Rifle Company at Uri, to remain uncommitted in Baramula and ready for a quick move. Yet another Rifle Company relieved the 4 Kumaon Company that had been located in Rampur, and enabled that battalion to concentrate at fall strength in the Mahura area. The remainder of 1 Madras was stationed in the Heman Buniyar Nullah, and 1 Sikh relieved of the commitment of having to move from Srinagar to Baramula, when 3 Garhwal moved out to Heman Buniyar.

1 Madras was a young and relatively inexperienced unit, having been raised at the outbreak of World War II. As such, its employment had to be carefully considered, and its roles tailored so as to be within its capabilities. This was purely an initial measure, as the standard of training attained by the unit was not known, as its true ability could only be assessed after having seen it operate. The Commanding Officer of 1 Madras, Lt. Col. Menon, who had been decorated with the Military Cross in World War II, and was as brave and gallant an officer as one could wish to serve alongside, was, however, champing at the bit to get at the enemy. When assigned what appeared to be a defensive role, he showed distinct signs of disappointment, but felt much happier when it was explained to him that his role could very easily turn in a matter of minutes to an offensive one, and was promised that the battalion would be soon given an opportunity to cross swords with the enemy.

Following close on the heels of 1 Madras came Major General Lakhinder Singh. The Duty Officer at Headquarters Jak Force telephoned Uri and stated that Major General Lakhinder Singh would be arriving by air at Srinagar at ten o'clock the next morning and that I was required to meet him at the airfield. He was unable to enlighten us on the purpose of the visit. I received Major General Lakhinder Singh at the airfield and drove him to Rear Headquarters 161 Infantry Brigade in Srinagar. When he had settled down, he informed me that he had been appointed the General Officer Commanding The Fifth Infantry Division (5 Div), and that the Division was moving into the Valley. 161 Infantry Brigade, as one of the original Brigades of the Division, would revert to its parent formation. This was great news, and I informed Lakhinder Singh that the Brigade would be delighted when this information reached it.

When he said that he was staying on in Srinagar and wished to establish his Headquarters as quickly as possible, immediate steps were taken to set up an *ad hoc* Divisional Headquarters. As he had only one Staff Officer with him, a certain number of officers were withdrawn from the administrative unit in Srinagar and Rear Headquarters 161 Infantry Brigade was ordered to evacuate a certain number of rooms in order to accommodate Headquarters 5 Div. By four o'clock that afternoon, a skeleton Headquarters 5 Div had been established and had commenced functioning, taking 161 Infantry Brigade under command. I suggested to Lakhinder Singh that he pay a visit to Uri the next morning, so that I could brief him on a map and then show him the piquets on the ground. This agreed to, it was decided that I meet him at Baramula at nine o'clock and drive him to Uri.

The next morning I picked up Lakhinder Singh at Baramula and drove him to Uri. I mentioned to him that on my way from Uri I had not been sniped at, but warned him that on the way back we might be subjected to sniper fire, but if a dash was made over the normally active areas, the chances of being hit were very slight. The snipers were probably having an off-day, as the drive to Uri was undisturbed by them. After a short break, in order to allow the effects of the drive to wear off, I took him into the Operations Room and commenced a briefing with the aid of the Situation Map. Having first pointed out the enemy concentrations in the Uri area, I explained very carefully the deployment of the troops on the various piquets and those in the Uri bowl. I then took him out to a vantage point from where most of the piquets could be seen, and pointed them out to him, and indicated where those which were not visible were located.

Lakhinder Singh had asked no questions and advanced no views up to this stage, and I inquired whether he had any questions or comments. His answer was to the effect that he considered the defensive system to be weak. Assuming that he was referring to the lack of sufficient troops, I stated that Uri certainly required another battalion, but in view of the situation on the Mahura front, there was no spare battalion.

His reply to this was quite shattering. He stated that in his opinion there were ample troops at Uri; what he meant to convey was that full use had not been made of them, that he was not at all happy with what he had seen and heard, and that the complete defensive system was tactically unsound. When I asked him how he would conduct the defence of Uri, he brushed aside the question by saying that he had not had a chance to study the ground in detail, but would do so at a later date. What he desired, however, was for me to take immediate measures to bring the defences on a sound and solid basis.

It being pointless to start an argument, I decided to drive him to Fort piquet, where Lt. Col. Kalaan, the Commanding Officer of 6 Rajrif was awaiting us. Introducing him to Kalaan, I asked Kalaan to show him around the piquet. From the remarks made it was clear that there was nothing right with the piquet, but when the final observation was made that Fort piquet was badly sited, badly constructed and would be incapable of standing up to even a feeble attack, I decided to step in and save a rather shattered Commanding Officer from any further gibes. Leading Lakhinder Singh away from the piquet, I drove him about fifty yards, stopped, and reminded him that only a few minutes previously I had explained to him in minute detail the wonderful action fought by Fort and its linked piquet Jitter. I had expected him to congratulate the Commanding Officer and his very gallant men, but all they had received for their fine effort was a strafing. Lakhinder Singh was not one bit repentant, and he repeated that he considered the siting and layout of the piquet tactically unsound. Although it had been my intention to take him to some other piquets and units, I decided to head for the Mess.

After a quick lunch, I drove him back to Baramula, saying to him as we approached a sniper's paradise that we might be shot at by a light automatic but I would speed through the area and the chances of being hit were negligible. Unfortuntely, a sniper did open fire as we rushed through the danger area, and this brought a tirade against 4 Kumaon: the battalions must be thoroughly inefficient to permit this state of affairs. I was instructed to convey to the Commanding Officer his displeasure. Having reached Baramula, he got into a jeep that was awaiting him, and

I returned to Uri, wondering whether what had happened was true or just a nightmare. Whichever it was, I decided that in the interests of the Brigade it would be best to treat the whole thing rather light-heartedly.

The next morning, Major Khare reported to me in Uri with a letter from the Divisional Commander. The letter stated that he had found Khare to be a thoroughly inefficient officer, that he had been relieved of his appointment, and that immediate disciplinary action should be taken against Khare, the sentence to be demotion to the rank of Captain from Acting Major. The verdict on Khare shattered not only the Brigade Headquarters Staff but also the unit officers in the Uri bowl. Khare's performance as the Senior Supply Officer, even during the most difficult periods that the Brigade had faced, had been of an extraordinarily high standard. As I was debating with myself how best I could persuade the Divisional Commander to tone down his demand that Khare be demoted, Major Derek Bobb, the DAA & QMG, came into the office and informed me that numerous telephone calls were being received from the officers of the administrative units in Srinagar, pleading that their units be ordered to move out of Srinagar to Baramula. The Divisional Commander, it was stated, was finding fault with everything, and it was only a matter of time before they suffered the same fate as Khare, or were placed under arrest.

These were impossible requests to accede to, and the officers were told to stick it out. To have made any major change in the administrative set-up would have caused even more trouble with the Divisional Commander, and in any case, with the situation about to erupt on the Mahura front, it could have been courting a major breakdown at a time when it could least be afforded.

So far as Headquarters 161 Infantry Brigade was concerned, pinpricks from Headquarters 5 Div followed at varying intervals. Some created a certain amount of amusement, but to deal with them was time-consuming and distracted attention from far more important issues. What they were in aid of was difficult to fathom. The Brigade had never canvassed for bouquets, but it did not merit, nor did it expect, brickbats at a time when it needed all possible help to fight and win the impending battle.

It was sincerely hoped that the annoying incidents that had taken place were merely a passing phase. This was, however, wishful thinking, as a telephone message from Headquarters 5 Div to Headquarters 161 Infantry Brigade brought matters to a head. It contained an order that just could not be complied with.

The message from Headquarters 5 Div was dictated on the telephone by a Staff Officer and received by Headquarters 161 Infantry Brigade at three o'clock in the afternoon. It stated: "The following units of 161 Infantry Brigade will move to Srinagar forthwith and without relief. On arrival in Srinagar they will come under command Headquarters 5 Div. Ex Baramula, one troop field artillery, squadron 7 Cavalary and 3 Garhwal. Ex Uri, Mountain Battery. All moves will be completed as early as possible and not later than 48 hours from the receipt of this order. On arrival at Srinagar units will concentrate in Badami Bagh Barracks. Unit commanders will report to Div Headquarters for orders. Transport requirements will be submitted to Div Headquarters by 1700 hours today. Units in Baramula have already been issued a Warning Order. 1 Sikh already taken under command Headquarters 5 Div. Acknowledge."

This impossible order called for immediate action. The first was to inform the units in Baramula that no action would be taken by them on the 5 Div Warning Order without further orders from Headquarters 161 Infantry Brigade. The second was to get in touch with Headquarters 5 Div and request an immediate conference with the Divisional Commander. The first was very quickly completed, but the second was subjected to inordinate delay. Lakhinder Singh was not available, having gone out, and his Staff was unable to state where he could be contacted or when he would return. Periodic telephone calls met with a similar fate, until at five o'clock in the evening, Headquarters 5 Div was informed that I was leaving for Srinagar immediately, and on arrival, which would be in about two hours, would report at the Divisional Commander's office and await his return, it was to be stressed to him that the matter I had for discussion was one of immediate operational importance and could not be postponed to the next day.

On arrival in Srinagar, almost on the stroke of seven o'clock, I drove to Headquarters 5 Div and went to Major General Lakhinder Singh's office and found him awaiting me. He opened the conference by informing me that if I had come to Srinagar with the intention of having the move order cancelled, I was wasting both my time and his. The orders were firm and final, and had been decided upon after very careful consideration of all the factors affecting the security of Kashmir. They would stand, and he wished the moves to be completed without delay. If there were any other subjects for discussion, he was ready to listen to me.

I informed Lakhinder Singh, very quietly but very firmly, that I had come in to discuss only one subject, the one that he had just tabooed. This order, if implemented, would result in the weakening of the forward areas to such a degree that there would be every danger of the Valley being faced with a threat identical to that which existed in October and November 1947. Stating that I would prove it to him, I walked across to a map affixed to a wall in his office, and was about to explain the situation in detail when I was cut short. Lakhinder Singh remarked that he was well aware of what was happening, needed no briefing whatsoever, and if that was the only subject for discussion I could take it that the conference was terminated.

This was quite unacceptable to me, and I asked permission to explain to him the Operational Plan to combat the threatened encirclement, which I stressed was known neither to Headquarters Jak Force nor to Headquarters 5 Div. I had started to tell him about it on his visit to Uri, but he had not wished to get involved in planning operations at the time, as he was not settled in; perhaps, I suggested, if he heard it now, he would be in a better position to appreciate the grim situation facing the forward areas. To my utter surprise, he said that he did not wish to listen to the plan, as he was convinced that the troops which would remain in the forward areas were far in excess of the requirements to meet any threat that was in the offing. What he was more interested in, and what was far more important, was the security of Srinagar, the defence of which had been grossly neglected. That glaring error had to be rectified immediately, and the troops that had been ordered to report to Headquarters 5 Div were required for that purpose.

Although I realised that I was hitting my head against a brick wall, the situation on the Uri and Mahura fronts was so critical, and the stakes so high, that I returned to my chair at his desk and resumed the charge. I informed him that the defence of Srinagar had neither been in the past, nor was it now, neglected grossly as he had put it. The safety of Srinagar and the Valley was entirely dependent on the ability of 161 Infantry Brigade to hold Baramula, Mahura and Uri. As long as these areas were held firmly, there was little chance of Srinagar being seriously threatened. The enemy, I admitted, had once attempted to enter the Valley via Handwara, and he could also come via Gulmarg, but the administrative difficulties that would face him would, limit these threats both in scope and intensity. With the Banihal Pass now open to traffic, and weather conditions making movement by air and the provision of fighter cover possible, the Valley could be speedily reinforced, and a threat to Srinagar, if he still visualised one, which I certainly did not, could be easily defeated.

A reverse in the area between Baramula and Uri would, however, I continued, have a direct bearing on the safety of the Valley, and to strip this sensitive area of troops was inviting trouble. It would only be justified if it was considered that it was impossible to hold the enemy in the forward areas. In that case, in preference to being weak everywhere, 161 Infantry Brigade should be withdrawn and deployed to hold the line Handwara, Baramula and Gulmarg. This I considered would be the obvious way to defend Srinagar and the Valley, and not what I had been given to understand by his Staff was the intention, to man the defences held by the Brigade in the Battle of Shalateng (they had asked me for the layout over the telephone). In concluding, I stressed the 161 Infantry Brigade could and would hang on to its forward area defences regardless of the threats poised against it, but this would be possible only if it was left intact. To whittle down its strength would be to play into the hands of the enemy.

Lakhinder Singh was either unimpressed by the arguments advanced, or in an irreconcilable state of mind. He continued to doodle with his pencil on the blotting paper, and then said that my assertion that 161 Infantry Brigade could not spare any troops was factually incorrect. If the Brigade was short of troops and needed every man, why, he asked, was a large party sent off to Leh on a "wild goose chase", and "without obtaining the permission of HQ Jak Force"? Also, if the enemy had attacked before the arrival of 1 Madras, how would 161 Infantry Brigade have coped with the situation? He was satisfied that the moves ordered could be effected without prejudicing any actions that I intended conducting. The conference was over, his previous decision was final and irrevocable, and he wanted the units to be in Srinagar by the next day.

There was now only one way through which the implementation of this disastrous order could be nullified, and I decided to take it. Asking Major General Lakhinder Singh if I could use the telephone, and receiving his assent, I asked the Signal Exchange to put me through immediately to the Commander Jak Force, Major General Kulwant Singh. Lakhinder Singh's reaction was retarded, as he had obviously been taken by surprise. When he recovered, he reacted violently, demanding to know what I meant by approaching the Force Commander over his head. I explained to him that I was not doing anything of the sort. I had had neither verbal, nor written, nor signal instructions from Headquarters Jak Force to the effect that 161 Infantry Brigade was under Headquarters 5 Div. I had accepted the position as he had stated it to be. Over the last few days, the Brigade had been receiving communications from both Headquarters Jak Force and Headquarters 5 Div. It was essential that the command and control position was clarified, and that I knew exactly to whom I was answerable for my actions. The present state of affairs could and would eventually lead to confusion. If 161 Infantry Brigade was under Headquarters 5 Div, his orders would be implemented, but I had a right to inform Headquarters Jak Force of the possible consequences. I had barely finished saying this to Lakhinder Singh, when the Commander Jak Force came on the time.

Major General Kulwant Singh was obviously in very good heart. He greeted me most cordially, inquired whether the Brigade was in good shape and then asked what problem I had for him. I told him that it was a simple one: Headquarters 161 Infantry Brigade was receiving instructions from two major Headquarters, and I would like a firm decision on which Headquarters I was answerable to—was it Headquarters Jak Force or Headquarters 5 Div? If confusion was to be avoided, I concluded, the Brigade should be responsible for its actions to only one master.

It was obvious that Kulwant Singh was baffled by my statement, as there was a very distinct pause before he said: "5 Div? What orders have you received from 5 Div?"

"An order to move back certain units from the forward areas." I replied, and then added, "which, if compiled with, could be disastrous."

"An order to move back units?" said Kulwant Singh, emphasising each word. Then, as if a light automatic was barking with rage, came the questions: "How did you get this order? Where did it come from? Who gave it to you?"

"HQ 5 Div sent it to me over the telephone this afternoon," I answered, "and it has been confirmed by the Divisional Commander."

"Divisional Commander?" stormed Kulwant Singh, his rage increasing with each second that passed, "What Divisional Commander? What's his name?"

I was, by this time, beginning to wonder whether sanity had deserted me, but managed to blurt out, "Major General Lakhinder Singh."

"Major General Lakhinder Singh?" roared Kulwant Singh, emphasising the rank, "Major General? Who said he is a Major General?"

"He says so," I replied, "he's the General Officer Commanding 5 Div."

This was evidently too much for Major General Kulwant Singh. A volcanic eruption must have shaken his office. His next few statements, although spoken into the mouthpiece of the telephone, were not intended for me. He was evidently thinking aloud. Then he roared: "Where is Lakhinder?" When I said he was sitting in front of me, I was ordered to hand him the telephone immediately. For the next three minutes I saw Lakhinder Singh wilting under the explosive attack.

The telephone was then handed back to me, and Kulwant Singh, apparently well satisfied with his work of destruction, said in a clear and authoritative tone: "There is no 5 Div in the Valley, and Lakhinder is not a Major General. He is a Brigadier. He has had no authority from me to command anything in the Valley, or to give orders to anyone. Now are you clear under whose command 161 Infantry Brigade is?"

"Yes," I answered quietly, and bidding him a Good Night, replaced the receiver.

It had been a nauseating experience. I had not visualised that my telephone call to the Force Commander would produce such a devastating result. Although it had been a fact, it seemed more like fiction that a Divisional Headquarters could set itself up in the Valley and take over operational control, without the knowledge of Headquarters Jak Force. Why, or how, it happened was too delicate a subject to be probed into, nor was it desirable to do so. Inevitably, however, it became a topic of conversation among the young officers, and the rank and file could not understand how a Div Headquarters could come into existence one day and shut down almost overnight. The whole episode reflected poorly on whosoever was responsible for what can be best described as a first class bit of nonsense.

Headquarters 5 Div never moved into the Valley. If orders for its move had been issued, they must have been cancelled as it remained at Ranchi in Bihar. When a Division was formed in the Valley about a month later, it was not Lakhinder Singh who was selected to command it, but Major General K. S. Thimayya.

The next morning, after my return to Uri, a signal was received from Headquarters Jak Force. It announced that "Zebra" Brigade had been raised in the Valley with Brigadier Lakhinder Singh as its commander. The new Brigade was to take over 1 Sikh and certain administrative units located in Srinagar, and would be responsible for the Valley and Handwara, but excluding Baramula which would remain the responsibility of 161 Infantry Brigade. I was asked to submit my recommendations as to what other combat units could be transferred to the new Brigade, without prejudice to the security of the forward areas. Headquarters Jak Force was informed that nothing could be spared at the moment, but a firm list would be forwarded as soon as the situation stabilised.

Chapter 18

The Limber Nullah Battle

THE equipment demanded by the enemy commander, Brigadier Khalil, was evidently materialising faster than he anticipated, as his signals had a much more chirpy air. Movements of personnel from the west to the east reported by agents and confirmed by 4 Kumaon were found to have diminished quite considerably. The obvious deduction was that the enemy concentration was either complete or fast approaching that stage. The long awaited attack was, therefore, imminent, and 161 Infantry Brigade's plan to combat it was put into motion.

Shielding from the enemy the fact that 161 Infantry Brigade was aware of his intentions had always been an essential ingredient of the plan. This had necessitated many surreptitious actions being taken over a period, none of which it was hoped, even if noticed, would give rise to suspicion. These essentials were completed by 7 April, one week before the forecast date of the attack. A party of troops, ostensibly on a pleasure jaunt, had arrived in a vehicle near a deserted house in Rampur and tried their hand at fishing in the river. When they left, about three hours later, the house, which was ideally located as a Tactical Headquarters for the Brigade, commanding an excellent view of the terrain to the north of the Jhelum River, had been equipped with wireless sets, a telephone exchange and the necessary maps. The small party of troops that remained behind to man it were instructed not to expose themselves during the hours of daylight.

A party from the field artillery in Baramula went to picnic in the area of Naushara, and while doing so chose suitable gun sites and carried out silent registration of targets on the north bank of the river. A group of men from the Mountain Battery in Uri also visited Mahura and carried out silent registration of targets in the area. The main target was the Kopra feature. The gun sites having been selected, the ammunition was brought forward from Srinagar and stacked in a suitable area under the protection of 4 Kumaon.

Major Rajan Raju of the Madras Engineers and a party of his men, travelling in a covered vehicle from Uri to Baramula, staged frequent breakdowns of their truck in the area between Rampur and Naushara. The scene, if viewed by the enemy, would have presented a case of a serious mechanical defect which kept recurring and necessitated the driver having to open the bonnet and carry out repairs. Concealed in the vehicle was an engineer group carrying out a field glass reconnaissance of the river banks. The object was to select a suitable site for a "Flying Fox" type of ferry. When a suitable spot was located, the vehicle stalled and two men equipped with buckets moved to the river, ostensibly to collect water. While doing so, they surveyed the banks and made an estimate of the water gap. It was an ideal spot with two stout trees facing one another on the opposite banks. Returning to the vehicle, they poured the water into the radiator and the truck moved off in the direction of Baramula. The necessary material for the ferry was collected and deposited in the custody of 1 Madras in the Heman Buniyar Nullah.

With 3 Garhwal patrols to Ijara continuing to educate the enemy and drawing no fire, and 4 Kumaon tiger patrols probing Kopra and

SKETCH SHOWING
THE LIMBER NULLAH BATTLE

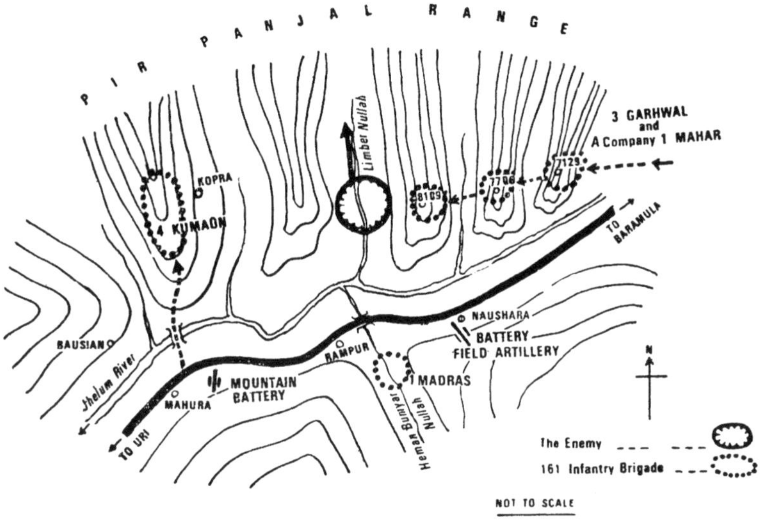

the route to it by dark, 161 Infantry Brigade's counter-measures were ready for implementation. Only one problem remained, the timing of the Brigade's attack. This, unfortunately, was dependent on the enemy commander's decision, and it still remained a closely guarded secret in his possession. Try as we did, we could secure no positive indication, but if the operation was to be a complete success, knowledge of this most important factor was essential. It was appreciated that Brigadier Khalil, convinced in his own mind that 161 Infantry Brigade was fast asleep, and with his attention focused on the crossing of the river, would not have catered for a contingency such as an attack from an unexpected quarter. When this materialised it would throw him off balance. His indecision if fully exploited would turn into confusion, and before he could recover from this state, added threats would turn it into a rout.

Our planning, however, had to provide for two widely divergent situations. Plan "A" was based on the Brigade launching the attack and was naturally the easier to operate as the initiative rested with us. Plan "B" was not a plan as such, but in the nature of a list of situations that could arise should the enemy be successful in crossing the river and occupying the hills to the south of the road, and of action that could be taken to contain him. It would be dominated by the tactical situation existing at the moment. Plan "B" was, therefore, not passed down to unit commanders.

Plan "A" was divided into three distinct phases:

Phase I.

3 Garhwal, composed of a Tactical Headquarters, three rifle companies and the mortar platoon, and with one section of "A" Company The 1st Battalion The Mahar Regiment (MMG) under command, was to move out of Baramula and capture as its first objective point 7129. The battalion was to be self-contained for 48 hours.

The battery field artillery was to move from Baramula to Naushara and be in position to support 3 Garhwal from its already reconnoitered position.

The armoured car Squandron of 7 Cavalary was to patrol the road between Naushara and Uri, the reserve troops being located in the Rampur area.

1 Madras, less its rifle companies at Baramula and Rampur, was to remain in the Heman Buniyar Nullah as the Brigade reserve. Transport had been attached to this battalion to make it mobile.

Phase II.

3 Garhwal to capture point 7706 on orders from Brigade Headquarters.

Phase III.

3 Garhwal to capture point 8109 on orders from Brigade Headquarters.

4 Kumaon to occupy the Kopra feature on orders from Brigade Headquarters.

The timings of the phases of Plan "A" could not be laid down. They had to be elastic as there were many unpredictable elements. Most important of these was the enemy's reaction to the advance by 3 Garhwal. There was a live possibility that the enemy might react violently, in which case 1 Madras would have been rushed to Mahura to take over from 4 Kumaon,who would have been used to pose a threat to the enemy concentrated in the Limber Nullah from the west, in order to ease the pressure on 3 Garhwal. If events took this turn, then Plan "A" would be scrapped and the battle fought in accordance with the situation that presented itself. Every eventuality was carefully considered, even that of a partial success of the enemy's encirclement plan being coordinated with an attack on Uri. The atmosphere was charged with dangerous possibilities, but 161 Infantry Brigade remained calm and waited confidently.

Meanwhile, commencing 3 April, there had been a marked change in the signals despatched from Khalil to Jamil. Whereas in the past they had tended to complain about the slowness in arrival of the equipment and offered reasons why he could not accelerate the date of the attack, they now exhibited a rather grandiose air. It was evident that Khalil realised that the eyes of everyone who mattered were now focused upon him, and he was not going to miss the opportunity of exploiting his position to the fullest degree. He was, in fact, "the man of the moment", and it was clearly his intention that the higher authority should take cognizance of it. There was a marked increase in the signals that he despatched to Jamil, the majority relating to the very high morale of his force, and anecdotes of how he had completely bamboozled the enemy. As his stature increased in his own estimation so did his security-mindedness diminish in actuality. He was rapidly moving towards making a thundering blunder, and it happened in the afternoon of 10 April.

Incredible and puerile though it may seem, he sent Jamil a personal signal, in clear, the words used being in Urdu, and evidently in his opinion adequate to disguise the actual meaning. It was, however, unlikely to deceive even the most dull-witted individual. Short and simple, the intercepted message read, "Tomorrow night I shall change the map." This was what 161 Infantry Brigade had striven so hard to obtain, and the enemy commander had presented it to us on a silver salver. Brigadier Khalil was to pay very, very dearly for this glaring error; on intercepting the message, "Lal Lotus" (Red Lotus), the codeword for the immediate implementation of Plan "A" was flashed to all units of the Brigade.

Appointing Lt. Col. S. S. Kalam of 6 Rajrif as the Commander of Uri, and having ordered the staff who manned the Tactical

Headquarters at Rampur to move out of Uri soon after darkness set in, I proceeded to Mahura in my jeep. Here I had a conference with Lt. Col. Man Mohan Khanna of 4 Kumaon, and having satisfied myself that there were no problems relating to the part 4 Kumaon would be called upon to play in the battle, moved on to Heman Buniyar to check on the Brigade reserve, 1 Madras, and finally arrived at Baramula at half past five in the evening. I found all the units were ready and merely awaiting the order to move. A short conference was held, and having ensured that there were no doubts in anyone's mind, the firm timings for the various moves were handed out. 3 Garhwal was to commence moving out from Baramula at seven o'clock that evening, the squadron of armoured cars at six o'clock the next morning, 11 April, and the field battery at half past six.

On the stroke of seven o'clock, when darkness had set in, 3 Garhwal and the section of medium machine guns of A Company 1 Mahar, began moving out of Baramula, one company at a time and with a reasonable interval in-between each company. Crossing the bridge over the Jhelum River at Baramula, the companies headed for a rendezvous about three miles to the west of Baramula. To an enemy agent or a casual observer these moves would not be suspicious as they had been made a daily habit. When the last element of 2 Garhwal had moved out of Baramula, I drove to the Tactical Headquarters at Rampur. It was so well "blacked out" that, with the jeep lights extinguished, I experienced a certain amount of difficulty in locating it, and very nearly plunged into a ditch with steep banks.

Having concentrated at the rendezvous, 3 Garhwal set off for point 7129. It had neither animals nor porters to assist in carrying the three-inch mortar barrels and base plates, the medium machine gun barrels and tripods, and the connected ammunition. Yet the rate of advance was steady, and remarkably good considering that the column was moving in the dark, over unreconnoitred country, and without guides to ensure that it was on the correct bearing. At seven o'clock the next morning, 3 Garhwal was within striking distance of point 7129, and the Commanding Officer decided to take the feature with two companies. Although movement had been observed on the feature, and was presumed to be hostile, the enemy, if he had been in occupation of point 7129, withdrew, as the Companies captured the objective without opposition. The remainder of the 3 Garhwal column then moved forward and consolidated the position.

Meanwhile, the squadron of armoured cars which was patrolling the road between Naushara and Uri reported everything quiet, and at eight o'clock the battery of field artillery reported that it was in position and ready for action. 3 Garhwal was now ordered to move forward and take point 7706, but the Commanding Officer suggested that as the advance to this point would be over open ground, and there were definite signs that the feature was being held in strength, the attack be postponed until after dark and the feature be first softened up by the field artillery. This was agreed to, but it was decided that the softening up of point 7706 by the artillery would not take place until the hours of darkness, as it was necessary that Brigadier Khalil should continue to live in a state of bliss for as long as possible, preferably up to just before his selected hour of attack.

The enemy had come to the conclusion that the occupation of point 7129 was no more than a strong patrol action. This became apparent when an intercept message reported that two companies of "Gorkhas" had appeared on the scene and had moved on to point 7129. In the interests of secrecy, they had been permitted to do so, and they had discovered nothing and would withdraw during the course of the day. When, however, the occupation of point 7129 continued throughout the afternoon and into the evening, Khalil must have become perturbed. It was a nasty thorn in his side, and could embarrass his crossing of the river, if not by fire most certainly by passing information. With his own "H" hour fast approaching, he had to do something, and there were two alternatives. He could attack point 7129 and drive the patrol away, but this would have awoken 161 Brigade from its slumber and negatived in a matter of minutes what he had spent weeks to achieve, the secret concentration of his force. Or he could reinforce point 7706 and prevent the patrol from interfering with his river-crossing. He chose the latter alternative and at about five o'clock started reinforcing point 7706, which was immediately reported by 3 Garhwal. Although premature by a few hours, 161 Infantry Brigade decided to show its hand. Directed by the artillery Forward Observation Officer with 3 Garhwal, the battery of the field artillery came into action. It had an excellent shoot, and taking the enemy completely by surprise, spread confusion into this ranks.

Khalil, his bluster of the previous day vanishing like ice in a desert, signalled Jamil that he was being heavily shelled and in danger of being attacked, and demanded immediate reinforcements. Jamil reacted by informing Khalil that he must attack the "Gorkhas" immediately and also the gun areas. In order to embarrass Khalil even further, the field artillery was ordered to shell the Limber Nullah area. This produced a vitriolic effect, Khalil demanding that as many reinforcements as were possible should be rushed to him immediately. Their movement forward was observed by 4 Kumaon at Mahura and reported to Brigade Tactical Headquarters. But it had become obvious that Khalil's boast of changing the map that night would not materialise. He would have to choose another date, if he was in a position to do so.

The field artillery continued a sporadic shelling of point 7706 and the Limber Nullah throughout the night of 11 April and during the early hours of the 12th morning, only lifting its fire from point 7706 when the 3 Garhwal attack on the feature entered its final stage. The enemy on point 7706 put up a weak form of resistance and withdrew. Two counter-attacks were then launched by the enemy to recapture the feature, but were thrown back. The Garhwali casualties during this period had been extremely light, one killed and three wounded. The beating back of the counter-attacks resulted in Khalil reacting even more violently, on the wireless set. He demanded further reinforcements, and 4 Kumaon confirmed that they could be seen rushing forward.

With the capture of point 7706, the Madras Engineers came into action. A platoon of 3 Garhwal was ordered to move to the spot selected on the north bank of the Jhelum river. On its arrival, a two-inch mortar bomb had its cap pierced and a triple signal cable was laced into it and fired across to the north bank. To the signal cable was attached a wire hawser which was pulled over and wrapped firmly around the tree on that bank. Then, with the assistance of the company of 1 Madras which was located on the south bank, a pulley was attached to the wire hawser whose other end was now affixed to the tree on the south bank. With a platform attached to the pulley, the "Flying Fox" was ready for operation. The 3 Garhwal company retained in Uri had been called back, and was ferried across the Jhelum river to rejoin the battalion. With the troops of 1 Madras carrying forward ammunition, especially three-inch mortar bombs, 3 Garhwal was replenished. The "Flying Fox" bridge had provided the unit with an excellent line of communication, and the battalion was no longer out in the blue.

With point 7706 firmly consolidated, the Garhwalis were left with only one more objective to capture, point 8109. With the capture of this feature and the sealing off of the Limber Nullah concentration by 4 Kumaon occupying Kopra, phase III of the plan would be implemented. This would be the coup de grace.

The engagement taking place in the Limber Nullah area produced no reactions on the Uri and Mahura fronts, not even an enemy patrol testing the defences. This, from 161 Infantry Brigade's point of view, was agreeable but not altogether so since it could be the lull that precedes a storm. Fortunately, the storm did not break, and the Brigade was able to concentrate on the job it had in hand without having to divide its attention.

There are three possible reasons that might have fostered the enemy inactivity. Firstly, Khalil's initial message informing Jamil that a strong patrol of Gorkhas had stumbled into his outpost position at point 7129, and suggesting that it would withdraw during the course of the day. This did not call for any action on the other fronts. Secondly, when the Garhwalis (Gorkhas to the enemy) remained on point 7129 and the field artillery engaged point 7706, Jamil might have assumed that the artillery fire had been ordered to enable the patrol to extricate itself. Khalil, it is true, had called for reinforcements, but Jamil might have arrived at the conclusion that he required these troops to engage the patrol, thus obviating the need to use units already earmarked for the river crossing plan. Thirdly, the essence of the overall plan was the encirclement and annihilation of the units in the Mahura area, the investment of Uri following in due course. It was, therefore, necessary that the Brigade was not roused, as it might have resulted in the rushing forward of units from Srinagar and Baramula; and in moving forward they might have stumbled into the river crossing operation while it was still under way.

Whether these assumptions and thoughts ever entered Jamil's head is mere conjecture, and perhaps there were other reasons which made him stay his hand. From the enemy's angle it was, however, a tactical error, as it made possible the movement from Uri to Mahura of the one unit on which every piquet in Uri was dependent for its defensive fire, and which was urgently required to support the 4 Kumaon attack on Kopra, the Mountain Battery.

The Mountain Battery had, through its excellent performances, earned for itself the title "Sharpshooters of the Kashmir Valley". So confident were the gunners that they could engage with pin-point accuracy any target within the range of their guns, that to ask them whether they could engage a given knoll, which was within range, would draw pained expressions on their faces. They would say: "Tell us which particular pebble you want hit and we will do it for you." Warned that the battery might be required for a role at Mahura, wooden "mock-ups" of the guns had been prepared and kept handy, to take the place of the actual guns when they were moved out. This substitution took place in the evening of 12 April, the stripped mountain guns being placed in the trucks which arrived in the unit lines as ammunition replenishment vehicles. The personnel to man the guns embussed in the vehicles when they had returned to the eastern sector of Uri, out of sight of any enemy on the Salamabad feature, and the trucks sped to Mahura. Here the guns were unloaded and assembled and drawn to the gun pits that had been prepared in advance; the ammunition had already been stacked at the site. By 5 pm the Mountain Battery was ready to support the 4 Kumaon attack on Kopra.

At 8.00 that night, the Dogra Company of the 15th Punjab Regiment, which had been serving with 4 Kumaon ever since its arrival in the Valley as an Independent Rifle Company in November

1947, moved forward to patrol the north bank of the Jhelum River. One platoon was to move westwards and another platoon eastwards, the Company Headquarters and the third platoon forming the patrol base and being located to the north of the bridge. The Company Commander had been instructed that 4 Kumaon would start moving forward to Kopra at 10 pm and that his company must not return to the bridge site before 11, as otherwise there might be a clash in the dark. On return to the bridge site, he was to take up a position in its vicinity and protect it.

There was peace and quiet in the area until twenty minutes to ten o'clock, when there was a burst of firing from the east. The platoon sent in that direction had encountered enemy and engaged them. Lt. Col. Man Mohan Khanna and I, standing near the "Start Line" of 4 Kumaon, were cursing our bad luck, when a bren gun with the leading platoon of 4 Kumaon at the bridge site opened fire and there was a shout from someone who had been hit. A few minutes later, a rifleman from the Dogra Company of 15 Punjab was led to us. He reported that the platoon that had moved to the east had bumped into an enemy patrol and had engaged it, and that his section commander, another rifleman and himself had been ordered to return and warn 4 Kumaon of the presence of the enemy. The section commander and the other rifleman had been wounded by the fire from the Kumaon bren gun.

The two casualties were brought in. The section commander had been killed and the other rifleman seriously wounded. It was an unfortunate and an avoidable incident. For these men of the Dogra Company of 15 Punjab to rush back in the dark, despite the very clear orders that the company was to stay clear of the bridge site until 11 pm was courting disaster. That they had done so in order to help their comrades of 4 Kumaon is undeniable, but the battlefield has certain tenets whose violation, more often than not, inflicts a very heavy penalty. The heat and excitement of battle, however, often makes even the best trained troops forget the tenets until they are brought home to them with a tragedy.

The firing in the area to the east of the bridge continued until five minutes to ten and then died away. The patrol clash could not have occurred at a more inopportune moment. When the firing ceased, the "Start Time" of 4 Kumaon was exactly five minutes away. That the enemy piquets on Kopra and the nearby features would have been alerted was accepted as being automatic, and with their senses sharpened, the possibility of 4 Kumaon making Kopra undetected would now be nothing short of a miracle. It was possible to defer the start by an hour in order to let the enemy settle down, but there was grave danger of a clash in the dark with the 15 Punjab Company which was observing wireless silence. A postponement by 24 hours was the other alternative, but this would disrupt the whole operation. It was, therefore, decided that whether the enemy was milling about on the route or not, and even if the piquets on Kopra had been alerted, the risk had to be taken. At 10.00 pm the leading element of 4 Kumaon rose from the ground and moved forward very slowly and very quietly, the remainder of the battalion following close on its heels.

4 Kumaon reached the base of the Kopra feature without encountering the enemy, and then commenced the long climb to the peak. The sentry of an enemy outpost, about a section in strength, and positioned on one of the lower slopes of the feature, assuming that the sounds of approaching footsteps were those produced by his own comrades, called out softly in order to guide them to the post. The section was silenced with the bayonet. The advance continued without further incident, and by seven o'clock in the morning of 13 April, Kopra was firmly in the hands of 4 Kumaon. The battalion signallers, laying a signal cable as they advanced, enabled the battalion to report its progress by telephone at regular intervals, thus ensuring both rapid communications and the maintenance of wireless silence.

Reports received from various sources had indicated that the Pathan tribesmen responsible for manning certain piquets had adopted the habit of evacuating them after dark, and having spent the night in a village at the foot of the feature, returning to occupy them after first light. In so far as Kopra was concerned, this proved to be wholly accurate. All the piquets, with the exception of the one encountered and which was manned by a section of an AKP unit, were found to be unoccupied. 4 Kumaon settled into them and awaited the arrival of the garrisons. Soon after first light they were observed moving towards Kopra, apparently in no particular hurry. Unaware of what was awaiting them, they adopted no semblance of any tactical formation during the climb, and, having reached the top, strolled very casually towards their sangars. They were swiftly mown down, not a single individual escaping. This sharp burst of firing, it was expected, would indicate to the enemy that Kopra was in hostile hands, but oddly enough it did not. There was no reaction whatsoever. It is not improbable that the sound of firing was attributed to the tribals engaging in a bit of shikar.

At ten o'clock , a civilian porter train, carrying three-inch mortar ammunition destined for the Limber Nullah, was observed approaching the feature. A reception was immediately laid on, but when the porters realised that the troops on the feature were neither AKP nor tribals, they jettisoned their loads and bolted. They were not fired at, and this perhaps led whomsoever had sent them forward to discount their story, if they carried it back, that Kopra was occupied by enemy troops. Brigadier Khalil, in the Limber Nullah, was quite oblivious of the fact that his line of communication had been cut. He was busy trying to force 3 Garhwal to evacuate point 7706 by engaging the unit with mortar fire, while his own force was being subjected to counter-mortar fire from the Garhwal mortars and shelling by the field artillery.

About mid-day, a rifle company from the 4 AKP battalion approached Kopra from the direction of the Limber Nullah. It is more than probable that, with the mortar ammunition requiring urgent replenishment, it had been sent out to contact the porter train and speed up its progress. This company was engaged by 4 Kumaon and forced to withdraw. Rushing back to the Limber Nullah, it must have reported that Kopra was being held in strength and that the line of communication had been cut, as at about 2 pm there were definite signs of uneasiness in the enemy rank and file in the Limber Nullah.

Khalil was now confronted with a most unsavoury situation. While the 4 AKP battalion might have stood firm, once the information relating to Kopra filtered down to the Pathan tribals, two thousand five hundred in strength and forming the major portion of his force, there would be serious trouble. The tribals' fear of being surrounded would rise to the surface and result in panic. He had to take immediate action to avert this, and he had four options from which to make the choice. He could either fight the Garhwalis and attempt to break out to the east, or try to re-establish his line of communication which would entail battling with 4 Kumaon. The launching of the encirclement plan was the third choice, but in view of the fact that the crossing would be engaged by artillery, armoured cars and infantry, all of which he could now see quite clearly on the south bank of the river, his chances of success were nil. His final option was to attempt to escape to the north, which was not sealed off by 161 Infantry Brigade but barred by the 13,000 ft. Pir Panjal Range, its crest covered by deep snow.

From almost the moment that 4 Kumaon reported its engagement with the rifle company of the AKP battalion, a battery of binoculars was trained on the Limber Nullah to watch for the reactions. Their manifestation took some length of time because the AKP company was probably not in wireless communication, but about the time that it would have taken to scurry back, there were definite signs of restlessness. This was accentuated after an attempt to dislodge 4 Kumaon from Kopra, by elements of either the 3rd or 5th AKP battalions, was hurled back through accurate shooting by the Mountain Battery and solid defence by 4 Kumaon. Khalil was now given very little time to ponder over which of the four courses open to him he would adopt. The field artillery was ordered to step up its rate of fire, and the enemy in the Limber Nullah soon found himself subjected to a murderous and well directed shoot. Simultaneously, 3 Garhwal was ordered to mortar point 8109 heavily, and with the activity on point 7706 increasing, Khalil must have been convinced that a battalion attack was imminent, and would probably synchronise with something advancing on the Limber Nullah from the direction of Kopra.

Whether Khalil issued any order, and if so what it was, is not known, but it was evident that his previously well disciplined force, having become aware that Kopra was being held in strength, degenerated into a rabble. The enemy ranks, who had shown a remarkable sense of obedience to all orders relating to security and concealment, kicked over the traces in a matter of minutes. Throwing caution to the four winds, they began revealing themselves by rushing all over the place in an effort to escape from the devastating fire of the field guns. Then, perhaps assuming that the hills in which they had lain concealed were the main targets of the guns, they streamed into the open bed of the Limber Nullah, which was soon filled with a mass of humanity. It presented an amazing sight and a perfect target, and the field artillery and the Garhwal mortars were on to it in a flash. There was now only one way to escape destruction, and the enemy took it, a mad rush commencing up the Limber Nullah towards the forbidding Pir Panjal Range.

As the fleeing enemy scrambled out of the range of the field guns, a fighter aircraft arrived overhead and was directed to the target with a round of blue smoke. It immediately dived into the attack, being joined a few minutes later by a second fighter. It must be admitted that the use of aircraft had never formed a part of Plan "A", and as such there was no VHF wireless set, for communication with aircraft, with 161 Brigade Headquarters. It was not because an air effort would have been valueless, but for the fact that the Air Force had evacuated Srinagar on the advent of winter and based itself in Jammu. With the Pir Panjal Range intervening between the Kashmir Valley and Jammu, and weather conditions still unpredictable, it would have been unrealistic to incorporate an air effort into the plan with any certainty that it would materialise at the required moment. Further, the distance to be covered by an aircraft from Jammu to the battle area would only permit it to be over the target for about ten minutes, and it was impossible to predict when the particular ten minutes of value would arise. The arrival of the two aircraft at the propitious moment was purely by chance, and was a stroke of good fortune. The air attack, had it been planned, could not have been launched with a greater approximation to split-second accuracy in timing.

The battle of the Limber Nullah was over by half past four in the evening. It had been won at a negligible cost in casualties, with the very strong enemy force offering only slight opposition as compared to what had been expected, a stiff and savage battle. It had, in fact, been almost a repetition of the Battle of Shalateng. No one was more surprised at the relative ease with which a dangerous threat had been completely liquidated, and a powerful enemy force put to flight, than the officers and men of 161 Infantry Brigade.

With the enemy streaming toward the Pir Panjal Range, 3 Garhwal advanced and occupied point 8109 in the evening of 14 April. During the night, neither 3 Garhwal nor 4 Kumaon was subjected to any type of activity by the enemy. 15 April was devoted to extensive patrolling of the area and the adjustment of the defences. On the morning of 16 April, 3 Garhwal was ordered to advance from point 8109 and to search the area in-between the Limber Nullah and Kopra, and to come into reserve at Mahura. No enemy was met by the battalion during the sweep, but it reported enemy dead and a large amount of equipment, arms and ammunition lying in scattered dumps in the area. D. P. Dhar was contacted and asked whether he could assist with a team of National Conference volunteers to clear the battlefield. He complied with the request immediately, and five hundred volunteers were moved forward in buses to the site of the "Flying Fox" ferry. Transported to the north bank of the river, and with two companies of 1 Madras providing local protection, they did an excellent job of work over the next three days. Eventually fetching up at Mahura, they were embussed and returned to Srinagar.

The enemy equipment and material collected was varied in range. It included the Headquarters Office of the 4th AKP battalion, some of the correspondence in the files making very interesting reading. The existence of a large Reinforcement Camp at Muzaffarabad was placed beyond dispute, and the reports and returns to and from this Reinforcement Camp showed that they had not been prepared by amateurs. Gallantry decorations had also been instituted, and judging from the sharp reminders in the file, the Battalion Commander had apparently shown slackness in forwarding the citations. Some of the citations, lying ready for despatch, were neither of historic nor of intelligence value. They only indicated that the person who had written them had a very fertile imagination and a flair for fantasy. More interesting were the expedients prepared and assembled for the river crossing. They included large quantities of already inflated goat skins, a few "Mae Wests", presumably for the more senior officers, light rafts made by lashing pieces of timber together, and numerous lengths of rope of varying thicknesses.

The bulk of the equipment had been placed in caches almost opposite Rampur, and the selected crossing site must have been in this area. Whether the enemy crossing would have been successful or not is problematical, as this area had been under close surveillance by 161 Infantry Brigade. The chances are that it would have been detected almost immediately, and it would have developed into a race as to how many of the enemy could have been ferried or swum across the river before 1 Madras from Heman Buniyar appeared on the scene, to reinforce its company that was located in the Rampur area. It would have been a tricky operation for both sides, as it would have been fought in darkness.

With Mahura now rid of the threat of encirclement, attention was turned towards the 3rd and 5th AKP battalion and the five hundred tribals who had been deployed in the area of Bari Baikh and Goshar. It was decided to engage them with two battalions, 3 Garhwal and 4 Kumaon. Both battalions were to operate with three rifle companies, one from each being left behind to protect Bausian and Mahura. 3 Garhwal was to attack Bari Baikh and move forward to point 9960, and 4 Kumaon to capture point 7760 and Goshar. The field artillery from Uri was to be in support of 3 Garhwal, and one section of the Mountain Battery in support of 4 Kumaon. Although the situation on the Uri front had remained peaceful, it was not considered prudent to continue the risk of denying the piquets gun support, and one section of the Mountain Battery had therefore been returned to Uri.

The education of the enemy was immediately taken in hand. Contrary to the very strict secrecy that had been observed prior to the Limber Nullah battle, there was now loose talk both in Baramula and Srinagar that an attack was going to be launched on Lachhipura by advancing over the hills from Uri. The "Mahura battalions", it

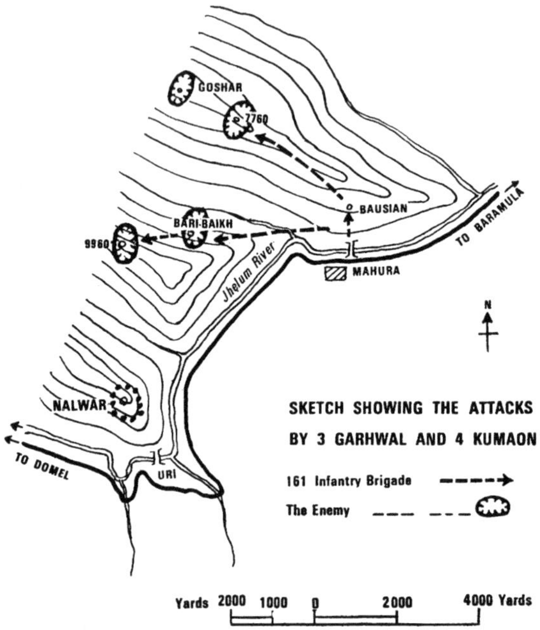

was stated had done their bit and were tired. They would be utilised to pose threats, but the main assault would come from Uri. Whether these rumours filtered down to the enemy or not is unknown, but subsequent events would lead one to believe that they did. In addition to the rumours that were spread there were some flagrant breaches of signal security, almost as bad as Khalil's "changing the map" signal.

During the next two days, both 3 Garhwal and 4 Kumaon made feint attacks towards their objectives, during the hours of daylight, pulling back hastily when the enemy opened up with long range fire, and by night they harassed the enemy with jitter patrols. There invariably produced a 'Brock's fireworks display' from the enemy. Meanwhile at Uri, Lt. Col. S. S. Kalaan, with one company of 2 Dogra and two platoons of 6 Rajrif, was busy preparing an equally good demonstration, to be staged on Nalwar piquet half an hour before the attacks by 3 Garhwal and 4 Kumaon were scheduled to commence.

Heavy rain, which commenced in the early hours of the morning and continued throughout the day and into the night, when the attack would have been launched, enforced a postponement. It rained throughout the next day, and in the evening changed to a steady drizzle. Conditions were by no means ideal for launching the troops, particularly as they would have to negotiate the slippery mountainsides, but it was decided not to postpone the operation any further. Half an hour before the Garhwalis and Kumaonis, who had moved forward to their concentration areas soon after darkness, were due to move forward, the troops on Nalwar piquet began to demonstrate. They created a most awful noise, and it certainly attracted the enemy's attention. He was probably led into believing that the feint attacks from Mahura were designed to distract his attention from the main threat, which now appeared to be coming from Uri. As we discovered later, he hastily readjusted his defensive layout.

4 Kumaon, on its way to point 7760, found a previously held company position to be garrisoned by a platoon, which was scuppered. The battalion then made its way to Goshar, and although the enemy tried to rectify his mistake, by rushing forward troops to man the well-sited trenches that had been evacuated, the Kumaons were in irresistible form and went in with the bayonet while the enemy was trying to settle in. An enemy company was caught out in the open and withdrew hastily, one of its platoons making a bold attempt to arrest the advance of 4 Kumaon but having to pull back under pressure. Moving steadily forward, the Kumaonis liquidated post after post, until eventually Goshar was captured.

3 Garhwal was, meanwhile, having a more difficult time. The feature that the battalion had to climb was very steep and now also slippery on account of rain. It fought its way forward, but at first light was well short of its objective, Bari Baikh. A battle of attrition followed. Despite stiff resistance the Garhwalis worked their way forward, and took Bari Baikh at 3 in the afternoon. The enemy counter-attacked, but in a half-hearted fashion and was easily repulsed. The battalion consolidated its gain, and continued its advance in the early hours of

the following morning. With enemy resistance weakening, 3 Garhwal captured point 9960 soon after first light.

It had been a most successful operation, fought under very difficult conditions. Both 3 Garhwal and 4 Kumaon had performed magnificently, and the mountain and field gunners had answered their every call with speed and great accuracy. The Mahura front, which till a few days earlier had been bristling with enemy activity, and which over a period of months had been a continuous source of worry to 161 Infantry Brigade, had now become quiet and peaceful. The road between Baramula and Uri was now safe, all sniping at it having ceased.

The section of the Mountain Battery which had been retained in Mahura to support 4 Kumaon was now returned to Uri. The expected attack on Uri could not be far off, especially in view of the reverses that had been suffered on the Mahura front. The enemy commander, in order to bolster up the morale of his mixed force and to save face with the locals, would have to do something spectacular in the very near future. By a process of elimination, and in view of the enemy concentration in the Bhatgiran area, it was considered that either the Ashok or Subhas piquet would be the target. Both piquets were manned with similar strengths, fully protected by wire and anti-personnel mines, and each had an Artillery Observation Post manned by the mountain gunners.

Major Mohinder Singh, the Commanding Officer of the Mountain Battery, had received orders posting him to a unit in the Punjab, and asked permission to hand over command of the Mountain Battery to his Second in Command to enable him to visit Ashok and Subhas piquets to say farewell to his personnel manning the OPs. He also requested that he be permitted to spend his last night in Uri in one of the two piquets. Both these requests were granted, and when Mohinder Singh asked which piquet he should stay in, although there was little to choose between them, Ashok was suggested.

Climbing the steep mountain side, Mohinder Singh headed for Subhas, and having spent about an hour in that piquet, moved across to Ashok which he reached at about 5 pm and immediately informed Brigade Headquarters that he had arrived in the piquet. An extremely popular officer who had served the Brigade very well, he was subjected to much good-natured bantering by the Brigade Staff over the field telephone. Each one warned him to be careful, and advised him what to do if the enemy came. Mohinder Singh reported that he wished the enemy would come, and if they did, they would wish that they had not. His wish was realised at 10 pm as Ashok piquet was fiercely attacked in strength.

Creeping though the thick forest, the enemy, about two companies in strength, approached to within one hundred yards of Ashok piquet and brought it under heavy automatic fire. The Mountain Battery immediately went into action. Major Mohinder Singh decided to take the shoot himself, and as the enemy crept forward he brought in the artillery fire closer to the piquet, until eventually the shells were bursting within a few yards of the defensive wire. The battle raged for about two hours before the enemy withdrew. The next morning, twelve enemy dead were found about twenty yards from the wire and nine more about fifty yards further on. The blood in the area was a clear indication that many more had been wounded.

The troops in Uri were delighted. Night after night they had awaited the long threatened attack, and at last it had materialised, to be dealt with in a most successful fashion. On his return from the piquet Mohinder Singh was given a hero's welcome. He left Uri a few hours later with a hevy heart.

It was the last enemy on Uri. Although reports of various planned attacks continued to come in, and on one occasion even Poonch Brigade sent a flash message repeating an intercept that had been picked up, indicating a heavy attack on Uri, none of these threats materialised.

Bits and pieces of news now trickled into Uri relating to a new command and control set-up. A Division, it was rumoured, was to be located in the Valley, and fresh Brigades were under orders to move in. Uri was to be taken over by one of the new Brigades, and 161 Infantry Brigade to go into reserve to enjoy a well earned rest.

Chapter 19

An Offensive Without Teeth

WITH no immediate operations on hand, 161 Infantry Brigade readjusted its dispositions. 3 Garhwal returned to Baramula, and the 1 Madras rifle companies at Baramula and Rampur rejoined the battalion which remained concentrated, and in reserve, in the Heman Buniyar Nullah. While remaining watchful and carrying out the normal patrols, the units utilised the respite to replace worn out equipment and attend to other administrative matters which had been shelved owing to preoccupation with operations. The peace and calm which reigned over the area seemed odd. Not even a stray rifle shot disturbed the serenity of the atmosphere either by day or by night. The unfortunate incident that was to take place in the Heman Buniyar Nullah was therefore staggering. It was brought about by enthusiasm which blinded the individual concerned and led him to an act of unjustified rashness and stupidity.

One afternoon late in April, with the weather somewhat warm and humid, Lt. Col. Menon, the Commanding Officer of 1 Madras, went to his tent after lunch and stretched himself out on his camp bed to read a novel. Although his unit had not been given the opportunity to engage the enemy, Menon could not resist having a personal crack at them. During the days when the main road was under enemy fire he would, armed with a rifle, take up various positions along the main road in the vicinity of his battalion camp, and stalk the enemy snipers as and when they exposed themselves. When the sniper threat to the road was cleared, he evidently spent his spare time roaming about in the hills on either side of the Heman Buniyar Nullah, taking with him a few men, in the hope that he might be able to bag some wild game. It was this practice that probably came to the enemy's notice and led to the disaster.

At 2.30 an individual, professing to be a Forest Ranger, approached a post of 1 Madras and asked to be taken to the Commanding Officer for whom he had an important message. Lt. Col. Menon interviewed this individual outside his tent, and was evidently informed that a party of enemy, six in number, had been detected resting in a deserted hut about two miles up the Heman Buniyar Nullah. Menon needed no spur. Grabbing his rifle, he ordered the nearest available sub-unit, the battalion Intelligence Section of seven men, to follow him. Led by the informant, this small party hurried away up the Nullah.

About twenty minutes later the rapid firing of small arms was heard, and 1 Madras immediately stood to. The firing died away as quickly as it had started, and after fifteen minutes a man from the Intelligence Section came rushing back to the camp with the information that the Commanding Officer's party had been ambushed. The Second in Commnand of 1 Madras immediately despatched two rifle companies to the scene of the incident, but although they carried out a meticulous search of the area, they found no trace either of the enemy or the guide but only the bodies of Lt. Col. Menon and his men, stripped of their arms and ammunition.

I had been away in Delhi attending a conference, and on returning the next morning went straight to 1 Madras. I found a shattered and very depressed battalion. No one could offer any good reason why Menon, with a full strength and readily available battalion at his disposal, should have chosen to rush off into the blue with a handful of men. It was only after questioning the sentry who had escorted the pseudo Forest Ranger to Menon, the lone survivor of the ambush, and Menon's batman, that information on the various stages of the incident could be pieced together. The rest of the battalion had been unaware of the fact that the Commanding Officer had rushed forth to intercept an enemy party, nor had there been any sound of firing before the rattle of fire that had alerted the unit. As it was not abnormal for Menon to move out with a handful of men, those who had seen the small party set out had assumed that it was for another wild game shoot.

On 1 May 1948, the command and control in Jammu and Kashmir underwent a radical change. Headquarters Jak Force was dishanded, and two new Division Headquarters raised, one being made responsible for the operations in Jammu and Poonch and the other for Kashmir. The Div Headquarters in Kashmir was designated Sri Division (Sri Div), and Major General K. S. Thimayya was appointed its commander. It established its Headquarters at Baramula. Zebra Brigade also changed its designation to 163 Infantry Brigade, and Brigadier J. C. Katoch, originally the commander of 161 Infantry Brigade, took over its command.

With the raising of 163 Brigade, the infantry battalions in Kashmir were reallotted to 161 and 163 Brigades. 161 Brigade retained 6 Rajrif, 4 Kumaon and 2 Dogra, while 163 Brigade was formed of 1 Sikh, 3 Garhwal and 1 Madras. The supporting arms were also subdivided, 161 Brigade taking on its order of Battle one battery Field Artillery, The Mountain Battery, a squadron of armoured cars of 7 Cavalry and a field company of Madras Engineers. The administrative units, with the exception of 3 Light Field Ambulance which was later replaced by 60 Para Field Ambulance, were taken under the direct command of Headquarters Sri Div and given the role of administrating both Brigades.

The reorganisation did not come as a surprise to 161 Infantry Brigade. Rumours apart, Major General Kulwant Singh, the Commander Jak Force, when on a visit to the Brigade after the Limber Nullah battle had hinted that such a move was likely in the near future. He had also mentioned that more troops would be inducted into the Valley and that 161 Infantry Brigade would be relieved of its Uri commitment by 77 Parachute Brigade. On relief, he stated, 161 Infantry Brigade would be located in Srinagar as the reserve Brigade of the Division about to be formed. After a short spell in Srinagar, the Brigade would, on a further Brigade arriving in the Valley, return to Ranchi in Bihar to rejoin its parent formation the Fifth Infantry Division.

The move of 161 Infantry Brigade into a reserve role was by no means out of turn. From the day that its leading elements had arrived in the Valley, the six months that had followed had demanded constant mental alertness and severely taxed the physical capacity of both officers and men. The mental strain had been the more serious, as a single major error could be disastrous. A rest was, therefore, very welcome, but the thought of leaving the Valley and proceeding to Ranchi met with definite disapproval. Somehow, 161 Infantry Brigade had come to feel attached to and possessive about the Valley, and the very idea of having to sever connections with it did not seem possible or right.

On taking over command of Sri Div, Major General Thimayya summoned me to Baramula to brief him on all aspects of the situation in Kashmir and to discuss future operations. With the mine of information that had been collected by the Brigade from all possible sources, the briefing took the whole morning. The topography of the various areas, from Srinagar to Skardu and Leh via the Zoji La Pass and Kargil, Handwara to Tithwal and Muzaffarabad, and Uri to Domel, was covered in very great detail. This was most important as the mountains, the roads, tracks, bridges, rivers and streams would all have a direct bearing on the quantum of troops needed to mount an operation in a particular area, and the type of transport and equipment necessary to ensure adequate logistical support. The dispositions of our own troops and those of the enemy were easily seen on the marked map, but I drew Major General Thimayya's attention to one particular enemy position, the area of Chakothi–Chinari, in which I stressed there was a regular Pakistan Infantry Brigade. I informed him that I had regularly reported the existence of the Brigade to Headquarters Jak Force for the past two months, but it had not been accepted as being factual. I stated that two units had been identified, the 1st Battalion the 13th Frontier Force Rifles and the 4th Battalion the 16th Punjab Regiment. The third battalion was from the Baluch Regiment, and was either the 3rd or 4th. Major General Thimayya accepted my assertion.

The formation of Sri Div might give the impression that Kashmir was being heavily reinforced. It had for the last six months been held by just one Infantry Brigade, and now it was to have a whole Infantry Division. It is true that Zebra Brigade had been formed in the Valley, but it could hardly be classified as a Brigade, being composed of one infantry battalion, 1 Sikh, and a smattering of supporting arms that could be spared by 161 Infantry Brigade. It had, in fact, been formed merely to cope with an administrative blunder and to absorb Brigadier Lakhinder Singh into some sort of appointment in the Valley.

Sri Div consisted of: (i) 161 Infantry Brigade which retained three of its battalions—6 Rajrif , 4 Kumaon and 2 Dogra; (ii) the newly raised 163 Infantry Brigade, which took the place of the disbanded Zebra Brigade and comprised two battalions—3 Garhwal and 1 Madras—transferred from 161 Infantry Brigade and 1 Sikh inherited from Zebra Brigade; and (iii) the newly arrived 77 Para Brigade. The sum total of infantry battalions newly inducted into the Kashmir Valley was therefore just the three battalions of 77 Para Brigade.

If 161 Infantry Brigade had had to struggle desperately to contain the enemy both during winter and after the Banihal Pass had opened, with the six battalions then present in the Valley, it is difficult to understand how Army Headquarters expected Sri Div, with just three more battalions, to accomplish its stiff task: the capture of Domel initially, and the relief of Leh, in Ladakh, later. I stated to Major General Thimayya that if Army Headquarters was really serious about Kashmir, and agreed with the accepted principle that the ratio between attack and defence should be at least 3 to 1, then eighteen battalions were necessary to ensure success in the attack. All it had done was to send in one Brigade of three battalions. By juggling about with the battalions already with 161 Infantry Brigade and Zebra Brigade, it had formed a Division of three Brigades and conjured up the appearance of a strong force.

Of this Division, one Brigade, 77 Para, had been earmarked to take over the Uri–Mahura commitment. This left him with just two Brigades for operations. With the weather having changed and reliable reports coming in that the enemy was in the Tithwal area, in strength, he could not afford to neglect the Handwara–Tithwal area, especially as the enemy had once reached Handwara by that route during winter when the snows hampered progress on foot. It would require one Brigade to operate in this area. That left him with just 161 Infantry Brigade to move down the main road to Domel. With a regular Pakistan Infantry Brigade in position in the Chakothi–Chinari area, supported by AKP battalions and tribesmen, it was extremely difficult to visualise how 161 Infantry Brigade could break through. Even if by a stroke of luck it did, there was forty-five miles of road between Uri and Domel which would have to be protected, and that would call for another Brigade.

After a break for lunch we resumed the discussion. After Major General Thimayya had given me a broad idea of the operations that he wished to mount, I suggested to him that he make an immediate bid for three more Brigades, bringing up the Division's strength to six Brigades. One Brigade would be utilised to hold the Uri–Mahura area, two Brigades for the advance to Domel, one Brigade for the advance to Tithwal, and as the advances to Domel and Tithwal were so wide apart, he should have one Brigade in reserve for each front. I stressed to Major General Thimayya that he was launching a Divisional attack on two axes, and with only three Brigades he would be doing so without a reserve which was absolutely essential. General Thimayya said that he would "chew over" the problem for a day or two and then call me up for another conference.

Officers of various units now started arriving in Kashmir, and anxious to have a look at Uri and meet their friends serving in the area, made daily trips to the place. Among them was Major Thimayya, Major General Thimayya's younger brother. Hearing a dog bark, I walked out of the Operations Room and saw a terrier running about in the Brigade Headquarters area. As a number of stray dogs had met their death by running into the anti-personnel minefields around the piquet positions, strict orders had been issued that no animals were to be brought to Uri. I therefore gave instructions that the owner of the dog be located, informed that it was to be put on a chain immediately, and removed from Uri at the first possible moment. The terrier, I was informed, belonged to Major Thimayya, who caught his pet and chained it to the railing of the Brigade Headquarters building.

About half an hour later, Thimayya asked the Brigade Major for permission to visit Nalwar piquet, and on receiving permission set off with a friend who knew the piquet well. The dog, watching his master disappearing in the distance, apparently tugged at its chain in an effort to free itself, and slipping its collar, rushed after him. When the animal caught up with him, Thimayya and the officer accompanying him should have turned back at once, but they continued on their way. The terrier, enjoying his outing, rushed all over the place, and it was not until the two officers were reasonably close to the piquet that Thimayya was advised by his companion to take his dog up into his arms. The terrier permitted Thimayya to get close to him and then playfully bounded away, until both dog and master were perilously close to an anti-personnel minefield. Thimayya's friend shouted to him to come back, but in his anxiety to save his pet he made a lunge at it, and the animal leaping backwards set off an anti-personnel mine. Both master and dog were killed instantly, and it was my sad task to ring General Thimayya and give him the tragic news. Another life had been needlessly thrown away.

In the first week of May 1948, 77 Para Brigade, commanded by Brigadier P. S. Nair, having arrived in Kashmir, was sent forward to relieve 161 Infantry Brigade of its commitments in the Uri–Mahura sector. In order to eliminate any possibility of an enemy attack attaining an element of success before the units of 77 Para Brigade had settled down, the unit of 161 Infantry Brigade, on handing over the piquets, came into reserve in the Uri bowl and at Mahura. The operational command of both Brigades was also vested in Headquarters 161 Infantry Brigade, the Divisional Commander having decided that it should be so until the Commander 77 Para Brigade declared himself ready and happy to assume the responsibility. Headquarters 161 Infantry Brigade continued to be in operational command until 20 May, when it moved down the road towards Domel.

The reason for not handing over operational control until 20 May was not because the Commander 77 Para Brigade did not reach a state of readiness before that date. It had been mutually agreed between the two Brigades that as the opening phase of 161 Infantry Brigade's plan was closely interlinked with the firm base and piquets manned by 77 Para Brigade, and also the use of one of its units in the Mahura area, it would be wiser to have one operational commander. This arrangement naturally meant that Headquarters 161 Infantry Brigade could not avail itself on the ten days' rest that had been sanctioned for the Brigade by Headquarters Sri Div, but the arrangement was an operational necessity.

Planning for the Spring offensive proceeded apace. Major General Thimayya's bid for a total of six Infantry Brigades met with a refusal. He was told that he must make do with the three Brigades in the Valley, 161, 163 and 77 Para. This was an extremely shortsighted decision by higher authority and was directly responsible for the subsequent failure to achieve anything more than limited gains. If the reason for the refusal was non-availability of the three Brigades, then the directive to Major General Thimayya should have been amended to something more in keeping with the capability of Sri Div, in place of a task which from the outset had only slender chances of success.

Unassailable arguments had been advanced in support of the necessity for three more Brigades. The enemy had a numerical superiority of nearly three to one; the terrain in which the troops would have to operate, being mountainous and favouring defence, accentuated the numerical disparity even further; one Brigade would be static and the other two were required to operate on two widely separated axes, each demanding that the line of communication be protected; and in the event of either or both advances meeting with stiff resistance and being halted, there was no Divisional reserve that could be launched to influence the situation and force a breakthrough. In fact, once Headquarters Sri Div launched 161 and 163 Infantry Brigades on the Domel and Muzaffarabad axes respectively, it would degenerate into an Administrative Headquarters, because both Brigades would be operating as Independent Brigades and Headquarters Sri Div, other than providing the logistical support, would be incapable of assisting in any way.

Any one of the arguments advanced was in itself a good enough case for the provision of the extra Brigades, that is, if Army Headquarters was serious about the operations; collectively, they made the sanctioning of them absolutely imperative. The refusal, therefore, is not easily understood, especially as Headquarters Sri Div's directive remained unamended. It could have been that the Army Headquarters' assessment of the situation was diametrically opposite to that which had been stated by Headquarters Sri Div on the basis of the details supplied by Headquarters 161 Infantry Brigade, or there may have been some other reasons that had not filtered through the Banihal Pass. In any case, the failure to send three more Infantry Brigades into the Valley resulted in Sri Div's advance being bogged down, and India being denied the control of Kashmir up to Domel.

Perhaps this might have been averted had the British Government's order that no British officer would involve himself in the fighting in Jammu and Kashmir not been in force. General Sir Rob Lockhart having left, General Sir Roy Bucher had succeeded him. The order forbade the Commander in Chief of the Indian Army to enter a certain area in which the units of the Army which he commanded were engaged in operations. As such, he could never feel the real pulse of the situation, and in so far as operations were concerned, he was more a paper chief than the Commander in Chief. It was his responsibility to keep the Cabinet of the Government of India fully briefed at all times, but his briefings could not carry the authority or conviction which they might have if he had come to Kashmir, got a feel of the terrain and the difficulties that it imposed, and talked to the local commanders. Only then could he have arrived at his own assessment of the situation and advised Government correctly, and issued directives that were capable of being implemented.

The Sri Div plan was now formulated. 161 Infantry Brigade was ordered to advance towards Domel, 163 Infantry Brigade from Handwara to Muzaffarabad via Tithwal, and 77 Para Brigade was given the role of holding the firm base in the Uri–Mahura area. Every avenue was, meanwhile, being explored to find a means of slackening the enemy's grip in the Chakothi–Chinari area. It was suggested to Major General Thimayya that if higher authority could be persuaded to agree to pose a threat to Chikar Khas, or even Bagh, with a strong column from Poonch, it could produce the desired result. If Chikar Khas was made the objective, the enemy line of communication would be threatened. When debating the possibility of Poonch Brigade being able to mount such an operation, the various factors and the situation confronting that Brigade were given full consideration, and it was concluded that the plan was well worth pursuing, and that

THE SRI DIV PLAN

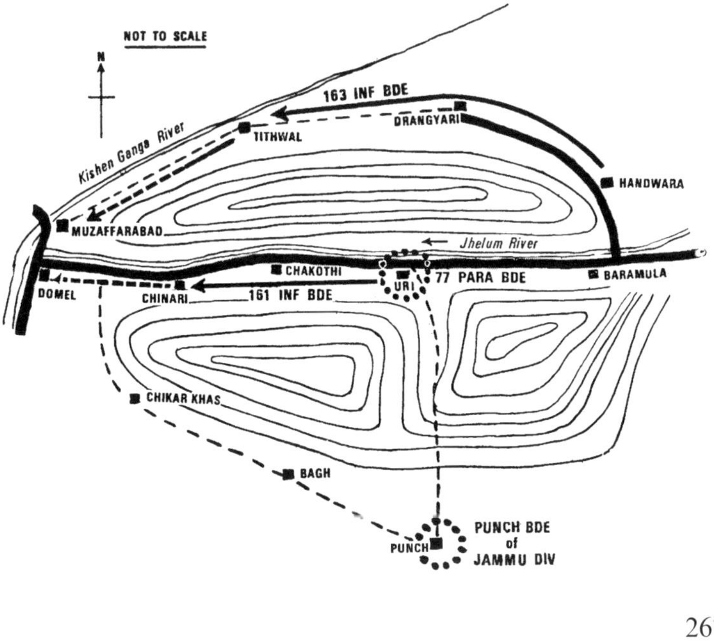

it would, if successful, have far-reaching effects. Given the attitude of Army Headquarters, however, it was neither unexpected, nor a disappointment, when the use of the Poonch Brigade was vetoed.

Headquarters Sri Div had now to produce its own diversionary threat. This was essential if the planned offensive was to have any hope of success. Major General Thimayya decided that the only possibility was for 163 Infantry Brigade's advance towards Tithwal to be launched two days before that of 161 Infantry Brigade towards Domel. It was hoped that the enemy might assume that the 163 Infantry Brigade's advance was the main threat. This was not wishful thinking, as 163 Brigade, unless halted, would arrive in Muzaffarabad which was almost next door to Domel, and the enemy would probably have to weaken his dispositions in the Chakothi–Chinari area in order to arrest it. Though this was a gamble, there was nothing else that could be done in the circumstances. 163 Infantry Brigade's attack was, therefore, scheduled to be launched on 16 May, and 161 Infantry Brigade's on 18 May.

163 Infantry Brigade's role was by no means an easy one. The Brigade was required to move from Handwara to Tithwal and thence to Muzaffarabad. Tithwal, it was known, had elements of the enemy, but its actual strength was unknown. The terrain over which the Brigade would have to operate was mountainous and presented many serious logistical problems, aggravated by its having to employ animals and porters when the motorable road ended at Drangyari. From Tithwal onwards to Muzaffarabad, the route ran through a gorge overlooked for its entire length by high hills. To expect just one Brigade to capture or even threaten Muzaffarabad was, therefore, placing one's hopes rather high. The task was, in fact, beyond the compass of any Brigade but, starved of troops, Sri Div could do no more than its best.

It was not surprising that 163 Brigade's advance was halted by stiff enemy opposition at Tithwal. Without a reserve with which he could break the stalemate, Major General Thimayya found himself placed in an utterly helpless position. Brigadier J. C. Katoch fell sick soon after the advance commenced and Lt. Col. Harbakhsh Singh, the Commanding Officer of 1 Sikh, took over the Brigade in the capacity of Brigadier.

In order to consolidate the impression that the main threat of the Spring offensive would be the one posed by 163 Infantry Brigade, various rumours were circulated regarding the future employment and location of 161 Infantry Brigade. It was freely voiced in Srinagar that the Brigade was returning to Srinagar en route to rejoining its parent formation in Ranchi, and many friends of the Brigade asked for suitable dates for farewell parties. It was agreed that the dates should be finalised after the Brigade had concentrated in Srinagar. This news, eventually and unfortunately, reached the ears of Bakshi Ghulam Mohammed who had returned to the Valley from Jammu. Hearing that I was at Headquarters Sri Div, at Baramula, he drove over and confronted me with what he referred to as a rumour. Knowing Bakshi as well as I did, I should perhaps have explained to him the truth behind the rumour, but unfortunately confirmed that 161 Infantry Brigade was pulling back, as it had undergone a very tiring and trying spell of duty.

Bakshi was most unhappy when the rumour was confirmed, and while agreeing that 161 Infantry Brigade was in need of a rest, argued that there were many lovely spots in the Valley where the Brigade could relax and enjoy itself. He then stated that he would never agree to the Brigade moving out of Kashmir, and would approach the Government of India on the subject. I hastily advised him not to do that, and suggested that he await Major General Thimayya's return, which was expected in a matter of minutes, and said I was certain that he could persuade Thimayya to retain 161 Infantry Brigade in Kashmir.

No sooner had Major General Thimayya joined us and sat down than Bakshi assailed him in a most determined manner, insisting that under no circumstances, and regardless of how many Brigades came to the Valley, was 161 Infantry Brigade to leave. Seeing that Major General Thimayya was flabbergasted, I quickly explained to him that Bakshi was most unhappy to hear that the Brigade was going to Ranchi, and that I had explained to him that he, Thimayya, was the authority to cancel the move and retain the Brigade in Kashmir. Major General Thimayya then dealt with the situation in his own inimitable way, and Bakshi Ghulam Mohammed left Baramula for

Srinagar a very happy man, having been assured that 161 Infantry Brigade would remain in the Valley and that the rumour was for the enemy's benefit.

In Uri, the deception plan covered two bridges. One was a wooden bridge not far from the eastern exit of Uri and on the road leading to the Haji Pir Pass. The other was a completely demolished bridge at the western exit of Uri, and about a hundred yards from Fort piquet. The wooden bridge on the Haji Pir Pass route had been partially burnt by the enemy during the winter, but as it was never used nor likely to be used by the Brigade, it had been left in its semi-charred state. It now received special attention. A small engineer party, with two companies of infantry affording local protection, visited the bridge site every day, and its repair was taken in hand. As the bridge was left unprotected by night, it was destroyed by the enemy when almost ready. Undeterred, the engineers proceeded to repair the damage, only for the enemy to repeat his act. This continued until 17 May, the date preceding the advance of the Brigade from Uri.

The bridge that mattered, the one at the western exit of Uri, received no attention that was visible to the enemy. It was reconnoitered in the hours of darkness and the span accurately measured. The engineers then marked out an identical gap in the Uri bowl and spanned it with a Bailey bridge. The prepared Bailey bridge was then divided into sections capable of being carried to the site on jeep trailers hauled by the infantry. Continuous practice during the hours of darkness enabled the engineer cum infantry team to reach a state of perfection, the gap being spanned in five hours without any noise to disturb the stillness of the night.

With the demolished bridge at the western exit of Uri receiving no attention, and the wooden bridge on the road to the Haji Pir Pass being reconstructed every time that it was destroyed, it is quite definite that the enemy was led into believing that an assault was about to be mounted against the Haji Pir Pass. Reports poured in of strong enemy reinforcements, mostly Pathan tribals, moving to and concentrating in the Bhatgiran area and on the spurs running north from the Pass to Uri. While they could have engaged the Uri defences, they showed a disinclination towards any type of offensive action, presumably preferring to wait and see what would happen.

The Emergency Government, on its arrival back in the Valley from Jammu, decided to raise a Jammu and Kashmir Militia. This militia was formed from an element of ex-State Force personnel and a large number of raw recruits. On 14 May, when Major General Thimayya telephoned me at Uri and asked me whether I would accept one of the newly formed battalions of the J&K Militia for employment in the Uri sector, I very politely refused the offer. The militia was then only a few weeks old, and neither Major General Thimayya nor I had any doubts that it had no place in the battlefield in a combat role. Major General Thimayya had, in fact, made one stipulation, that if I did agree to accept the battalion, I was to ensure that it was employed in a role in which it would not be exposed to enemy fire or action. I suggested to him that 77 Para Brigade might have some suitable role, such as garrisoning Baramula or guarding the bridges in-between Baramula and Heman Buniyar. This, I added, would meet his stipulation as it would be well out of harm's way. 77 Para Brigade, however, also declined the offer.

The same evening, Major Geneal Thimayya spoke to me again about the militia battalion, and asked me to reconsider my refusal. He said that he was being pressured to associate the militia with the fighting, and his argument that they were totally unfit to take any sort of active part in combat was falling on deaf ears. He requested me to relieve him of his embarrassment and to accept a battalion. Very reluctantly I did so, and Major General Thimayya again asked me to ensure that the unit was not exposed to any form of threat. I decided to postpone my decision as to what role I could allot the unit until I had seen it. It arrived in the morning of 18 May in Uri.

Uniformed, equipped with rifles and a few light machine guns, and the major portion having fired a few rounds on a rifle range, the battalion could march in step, and that was about all. It totally lacked tactical knowledge, and the training that it had received was so puerile that it did not even reach the average section level. The unit was, in fact, nothing more than a body of uniformed and armed individuals, unfit for combat duties. I offered them to 77 Para Brigade, but they had seen exactly what I had, and refused emphatically to take them on strength. I therefore decided not to use the unit unless I found a completely safe area, if such a thing exists in a combat zone, and the role would have to be such that it would not divert my attention from the operations to be conducted by 161 Infantry Brigade, and that I would not suffer from a constant nightmare wondering what was happening to the Militia battalion.

This is no reflection on the rank and file of the militia battalion. They were very keen, but whosoever had trained them was apparently ignorant of the requirements of the battlefield. Keenness does not suffice in a combat zone, and ignorance could and would lead them to their deaths. That the battalion should have been permitted to approach a battle area was unfair to Major General Thimayya, unfair to 161 Infantry Brigade since it could have been a serious embarrassment to the security of the Brigade, and, worst of all, unfair to the men of the battalion who were being asked to face possible situations which, had they arisen, would have resulted in the unit being decimated.

A few days prior to 18 May, 161 Infantry Brigade was allotted a fourth battalion, the 7th Battalion The Sikh Regiment (7 Sikh), which had arrived in the Valley. This extra battalion was essential as the 161 Infantry Brigade plan envisaged one of its battalions advancing as a right flank guard, and well away from the main axis of advance, thereby reducing the striking force down the main road to two battalions. It was a workmanlike outfit, full of confidence and with a high percentage of World War II veterans. In the actions that it fought, this unit certainly lived up to the high impression formed of it at first contact. Although strange to the Brigade, and with little time to marry up with the supporting arms, it dovetailed into the Brigade in a matter of hours and became a valuable member.

2 Dogra was, meanwhile, taken over by a new Commanding Officer, Lt. Col. Thakur. A posting order asking him to proceed to Delhi to set up the National Cadet Corps had resulted in Lt. Col. G. G. Bewoor having to hand over the battalion. This change of Commanding Officer at a critical juncture was most unfortunate, especially in the case of

a battalion such as 2 Dogra which was just beginning to find its feet. Bewoor had got to know the unit well and realised its weaknesses, and this enabled him to command it with a rare mixture of sympathy and firmness. Under its new Commanding Officer, 2 Dogra, given what was considered to be the simplest of roles, faltered very badly. It caused utter confusion at the outset of the advance to Domel, completely jeopardising the Brigade plan and nullifying all the strenuous efforts that had been made to achieve the surprise.

* * *

The plan shaped by 161 Infantry Brigade envisaged a two-pronged thrust. One was to be delivered by 4 Kumaon acting as a right flank guard, and necessitated an advance from Mahura along the crest of the Kazinag Range to Pandu and point 6873. The feature formed a part of the Pir Panjal Range, and ran parallel to the main road along the north bank of the river Jhelum. Although its official name is not the Kazinag Range, it was given this designation by 161 Infantry Brigade for convenience, as its highest point was Chhota Qazinag. The other thrust was to be launched by the remainder of the Brigade along the main road from Uri to Domel.

Both advances posed diametrically different problems in the field of logistics. 4 Kumaon's route lay across a high mountain range with numerous cols, sharp peaks and precipitous slopes. Reliance for its maintenance had, therefore, to be based on a very large porter train. Pack ponies were also made available, but these stout-hearted little animals were incapable of negotiating the trackless route taken by the battalion, much of it being up steep mountain sides. They were therefore employed in ferrying stores forward from Mahura to a supply dump located at the base of the feature, from where the porters hiked the loads forward to the unit. The main thrust had the use of a first class tarmac road, bordered along its complete length by the river Jhelum on the north, and mountain spurs running up to the heights of the Pir Panjal Range flanking it on the south.

To make matters more complicated and capable of leading to serious confusion, the map sheets depicting the route from Srinagar to Domel underwent an extraordinary change at Uri. In one sheet, the milestones commenced at Srinagar and ended at M.S. 64 which was the bridge site at the western exist of Uri. On the continuing sheet, a second M.S. 64 appeared about four miles further to the west of Uri, and the milestone numbers decreased until Domel was shown as being M.S. 19. The use of milestones, in all the communications had, therefore, to be carefully watched, as, for example, M.S. 60 could be either between Mahura and Uri, or to the west of Uri at Urusa, a variance of twelve miles.

Along the forty-five miles of road from Uri to Domel were twenty-two bridges, of which eight were of wooden structure, three with masonry arches, and eleven of steel girders. As past experience had shown that the enemy was adept at bridge destruction, and had invariably resorted to this practice in an endeavour to slow down or halt an advance, it was fully expected that he would not hesitate to demolish the bridges if the occasion demanded it. The possibility of having to create diversions was therefore given serious study, and the advice of the engineers in the service of the Government of Jammu and Kashmir, who had been responsible for the construction and maintenance of these bridges, was obtained. The engineers stated that diversions could be created around most of the bridges with relative ease, with the exception of the bridges at (the mile-stones quoted are those shown on the map sheet covering the area from Uri to Domel) M.S. 58, M.S. 45, and M.S. 42, where the diversions would take some amount of time and labour. The bridges at M.S. 60, M.S. 28 and M.S. 18 would, however, present a very difficult problem. From the point of view of operations, in which speed was essential, the only answer was assault bridging.

Assault bridging had been brought into the Valley and stocked in Srinagar, but the total length available fell far short of the estimated requirement. With the logistical support of the units advancing along the main road based on the use of mechanical transport, and therefore dependent on the state of the bridges, in order to counter the possibility of the advance coming to a grinding halt at a damaged or destroyed bridge, each infantry battalion was allotted forty-two pack ponies for use if and when required.

The smooth functioning of the logistics was naturally dependent on the protection of the supply columns and the bridges. The route was very vulnerable and presented excellent opportunities for attack by enemy raiding parties, and as this was a live possibility the problem was discussed at length with Headquarters Sri Div. It was argued that 161 Infantry Brigade would find it very difficult to fight an enemy far superior in numbers, and in mountainous terrain, and also be responsible for the protection of its own line of communication. To attempt to do so would only result in dissipating the fighting strength of the Brigade, and would compel Brigade Headquarters to look constantly over its shoulders.

Major General Thimayya fully appreciated the points raised, but found himself helpless to assist with the problem. He pointed out that he had no reserve and hence no spare troops, and Army Headquarters had refused all his requests for extra formations and units. The militia units were available, but he was doubtful whether they would be able to cope with the task. I refused the offer of the militia stressing the point, with which Major General Thimayya agreed, that to employ the militia in a forward area would tempt the enemy to help himself to an on-the-spot arsenal. There was no solution to the problem. It was left to 161 Infantry Brigade either to protect its own line of communication from Uri westwards at the expense of its striking ability, or to leave the line of communication unprotected and accept any consequences that might arise through taking the risk.

161 Infantry Brigade's plan of action was finalised after taking into account the difficulties imposed by the terrain, the possibility of meeting with demolished bridges, the protection or neglect of the line of communication, and the enemy strength likely to be encountered—a Pakistan Regular Infantry Brigade, an AKP Brigade, and a large number of Pathan tribals. It was limited, in the first phase, to the

capture of Chinari. Subsequent phases, it was agreed by Headquarters Sri Div, would be undertaken should the first phase be successfully accomplished, and dependent on the situation prevailing at the time.

The plan in brief, was: –

(a) 4 Kumaon was to advance from Mahura, starting after darkness had set in on 17 May, and to concentrate at Sikkibat by first light on the 18th morning.

This preliminary move was necessary in order to enable the battalion to position itself on the Kazinag Range, to carry out its reconnaissances, and be poised to move forward as the right flank guard to the thrust down the main road.

(b) The Sawai Man Guards (a unit of the Jaipur State Forces, and now serving with 77 Para Brigade) deployed on Goshar and point 9062 was to come under command of 4 Kumaon when the unit arrived at Sikkibat. The Commanding Officer

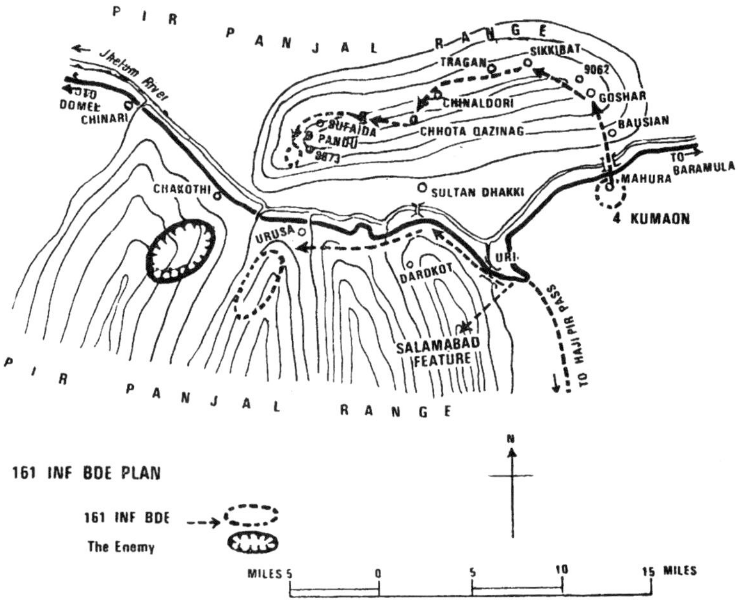

of 4 Kumaon was authorised to use the Sawal Man Guards to cary out a deceptive role, but not to weaken its hold on the firm base. When 4 Kumaon advanced, the Sawai Man Guards were to revert to the command of 77 Para Brigade.

(c) Commencing at 0200 hours on 19 May, 4 Kumaon supported by 11 Field Battery was to pass through the firm base held by the Sawai Man Guards and advance via Tragan, Chinal Dori, Sufaida and Pandu to point 6873.

As 4 Kuamon was carrying out what was an independent role, and it was quite impossible to gauge what difficulties it would experience in overcoming the enemy opposition and the terrain, the timings, objectives to be taken, and the rate of advance of the battalion, once it passed through the Sawai Man Guards, was left to the discretion of the battalion commander, Lt. Col. Man Mohan Khanna.

(d) 2 Dogra was to advance from Uri at 2200 hours on 18 May and capture the Salamabad feature by first light on 19 May. It was to be supported by 11 Field Battery and the Mountain Battery.

2 Dogra had been selected for this task, as it was considered to be reasonably easy and simple, and well within the capabilities of the unit. There was little danger of losing direction during the advance, as it would be a moonlit light and the feature to be occupied would be clearly visible from Uri. Although occupation of the Salamabad feature by a piquet had always been desirable, it had not been possible owing to the shortage of troops. It had nevertheless been a regular patrol task of 2 Dogra. The enemy had also not been attracted to it in any strength, an occasional platoon or observation post being noticed on it but withdrawing when a patrol from Uri moved out in its direction. To take possession of it now was essential. Not only did it command about eight miles of the road from Uri to Domel, but its occupation would deny to the enemy, particularly those in the Bhatgiran and Haji Pir areas, the ability to interfere with movement down the main road. The Salamabad feature had three distinct Pimples, and 2 Dogra was carefully briefed to take each Pimple in

turn, and to establish a company firm base on each Pimple before moving on to the next.

(e) The field company Madras Engineers was to proceed to the bridge site at the western exit of Uri at 2300 hours on 18 May, and to complete the launching of the Bailey bridge by 0400 hours on 19 May.

(f) On 2 Dogra reporting that the three Salamabad Pimples were firmly held, one squadron armoured cars 7 Cavalry and one rifle company 7 Sikh, mounted in Bren Carriers, were to move forward on orders of Bridge Headquarters and deny to the enemy the use of the bridge over the Jhelum River near M.S. 68. (This M.S. did not appear on the map. It was the second M.S. 64 on the map, and as it was about four miles west of Uri, was referred to as M.S. 68 by the Brigade.)

The move was aimed at preventing a large body of AKP troops and Pathan tribals, who had been located on the north bank of the River Jhelum, from crossing over to the south bank. The bridge, which was almost opposite Sultan Dhakki, had been constructed by the enemy.

(g) 7 Sikh, less its rifle company with the armoured column, was to advance and link up with the armoured column on orders from Brigade HQ.

(h) 6 Rajrif was to be held in reserve.

(i) Brigade Headquarters was to be established in Fort Piquet at 1800 hours on 18 May, and its axis of advance was to be along the main road.

(j) Casualties from both axes were to be evacuated to 60 Para Field Ambulance in Uri.

(k) All units were to be on hard scale rations for seven days.

On 17 May, 4 Kumaon left Mahura at 1800 hours, and by 0600 hours on 18 May was concentrated at Sikkibat. The approach march, carried out over extremely difficult country and involving the climbing of several precipitous mountains, was achieved in good style and undetected by the enemy. The daylight hours were devoted to carrying out reconnaissances and ensuring that the logistical support was working smoothly. It was an excellent start to the Spring offensive, but was unfortunately to be short-lived.

* * *

Advancing from Uri at 2200 hours on 18 May, 2 Dogra headed for the Salamabad feature and Pimple One. The mountain was bathed in moonlight and stood out very clearly and majestically. Standing by to support the battalion at a moment's notice were the field and mountain batteries, while Brigade Headquarters, with a log night facing it, waited calmly in Fort Piquet. At 2300 hours, moving past Brigade Headquarters extremely silently, went the field company, Madras Engineers, heading for the demolished bridge at the western exit of Uri. A few moments later, a train of jeep trailers, loaded with prepared sections of the Bailey bridge, and propelled by a rifle company of 6 Rajrif, slid by equally quietly. On arrival at the bridge site, the sections of the Bailey bridge were unloaded and the jeep trailers returned to the Uri bowl. With one rifle company of 7 Sikh already in position on the far side of the demolished bridge to afford local protection to the bridging party, the Sappers commenced their task.

The sound of muffled thuds disturbed the stillness of the night, and to those listening carefully for any trace of sound, the noise seemed to be rather loud, but it was a case of anxiety sharpening the faculty of perception. That the sound waves did not carry as far as the enemy who might have been lurking in the area is reasonably certain, as there was no hostile reaction. The work continued into the early morning, and at 0300 hours, half an hour before the scheduled time, the engineers reported that their task was completed. It had been a superb performance, conducted with speed, silence and efficiency.

The progress made by 2 Dogra was unknown. Wireless silence was being observed to be broken only in the event of the unit encountering the enemy in strength and requiring artillery support, or at first light, by which time the occupation of the Salamabad feature should have been completed. No news was, therefore, good news and in consequence no cause for anxiety. The maintenance of wireless silence was, in fact, being interpreted as indication of an unopposed success. This feeling of self-satisfaction was, however, rudely shattered at 0420 hours, when an extraordinary spectacle presented itself. It was a sight that has rarely, if ever, been witnessed on a battlefield in the modern era, and is unlikely to be seen ever again.

Without any indication or warning, the ridge running north from the Haji Pir Pass towards Uri burst into flames. As the area was thickly wooded, it was assumed that it was a forest fire which appeared to be spreading rapidly. The flames then formed themselves into long columns and snaked their way up the slopes towards the Haji Pir Pass. After a few moments it became apparent what was happening. The enemy concentrations, in the Bhatgiran and other nearby areas, had obviously received warning of the move on to the Salamabad feature. It had probably been interpreted by the enemy as being an attempt to encircle the personnel in that area. This was understandable, as a continuation of the Salamabad advance would have landed 2 Dogra on the Pir Panjal Range in the vicinity of Ledi Gali, and cut the line of communication of those in the Haji Pir Pass area. To aid them to attain speed in their flight, the enemy had lit torches made of faggots, and had not been conservative in the numbers that were gathered and lit. The torchlight column were, unfortunately, because of crest clearance, incapable of being engaged by the field artillery, and a wonderful target had to go unpunished. It was most frustrating, but nothing could be done other than to watch the Torchlight Tattoo move further and further away and eventually disappear.

The obvious deduction drawn from the pageant that had been viewed was that on the Salamabad feature there was either an enemy observation post or perhaps a platoon patrol. Any doubt that this was so was soon removed, as a section of 4.2-inch mortars started shelling Uri from a position somewhere near the main road. The fire, very definitely ordered in haste, was not directed at any particular target and in consequence was inclined to be wild. A few lucky shots did, however, land close to the gun area and a few yards to the east of Fort Piquet, and inflicted three casualties. Although the location of the enemy mortar section had not been spotted, the Mountain

Battery was ordered to engage various areas on the road and near the base of the Salamabad feature, and had greater success. A chance shot knocked out one of the mortars, which was found next morning in a badly damaged condition. This must have acted as a deterrent to the mortar section, as the firing ceased almost as quickly as it had started.

The continued presence of the Pakistan Regular troops in the Chakothi-Chinari area was firmly established. The AKP units had been equipped with three-inch mortars and had used them, but never the 4.2-inch mortars. The advance of 163 Infantry Brigade towards Tithwal, which it was hoped would result in the Pakistan Regular Infantry Brigade being withdrawn, had not achieved that object. 161 Infantry Brigade, when it moved forward, had therefore to contend with a head-on clash against this Brigade, in a well entrenched position, and in terrain which was eminently suited to defence. This observation, supported by the fact that Uri had been shelled by 4.2-inch mortars, was sent to Headquarters Sri Div and eventually reached Delhi.

It was given no credence. An immediate rejoinder to Headquarters Sri Div ordered it to inform Headquarters 161 Infantry Brigade that it was to cease making wild statements. In order to prove that the report made was no exaggeration, Rear Headquarters 161 Infantry Brigade, which had been moved forward toUri, was ordered to collect the tail fins of the 4.2-inch mortar bombs that were lying in the area and to dispatch them to Headquarters Sri Div for delivery to Delhi. Accompanying the package containing the tail fins of the mortar bombs was a note to the effect that neither 161 Infantry Brigade nor 77 Para Brigade was equipped with the 4.2-inch mortar, nor had it formed part of the J&K State Force armoury. The AKP units and the Pathan tribals had not been equipped with this weapon in the past, and it was most unlikely that it now formed part of their arsenal. Despite what was unassailable proof of Pakistan's active participation in the Kashmir operations, her regular troops being deployed in the area, Army Headquarters' insistence that it was nonsense continued, but only for a few more days till they were presented with still further evidence, this time in the shape of a prisoner of war.

At dawn, 2 Dogra broke wireless silence and reported that its leading company was one thousand yards away from the final objective, Pimple Three, and advancing against no opposition. Although the final objective was required to be taken by first light, which would now be delayed by about half an hour, or at worst forty-five minutes, the situation was satisfactory. The armoured column of one Squadron 7 Cavalry and the rifle company 7 Sikh in Bren Carriers, was ordered to stand by to move at short notice, on receipt of orders from Brigade Headquarters. Its move to the area of M.S. 68 had, however, to be postponed indefinitely, as almost immediately 2 Dogra reported that it had run into trouble.

The message, received on the wireless from Headquarters 2 Dogra, stated very bluntly that four of its platoons had been counter-attacked by the enemy and scuppered. It was impossible to get any further information as the set went off the air. Heavy firing of small arms could be heard on Salamabad, and frantic efforts to regain contact with the unit Headquarters succeeded only after a grim interval of twenty minutes. The next report stated that of the four platoons, only the company commander, one platoon commander, and two men had survived what was described as a fierce hand-to-hand battle. The enemy's strength was estimated at being over a battalion.

The Brigade plan had now been thrown completely out of gear, as until such time as the enemy battalion on Salamabad was evicted, and that would necessitate the launching of 6 Rajrif or 7 Sikh or even both into the assault, no advance down the road could be considered. Before committing either of these battalions into the assault, it was essential that a clear picture was available as to what features were in the possession of 2 Dogra, and which were held by the enemy. Reports from Headquarters 2 Dogra were, however, garbled and half-baked. Then, despite the fact that the Commanding Officer was unaware of the exact location of his rifle companies, he called for Artillery support without indicating which target he wished struck. When asked where his artillery Forward Observation Officer (FOO) was, he said that he did not know. The FOO was, in fact, within twenty yards of him. This Gilbert and Sullivan opera continued until 0800 hours. How to terminate it was a problem. To have moved on to Salamabad, and judged the position for myself, would have entailed my having to segregate myself from the rest of the Brigade as it involved a three hours' climb. This, with 4 Kumaon already on the move on the right flank, was impossible at what was a most critical juncture.

In order to get some idea of what features were held by 2 Dogra on the Salamabad feature, I demanded that the battalion commander give me his exact location on the ground, and the next moment I was completely shattered. Instead of being with his forward companies, he was with the reserve Company about eight hundred yards in front of Brigade Headquarters located in Fort Piquet. There was now no option but to take over command of 2 Dogra, and the first order handed out was for the Commanding Officer to move immediately on to the Salamabad feature, with the reserve company, and to join up with his forward companies. I informed him not to issue any orders to his forward companies without first obtaining my approval, and to tell his Companies to stay put wherever they were and not to wander about. The Battalion Headquarters would, in fact, be nothing more than a Post Office for the next three hours, the time it would take it to connect up with the rest of the battalion.

Then, taking a tremendous gamble—since I had no idea of the exact location of the remnants of the 2 Dogra Rifle companies on the Salamabad feature—I ordered the field artillery to shell the area in-between Pimples Two and Three. It was a dreadful thought that casualties might be inflicted on my own troops, but if the enemy was on the feature, that was his likely position. It was also reasonable to assume that when the first few rounds, which would be smoke, fell in the area, if it was in the hands of 2 Dogra there would be an immediate protest. As no signal of dissent was received after two rounds of smoke had been fired at the target, the field battery was ordered to plaster the area, which it did by observation from Fort Piquet.

At 0900 hours, Headquarters 2 Dogra reported that its forward companies had indicated that all firing had ceased in the area to which the four "lost" platoons had moved. It was still not possible to indicate the exact area, but there were unmistakable signs that the enemy was concentrating to launch a counter-attack against the remainder of the battalion. The ammunition had been almost expended and the reserve ammunition was urgently required. The ammunition, incidentally, was still lying within the unit lines in the Uri bowl.

With the situation moving from the sublime to the ridiculous, a completely fresh approach to the problem was necessary. With only five rifle platoons remaining from the nine that had mounted the feature, and they too with insufficient ammunition, the reserve ammunition was not going to materially alter the situation, particularly if, as had been reported, there was an enemy battalion on the feature. Salamabad had to be captured and cleared of the enemy. Although it was undesirable to commit the reserve battalion at this early stage of the operation, there was now no option. At 1000 hours, 6 Rajrif moved forward, with orders to pass through the elements of 2 Dogra, which would presumably still be on Pimple One when 6 Rajrif arrived, and to capture Pimples Two and Three.

Lt. Col. Kalaan and his men moved fast. That there were enemy on the feature there is no doubt as they tried to retard the progress of 6 Rajrif with long range sniping. It certainly was not a battalion, and probably a platoon or a very weak rifle company. 6 Rajrif reached Pimple One at 1230 hours, and spent the remaining hours of daylight collecting 2 Dogra and reorganising the battalion. Pimple One was then handed over to 2 Dogra and 6 Rajrif prepared to attack the other two Pimples. Advancing from Pimple One at 0400 hours on 20 May, 6 Rajrif took Pimple Two and then advancing to Pimple Three captured it without opposition, soon after first light. The next few hours were spent handing over the positions to 2 Dogra. When this had been completed, Lt. Col. Kalaan reported seeing hundreds of the enemy crossing the bridge at M.S. 68 and rushing back along the road towards Domel. He asked for permission to rush towards Dardkot over the hills, in order to intercept them. This was immediately agreed to, and 6 Rajrif swooped down on Dardkot, but the enemy had had too big a start, and 6 Rajrif was only able to fire into the tail end as it disappeared up the Nawa Rundan Nullah.

To return to 2 Dogra's escapade, which had completely wrecked the Brigade plan in so far as timings were concerned, and had necessitated

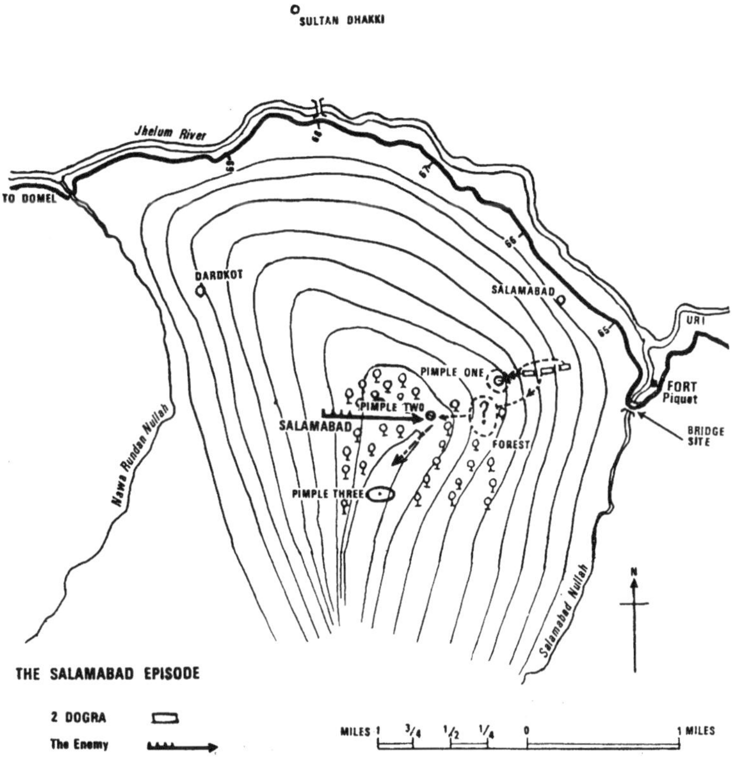

the premature commitment of the reserve: the details of what took place on the Salamabad feature were learnt from Lt. Col. S. S. Kalaan and later from the officers of 2 Dogra. It was quite clear that three factors contributed to the chaos: a total lack of command and control, an arbitrary decision to change an order, and the flaunting of the fact that a human being's sense of direction fails when in strange surroundings, particularly so in darkness.

2 Dogra had moved up the Salamabad feature, not as a battalion which had been the order, but as three rifle companies. Battalion Headquarters and the reserve company remained in an area hours away from the other companies, and with wireless silence imposed, the Battalion Commander surrendered his prerogative of exercising

command and control of his unit from the outset. Worse still, he left himself impotent to influence any battle that might demand the launching of his battalion reserve.

When the Battalion Commander decided to remain behind, it was essential that the operational control of the three companies moving forward rested with one commander. The actions of the three companies demanded very close coordination, each Pimple being firmly established before any move was made towards the next one. The operation was never designed to be implemented by three independent rifle companies, and it was the failure to ensure that this was clearly understood which started the rot. When the column was nearing Pimple One, the Company Commander of the company detailed to occupy Pimple Two, instead of following on to Pimple One and awaiting its consolidation, decided to save time by taking a short-cut to Pimple Two and peeled off with his company in that direction. This attempt to save time was fatal, as, quite apart from the fact that it was dangerous, it had slipped the Company Commander's mind that wireless silence had been imposed and there was no method by which he could indicate that he had reached Pimple Two other than sending personnel back to Pimple One in the dark, which could have been fatal. At the same time, the company earmarked for Pimple Three could not move forward, and very correctly did not because there was the perfect setting for an inter-company battle in the dark.

The company heading for Pimple Two very soon found itself in serious trouble as it entered thick jungle. Despite the moonlight, it lost all sense of direction. Meanwhile, the other two companies reached Pimple One, which was consolidated, and the company earmarked for Pimple Three stayed on Pimple One and awaited a report that Pimple Two had been consolidated. The Pimple Two company groped about in the dark for about two hours. At dawn it regained its bearings, found itself about one thousand yards from Pimple Two, and, moving towards it eventually consolidated the feature. Feeling guilty over the damage that he had done, and learning that the company earmarked for Pimple Three was still at Pimple One, the Company Commander at Pimple Two decided to rectify matters by taking Pimple Three himself. Almost at the same time he found that he had lost his haversack in which was the battalion Operation Order, which also included the Brigade plan in broad outline. He therefore ordered the senior platoon commander to take the company to Pimple Three, and with another platoon commander and two men went off in search of the missing haversack.

An enemy platoon, located on a flank between Pimple Two and Pimple Three, was watching the company on Pimple Two and, permitting it to go past, brought it under fire. Wireless silence was immediately broken, the company calling for reinforcements. The company which should have taken Pimple Three immediately sent forward a platoon. The "segregated" company, now four platoons strong, took up a defensive position and a fire battle commenced with the enemy. The Company Commander and his party, hearing the firing, gave up the search for the lost haversack but, finding it impossible to rejoin the company, worked their way back to Pimple One. That was how the report of the four "scuppered" platoons and the "sole survivors" emanated. When 6 Rajrif arrived at Pimple One, the enemy decided to withdraw and the four lost platoons worked their way back to Pimple One.

It was not the troops who were responsible for this sad turn of events but downright bad leadership. The men did all that was asked of them, and had there been proper command and control, and the orders as issued carried out, there is no question of doubt that 2 Dogra would have delivered the goods. The occupation of the Salamabad feature had never been viewed as a major military operation. It had been considered a simple and straightforward operation. It was a much easier assignment than that given to 2 Dogra on the return from Poonch, when the battalion, with only a few minutes' warning, had to rush back, climb the Pir Panjal Range and occupy the Haji Pir Pass. It had completed the task with speed and efficiency. Nor can the Salamabad action even begin to bear comparison with the brilliant achievement of the small body of officers and men of the battalion who had surmounted the dangerous Zoji La Pass and made their way to Leh. That the men of the battalion were capable and courageous, and if properly led could rise to great heights, had been amply demonstrated.

The battalion had, during the six months that it had served with 161 Infantry Brigade, gained much in experience, and had shown a marked improvement. The action of Salamabad is, therefore, somewhat incongruous, and when compared with its various past performances does not add up correctly. The conundrum is, however, answered if the missing factor, the plus value of leadership in operations, is taken into account. The column to Leh abounded with it and attained a magnificent result, while the same battalion, which had produced this column, started off with a leadership flaw at Salamabad which escalated with each step up the feature. The chaos that followed was inevitable.

Chapter 20

Limited but Precious Gains

THE withdrawal of the enemy from the north to the south bank of the Jhelum River, the moment 4 Kumaon's advance along the Kazinag Range became known to them, had been foreseen, and the Brigade plan had catered for this contingency with the formation of the armoured column. The Salamabad set-back, and the consequent loss of both time and surprise, had unfortunately presented the enemy with a clear run, and he had capitalised on it. What was worse, was that when the armoured column set out, in unison with 6 Rajrif's advance from Salamabad to Dardkot, it was halted by a burnt bridge.

An inspection of this bridge and of numerous other burnt wooden bridges on the road to Domel showed quite clearly that their destruction had been accomplished during the previous twenty-four hours. Had the column set out in accordance with the plan that had been formulated, it would not only have stymied the enemy's escape but also saved the engineers much hard labour.

The rapid advance of 6 Rajrif from Pimple Three on Salamabad to the Dardkot area was, however, not infructuous. Its appearance from an unexpected direction completely surprised a forward rifle company of Pakistan's 1st Battalion The 13th Frontier Force Rifles, located in a defensive position on a feature near Dardkot. The rifle company withdrew hastily. Some Pakistan Engineers who were busy preparing for demotion the steel girder bridge near Urusa were equally shattered and, leaving their task, followed the withdrawing rifle company. Having occupied the feature overlooking the bridge, a party from 6 Rajrif moved forward to the bridge, collected a large quantity of demolition stores, and having neutralised the work of the Pakistan Engineers, rejoined the battalion. The saving of this bridge from destruction was a great asset. Although a diversion would have been constructed in the course of time, it would have been, as the Kashmir State Engineers had stated, a herculean task.

Searching the area around its defensive position, 6 Rajrif found the Quarter Master's store of the 1st Battalion the 13th Frontier Force Rifles. This was located in a small red house not far from the eastern approach to the steel girder bridge. It was well stocked with rations, ammunition, blankets, clothing and the necessaries normally found in a Quarter Master's (QM) store. In addition there were sewing machines, bicycles and amenity stores. The orderly stacking of the various items, and the carefully maintained ledgers, left no shadow of doubt that the unit had been in the area for a considerable period of time. There was also evidence to indicate the QM's stores had orders to move back. This capture blew sky high Army Headquarter's obstinate insistence that Pakistan Regular troops were not in Kashmir. Consolidating its gains, 6 Rajrif awaited the arrival of the Brigade.

When 6 Rajrif moved from Salamabad to Dardkot, it was decided to utilise the services of the Jammu and Kashmir Militia battalion. As there was no intention of taking the unit forward, there was only one area in which it could be employed and that was the Salamabad feature. With the enemy in the Haji Pir Pass area having beaten a hasty withdrawal, it was now reasonable to assume that the Salamabad feature would not be subjected to action. Even if 161 Infantry Brigade had to piquet the feature, the maximum garrison would have been one rifle company, and with a whole militia battalion on it, the presence of such a large number of men would have deterred the enemy from approaching it. With 2 Dogra holding the area, all that the militia had to do was to climb the hill and take over. A promise had been made that the unit would be used, and here was the ideal opportunity to redeem it. Contact had been reported by 6 Rajrif with a regular battalion of the Pakistan Army, and it was safe to assume that a Pakistan Brigade was in the area. With only two battalions available, 6 Rajrif and 7 Sikh, the move forward of 2 Dogra had become a necessity, and this could most easily be achieved by handing over Salamabad to the militia. The militia battalion was, therefore, ordered to move on to Salamabad. It set out in fine style, moving in column of route and keeping in step.

This formation is normally used on a main road or on a barrack square, and never in an operational area. With no possibility of enemy intervention, and in order to avoid confusion by halting the unit and ordering it to adopt a tactical formation, which it probably did not know, it was permitted to proced undisturbed. Its tactical ability, which had always been suspect, was soon confirmed as being non-existent, as the unit began to climb the feature as if it was every man for himself. What was most disturbing was the total lack of physical fitness. With the packs and weapons getting heavier with each step, with only a quarter of the climb completed, the men of the militia started flagging and then came to a dead halt. It was obvious that they would never make the summit of Salamabad in any sort of condition, and it would serve no useful purpose to force them to move forward. Orders were, therefore, issued for the unit to return to Uri.

Efforts were made to try and persuade 77 Para Brigade to take them over and use them in some sort of role, but this failed, and Headquarters 161 Infantry Brigade had no option but to return the unit to Srinagar. Major General Thimayya, who was informed of what had happened, was not one bit surprised, and agreed that the unit should be returned. He had been pressured to utilise the militia. He could now state that they had been tried, and found too untrained to meet any requirement of the battlefield. It must have been most demoralising for the men, who were very keen, and had been led to believe that it was possible to turn a raw recruit into a combat soldier in two to three weeks.

On the right flank, 4 Kumaon, having completed its reconnaisances, rested at Sikkibat during the daylight hours of 18 May, and moved forward soon after darkness set in. In order to increase the fire power of the battalion, four medium machine guns, which had been captured from the enemy during the winter and were manned by the unit personnel, accompanied the unit. The mountains over which the battalion had to move were most forbidding, the heights ranging from 10,000 to 13,500 feet. At 0200 hours on 19 May, 4 Kumaon reached its forming up place, point 11505. In order to reach this position, the unit had carried out a wide encircling movement which enabled it to concentrate in the rear of the enemy holding Tragan, which lies to the North of the Maidan Pass. The enemy, one company in strength, occupying a well constructed defensive position, did not detect this move and was unaware of the fact that its well sited position was about to be struck where it was weakest. At 0230 hours, creeping forward as silently as was possible, the leading troops of 4 Kumaon closed with the enemy before he knew what was happening, and almost completely annihilated the garrison, only a handful, assisted by the darkness, managing to make their escape.

Consolidating its gain, 4 Kumaon began reconnoitering forward at first light and prepared for its next attack. The objective was an enemy rifle company entrenched at Chinal Dori, south of the Maidan Pass. At 1230 hours in the afternoon, one rifle company of 4 Kumaon, supported by 11 Field Battery and the unit mortar platoon, moved forward to get into a suitable position from where the attack could be launched. This again necessitated an encirclement move towards Chinal Dori, which was completed during the hours of darkness, and without rousing the enemy garrison. In position by 0400 hours on the morning of 20 May, the Kumaon company attacked at first light, and the enemy position fell after a savage battle. In order to distract the enemy's attention from the encirclement, one rifle company of the

Sawai Man Guards mounted a feint attack on the right flank of the enemy position, which apparently engaged his attention so closely that he was totally unaware of the danger that threatened his rear, until it descended upon him.

Chinal Dori was a brilliantly planned and executed action. The Kumaonis, moving skillfully and making full use of ground and cover, achieved surprise as complete as was possible. The supporting fire, delivered from an opposite direction to the attacking troops, pinned the enemy to the ground and then lifted as the attacking company closed with the bayonet. The enemy fought hard and well, many hand-to-hand encounters taking place, but the Kumaonis were in irresistible form and, pressing their attack, gained the objective. As at Tragan, very few of the enemy succeeded in making a getaway, the majority being buried in the trenches that they had fought so stubbornly to defend.

Chhota Qazinag, 10,657 feet in height, now faced 4 Kumaon. This peak completely dominated the area, gazing down on those below like a defiant giant. No one had any doubts that it was going to be a very hard nut to crack. There were two approaches to the position, one along the crest of the range and the other via the northern flank. The southern flank was absolutely sheer, and incapable of being scaled save by fully trained and equipped mountaineers. The route along the crest was the easier of the two possible approaches, but almost every inch of the ground was covered by enemy automatics which would take a heavy toll of casualties. The more difficult approach, from the point of view of terrain, was therefore selected. Nor was this the only problem that confronted Lt. Col. Man Mohan Khanna. The extreme sharpness of the crest placed a strict limitation on the number of sub-units that could be deployed when the ultimate attack was launched. The frontage could only accommodate about one platoon.

One rifle company was, therefore, detailed to assault the feature. Advancing at 0400 hours of 21 May, it worked its way around Chhota Qazinag until it reached a point due west of the feature. Once again, the enemy failed to detect this move and the Kumaonis were able to achieve surprise which was vital for success. Creeping up the slope leading to the enemy defences, the Kumaon company halted just below the crest and attacked as dawn was breaking. The enemy reacted violently and a savage battle commenced. The enemy company holding Chhota Qazinag, making quick adjustments to its positions, fired its automatics and hurled grenades at the advancing Kumaonis, in a desperate effort to arrest their progress. Determined and undeterred, the Kumaonis, using all their skill in groundcraft, steadily closed the gap and then rushed in with the bayonet. The battle reached a crescendo, the trapped enemy fighting desperately for every inch of ground. By 0900 hours, Chhota Qazinag had been captured. The enemy suffered very heavy casualties, the Kumaonis sustaining two killed and eleven wounded. With three quick spectacular successes notched up, 4 Kumaon were now on top of the world.

There was now no holding the unit. Sufaida was assaulted and taken and then Pandu was captured. But the enemy was certain to try and bar the path of the steam roller advancing along the Kazinag Range, and he made a determined bid to do so when 4 Kumaon approached point 6873. This feature was held by two companies of a regular Pakistan infantry battalion. Reconnaissances showed that it was a formidable defensive position, heavily bunkered and its frontage covered by medium machine gun fire. It was, therefore, subjected to a softening up by the field artillery. When the artillery fire lifted, at dawn on 24 May, two companies of 4 Kumaon moved forward to assault the position, but the attack was halted almost immediately by extremely heavy medium machine gun and light automatic fire.

Lt. Col. Man Mohan Khanna was not going to be denied his prize. Concentrating the light automatics and two-inch mortars of his two reserve companies, and forming them into an *ad hoc* Support Company, he placed this company on a flank. This *ad hoc* Company then proceeded to pour a devastating weight of fire into the enemy defences. As the enemy was still reeling under this, the two rifle companies which had been held up during the initial assault worked their way forward and assaulted with the bayonet. A fierce battle raged for about twenty minutes, and then the enemy broke and withdrew. The Kumaonis had inflicted very heavy casualties on the defenders, their own being four killed and twelve seriously wounded. With the capture of point 6873, the right thrust of the brigade plan had been a complete success. It had been achieved through skillful planning, dash, and unbounded courage, and 4 Kumaon had every reason to be elated. With the Kazinag Range firmly held, 161 Infantry Brigade's right flank was secure.

With 6 Rajrif holding the Dardkot ridge, and the armoured column held up at the first of a series of demolished bridges, the engineers were ordered forward and took in hand the construction of diversions. The squadron of armoured cars and the field artillery were ordered to work their way forward as soon as each diversion permitted them to do so, and Brigade Headquarters and 7 Sikh, the company in Bren Carriers having dismounted and returned the vehicles to Uri, set off for Dardkot on foot. Arriving just before 1400 hours, contact was made with 6 Rajrif, and 7 Sikh was immediately deployed on the left flank of that battalion, and ordered to send out patrols to the features adjacent to its positions. That the enemy, although he had not engaged 6 Rajrif, was very close was quite certain, and it was also clear that he was occupying a very strong defensive position in the area.

To attack a Pakistan Brigade of three regular infantry battalions, and one that had been in the area for some considerable time and was obviously well entrenched, 161 Infantry Brigade had two battalions, 6 Rajrif and 7 Sikh, one of which would not be available for an attack as it would have to hold a firm base. It, therefore, boiled down to a position where one battalion would have to evict three, a task which had slender hope of success. Had the enemy been composed of ill-trained troops or tribals it might have been possible, but not against regular troops occupying a strong defensive position, armed and equipped in a fashion similar to our own, equally well trained, and with the numerical odds of over three to one in their favour. Something, however, just had to be done, and if it was to have any chance of success, it had to be carried out with the minimum loss of time.

At 1700 hours, one of the Brigade jeeps arrived at Dardkot. In order to ascertain the chances of the squadron of armoured cars and the Field Battery moving forward, I drove back in order to obtain a first-hand idea of when this would be possible. The engineers had certainly done an excellent job, tackling all the demolished bridges simultaneously, and the diversions would, I was informed, be ready for the heavier vehicles within an hour. As there were only about ninety minutes of daylight left, and not wishing the squadron and the battery to be strung out along the road during the hours of darkness, I drove to the point where they were held up and ordered one troop of the armoured cars to move forward to Dardkot, when possible, and the remainder of the squadron and the field battery to return to Uri and await further orders.

As I was on the point of returning to Dardkot, with the light fading fast, I was informed that a 15 cwt Dodge truck had negotiated the diversion at the first demolished bridge. This was good news, and on reaching the diversion I congratulated the engineers, but also had to reprove them for not having carried out what I considered a very essential precaution. On my way down the road towards Uri, I had instructed each team of engineers working on a diversion to place an obstruction at either end of the demolished bridge, so that personnel, animals and vehicles, moving in the dark, would be warned and prevented from falling into the gap. This had not been done, but I was assured that the order would be complied with immediately.

Continuing my way back to Dardkot, on rounding a bend beyond which was the next demolished bridge, I was greeted with a sight that I had feared: the rear portion of a 15 cwt Dodge was sticking out of the gap. Inquiries showed that it was the party of engineers who, it had been reported, had moved forward. The vehicle had come shooting round the bend, and although the driver had braked hard on suddenly noticing the gap, the vehicle's momentum could not be arrested in time and it had plunged gently into the gap. Fortunately, those in the vehicle sustained relatively minor injuries in the form of broken ribs and fractures, but the accident had deprived the Field Company of the services of its two officers, at a time when they were most needed. A flash signal to Headquarters Sri Div, however, proved fruitful and two replacements arrived the next morning.

A troop of armoured cars arrived at Dardkot at 2000 hours, and tucked itself into a re-entrant on the side of the road. It was decided to use them as mobile pill boxes from the next morning. Meanwhile, a patrol from 7 Sikh had returned and reported that it had heard the enemy moving in strength towards the ridge overlooking the western exit of the steel girder bridge. This could not be permitted. It was essential that the bridge remained under our control, and the enemy who was moving forward under cover of darkness had to be stopped. 7 Sikh was immediately ordered to prepare to move on to the same feature, commencing at 2200 hours. Under normal circumstances, such an attack would not have been mounted, but speed and darkness were invaluable allies, and both would deny to the enemy the knowledge that he was stronger than we were, a fact that would become obvious the next morning if he was in possession of the feature.

With the object of achieving a certain amount of surprise, and at the same time creating an impression that a very heavy attack was being mounted, the troop of armoured cars was moved forward and placed in a position from which it could see the outline of the ridge overlooking the steel girder bridge. It was instructed to train the atomatics at the ridge, and commencing at 2200 hours, to rake the area with fire for fifteen minutes. This, it was hoped, would distract the enemy's attention from 7 Sikh.

At 2200 hours, the armoured cars opened fire and 7 Sikh moved forward to attack. After a few moments, enemy light automatics replied, aiming their fire in the direction of the armoured cars. While doing them no harm, it forced Brigade Headquarters, which had positioned itself near the armoured cars, to move to a more hospitable area. The fifteen minutes over, the armoured cars ceased firing and there was a roar as 7 Sikh rushed in the direction of the enemy. The enemy battalion did not accept the challenge; it withdrew hastily and 7 Sikh took the position without loss. It sent back as a prisoner of war a enemy rifleman, who stated that he was from the 1st Battalion The 13th Frontier Force Rifles.

During the morning and afternoon of 21 May, the enemy disclosed a certain number of his positions by resorting to long range, intermittent, medium machine gun fire. It was directed at the road, but because of the bends it was relatively simple to stay out of the line of fire and to move past the danger zone during a lull in the firing. 7 Sikh was also subjected to bursts of firing, but as in the case of the road, the damage done was negligible, the only casualty on the road being one rifleman of 7 Sikh who was wounded in the leg. Two other casualties, however, though not the result of enemy fire and slight from the medical point of view, were serious from the operational angle. While not self-inflicted, and not the result of carelessness, they were caused by what can only be termed as an act of god.

The two Engineer officers, who had reported for duty at 0800 hours on 21 May, as replacements for the two unfortunates who had crashed into the gap of the demolished bridge, were hors de combat by 2200 hours the same evening. Tired, after a grueling day's work, they fell asleep resting on the side of the road with their legs stretched underneath a Dodge vehicle. As the driver of the vehicle decided to move it to another spot, and did so, a rear wheel of the vehicle ran over their legs and fractured one of the officers' ankle and broke the other's shin. This was an expensive "writing off" of Engineer officers, and amused neither Headquarters Sri Div nor Headquarters 161 Infantry Brigade. Replacements from Delhi arrived in due course, and fortunately the hoodoo on Engineer officers ceased.

On the morning of 22 May, Headquarters Sri Div signalled that an air strike of two sorties would be available during the afternoon, weather conditions permitting. This, while very acceptable, would be much too light to do material damage of a major order to the heavily bunkered enemy defences, and was unlikely to alter to any great extent the situation facing 161 Infantry Brigade. It would, however, be useful from a psychological point of view. The VHF wireless set, for communication between ground and air, was ordered forward and arrived at about 1100 hours. Loaded on a mule, the set arrived at the foot of the Brigade Headquarters feature, and Captain D'Souza reported for orders.

With the hillsides steep and very slippery, D'Souza was given strict instructions to take the set off the mule and to have it carried to the Brigade Headquarters Command Post. The mule leader, however, anticipating that the wireless set would be required at the top of the hill, moved up a narrow track, and in a matter of seconds the mule came slithering back and crashed into a ditch at the bottom. The animal suffered only a few scratches, but the damage done to the set was unknown. It was now much too late to call forward a reserve set from Srinagar and to place it in position, and the only relief available to the Brigade Staff was to castigate the stunned Captain D'Souza. With no means of communicating with the pilots, the two sorties would be valueless as target indication would be impossible. D'Souza and his detachment sheepishly manhandled the equipment to the Command Post and, after setting it up, announced, much to their own and everyone's relief, that the set was undamaged.

The aircraft appeared on schedule at 1400 hours, and circled over-head while the pilots were being briefed. The initial target, it was explained, would be indicated with a round of blue smoke, and subsequent targets with various combinations of coloured smoke. It had been anticipated that the Pakistanis would try to confuse the pilots by firing similar coloured smoke at our positions, and in order to counter this, varying combinations of the colour of the smoke, and the intervals between them, were indicated to the pilots who were briefed to ignore all other smoke seen in the area. What was anticipated did in fact happen, but the pilots conducting the two sorties were not deceived, and the strikes were made on the correct targets. The air strike must have caused a certain amount of discomfort to the Pakistan Brigade, but it was too light to achieve anything more than that.

6 Rajrif and 7 Sikh had not sat back on their initial gains. Both battalions probed forward and occupied features closer to the enemy defences until 7 Sikh took up a position on a spur to the west of which, about one thousand yards away, was another spur with an enemy battalion, firmly entrenched and fully supported by medium machine guns and heavy mortars. The position occupied by 7 Sikh proved to be a most unhealthy one. The enemy, located on a higher spur, was able to look down on the unit and engaged it with medium machine gun fire throughout the day. 7 Sikh out in the open and digging hard, the inevitable casualties were inflicted on the battalion, and after fourteen men had been wounded over the next forty-eight hours, it

was decided to withdraw the unit to a position slightly further back. This was successfully accomplished, and the daily casualties which had been depressing, in that 7 Sikh could not reply effectively from its previous position, ceased.

A stalemate having resulted, it was decided to strengthen the Brigade position by bringing 2 Dogra forward. This was now necessary in order to give the Brigade greater depth in defence. It was fully realised that by evacuating Salamabad the line of communication between Uri and Urusa would remain unprotected and a serious risk incurred, but against this was a defensive position which very definitely demanded depth and this could only be provided by a third battalion. It was a choice between two evils, and it was the lesser of the two that was selected, since, if the road was cut, Headquarters Sri Div could employ the Para Brigade to re-open it.

Fantastic though it may seem, soon after 2 Dogra moved forward from Salamabad to the Dardkot area, Headquarters 2 Dogra "lost" its companies. The move was being carried out in broad daylight and over the same route that had been taken by 6 Rajrif, and how it happened is extremely difficult to understand. With Headquarters 2 Dogra feeling helpless, a rifle company of 6 Rajrif was sent back to search for the missing companies. It succeeded in locating them, after much hard work, and led them to their new locations. Confused map reading combined with companies moving forward independently must have caused the confusion, but it was definitely accelerated by Headquarters 2 Dogra closing down its means of communication with its companies and then being unable to regain contact. Handing over its commitments to 2 Dogra, 6 Rajrif moved forward to the Urusa ridge.

With no further advance possible or contemplated, 161 Infantry Brigade confined itself to consolidating its gains and patrolling vigorously. The squadron of armoured cars, based on Uri, was given the role of road protection duties during the hours of daylight. The guns of a troop of the field battery were manhandled up a track prepared by the engineers and placed in position on the Urusa ridge. From this location, all crest clearance problems were eliminated, and the gunners were able to shoot effectively.

The steel girder bridge further to the west, at M.S. 58, was found demolished, with the enemy occupying strong emplacements on the features overlooking the western exit of the bridge. The enemy medium machine gunners were found to be very trigger-happy, blazing away at any target. But, apart from imposing caution, they did no damage. The Pakistan Brigade made no attempt to recapture the territory that it had lost, and was in fact very subdued.

161 Infantry Brigade's Spring offensive had not been spectacular, with the exception of the effort on the right flank, but in view of the strong enemy concentration that it had encountered, it had been reasonable. To have tried to take Chinari, let alone Domel, single-handed and with the dice loaded heavily against it, was impossible. 4 Kumaon had gained useful ground and was firmly entrenched on the Kazinag Range, and nine miles of road territory had been gained by the main thrust, despite the misfortunes that had plagued the Brigade from the outset. It had, however, been a disappointing and to a certain extent a depressing experience, and one which could have produced quite a different result if Army Headquarters had responded positively to the request for another Infantry Brigade.

Chapter 21

Advantage Thrown Away

THE bridge constructed by the enemy over the Jhelum river opposite Sultan Dhakki, at M.S. 68, was invaluable as it provided a ready and valuable link between 4 Kumaon on the Kazinag Range and 161 Infantry Brigade in the Urusa area. Had it been destroyed, the immediately available route would have been via the bridge at Uri. The engineers would certainly have thrown a bridge across the river, but this would have taken time, and the evacuation of the Kumaon casualties and the carrying forward of ammunition and other stores would, in the meantime, have entailed a long trudge. Lt. Col. Man Mohan Khanna was now able to visit Brigade Headquarters without having to make the extra trek to Uri. He was bubbling over with confidence and was emphatic that he could hold on to his gains against any attempts by the enemy to dislodge him.

77 Para Brigade now felt that it should be given a more active role, and approached Headquarters Sri Div. Major General Thimayya posed to me the possibility of the Kazinag Range, together with 4 Kumaon, being handed over to 77 Para Brigade. While having no objection to 77 Para Brigade taking over the Kazinag Range, there was no reason why 161 Infantry Brigade should also have to hand over 4 Kumaon. This battalion could be very usefully employed in the Urusa area. The removal of 4 Kumaon from 161 Infantry Brigade was, therefore, stoutly resisted, and a counter-proposal was put forward for his consideration. I suggested that I was quite prepared to hand over the Kazinag Range to 77 Para Brigade, provided that it relieved 4 Kumaon with its most experienced battalion, the 2nd Battalion The 3rd Gorkha Rifles (2/3 GR). I stressed that I had laid down this stipulation as I could not afford to take a chance with the right flank of 161 Infantry Brigade. I would withdraw 4 Kumaon to Urusa when 2/3 GR was well settled in. The Commander 77 Para Brigade was not, however, agreeable to utilising 2/3 GR to garrison the Kazinag Range, and the idea was shelved.

The proposal that 77 Para Brigade take over the Kazinag Range with one of its own battalions was not unreasonable. When 4 Kumaon had passed through the Sawai Man Guards, who were holding Goshar and point 9062, and had captured the whole of the Kazinag Range, the holding of these two points was no longer necessary, and the Sawai Man Guards had been withdrawn to Uri, where they were in reserve. So for that matter were 2/3 GR, the Uri piquets, with 161 Infantry Brigade out in front, being manned by just one battalion. 77 Para Brigade thus had two battalions in reserve, while 161 Infantry Brigade was fully stretched.

7 Sikh was finding that its frontage tended to be too extended, not an unusual state of affairs in the mountains, where for every position occupied there is always a better one a bit further away. In the case of 7 Sikh, however, the position was very acute, as the battalion was located on the lower slopes of a spur which ran down from the lofty Pir Panjal Range. There was a live danger of the enemy occupying a higher feature on the left flank of the unit and overlooking its defensive layout. In

such an event, they could make the position untenable. With 4 Kumaon released from Kazinag, this threat could have been neutralised to some extent by locating the battalion in echelon on the left of 7 Sikh.

With the enemy showing signs of increasing activity, it was found essential to place something on the left flank of 7 Sikh, and Lt. Col. Man Mohan Khanna was asked whether it would be possible for him to release one company of 4 Kumaon for employment at Urusa, and to take in exchange one company of 2 Dogra. He readily agreed to this proposition, and the transfer was effected. The 4 Kumaon company was placed under command 7 Sikh and positioned on a knoll on the left flank. This company was to be faced with a situation so amazing that it is difficult to believe that it actually took place.

At 1000 hours on a sunny morning in the first week of June, a bugle call sounded in the enemy lines. This was abnormal, but was dwarfed by what was to follow. About fifteen minutes later, two rifle companies of enemy troops appeared on the skyline of the feature held by the forward battalion of the Pakistan Brigade, and began a descent to the nullah below. Here they halted and proceeded to adopt a battle formation. Well within the range of our medium machine guns and mortars they could have been scattered in a matter of minutes, but it was decided to leave them undisturbed until it became clear what their intentions were.

After the rifle companies had carried out movements that would have been appropriate if they had been performed on a parade ground in a peace station, a whistle blast was heard and an advance towards the feature held by 7 Sikh commenced. One enemy rifle company was deployed in front, the second following about three hundred yards to its rear. Crossing the nullah, the leading company began the ascent. The twenty minutes required to negotiate the climb gave 7 Sikh and the 4 Kumaon company ample time to make small adjustments to their positions to beat off what was now clearly intended to be an attack. For some unaccountable reason, the attack was unsupported by covering fire of any description. Had the enemy's idea been to gain surprise by not disturbing the defenders, it would have been understandable, but the attack was mounted in broad daylight and in full view of the defenders. And with bugle and whistle sounds to boot, there was no chance of attaining any surprise.

With their positions suitably adjusted, 7 Sikh and the 4 Kumaon company waited calmly to accord a suitable reception to the enemy. Before he had even neared the defences, it was perfectly obvious that the fate of the leading company had been sealed, and that is exactly what happened. As the two leading platoons neared the crest and were only forty yards away, they were subjected to a murderous frontal and flanking fire and a hail of grenades. They were almost decimated, as was the third platoon which attempted to run the gauntlet. The follow-up company turned and rushed down the hill and across the open nullah, suffering casualties from the medium machine guns and the three-inch mortars which now came into action.

An Identity Card retrieved from the pocket of the leading Company Commander disclosed that the unit was the 1st Punjab Regiment. What tempted this famous Regiment, the senior-most Infantry Regiment of the undivided Indian Army, to commit such an incomprehensible act is unfathomable. It could by no stretch of imagination be classified as an assault, it was sheer suicide. Not one person in 161 Infantry Brigade felt elated over this action. If anything, there was a general feeling of sympathy for the unfortunate officers and men who had been sacrificed, thanks to the idiocy of some grossly incompetent individual in command.

With 163 Infantry Brigade now firmly held up at Tithwal, Major General Thimayya, anxious to set the advance in motion again, suggested that the Kazinag Range be taken over by a battalion that had arrived in the Valley and which he would send forward. It was the 1st Battalion The Bihar Regiment (1 Bihar). General Thimayya's idea was that 4 Kumaon, on relief by 1 Bihar, should proceed to join 163 Infantry Brigade at Tithwal. His argument, in support of the change in units, was that Kazinag was such a strong feature that it could be held easily by a weak battalion. I disagreed with him, and stated that the Kazinag feature was a strong position and would remain so, but only as long as it was held by a strong and not a weak battalion. It was for this very reason that I had insisted, when it was proposed that

77 Para Brigade take over the Kazinag Range, that it would have to deploy on it its most experienced battalion. To entrust the feature to 1 Bihar, which he himself admitted was a young and inexperienced World War II raised unit, would be to take a grave risk. I emphasised that I would be most unhappy with the situation if he insisted on the relief being effected, and requested him not to force the issue. As a result of my arguments, Major General Thimayya withdrew his suggestion and 4 Kumaon remained in situ.

This bidding for experienced battalions in his formation, which Major General Thimayya was being subjected to, was hardly the position that one would expect a Divisional Commander engaged in a serious operation to be plagued by. He could only effect changes in the Brigades by strengthening one at the expense of weakening another, and as both 161 and 163 Infantry Brigades were facing difficult situations, it was a state of affairs that should never have been forced on him. Had 161 Infantry Brigade been able to assist by releasing any one of its experienced battalions, 6 Rajrif, 7 Sikh or 4 Kumaon, it would have done so gladly. But the situation facing the Brigade did not permit such generosity. Far from being in a position to hand out its experienced units at the expense of the Brigade, there was pressing need for further units, of a high caliber, to enable it to consolidate and hold the territory that it had gained.

The attitude adopted by Army Headquarters from the inception of Headquarters Sri Div. had been most extraordinary. There had been the initial flat refusal for any further formations to make the Division a reasonably strong one and capable of fulfilling its role. The despatch of 7 Sikh to join 161 Infantry Brigade had been made grudgingly, and only because it was very firmly stressed that with one unit in an independent role on the right flank, the striking force of the Brigade down the main road axis would be of two battalion strength which, in view of the opposition that would be faced, was totally inadequate. Then, when both 161 and 163 Brigades were bogged down, the inexperienced 1 Bihar was sent forward. The reinforcements asked for were for employment in the Tithwal area, and the battle envisaged was going to be a very stiff one. To have launched 1 Bihar into this battle was most inadvisable, and Major General Thimayya was trying to absorb this battalion into a role where its greenness would not be too apparent and the task within its capabilities. The holding of the Kazinag feature was, however, not in that category.

The company of 2 Dogra, sent to the Kazinag feature in exchange for a company of 4 Kumaon, was placed by Lt. Col. Man Mohan Khanna on a feature to the north of Pandu. It was of no particular importance, and although semi-isolated, the position was unlikely to be attacked. In order, however, to enable the Dogra company to further strengthen its defences, Lt. Col. Khanna had promised to give it a medium machine gun. Anxiety over the non-receipt of the weapon resulted in daily inquiries by the Dogra company as to when it would be delivered. These conversations were held on the wireless, and in clear. One afternoon, the signaller on the 4 Kumaon command set, perhaps exasperated by the continual inquiries, informed the Dogra company that the Commanding Officer was setting out the next morning with the medium machine gun. This unforgivable violation of security, which has been one of the main causes of loss of life in battle, was going to claim its price, and the cost was a heavy one. The enemy intercepted the message, and the stage was set for an ambush.

Soon after 1000 hours the next morning, Lt. Col. Man Mohan Khanna set out for the Dogra company position, taking with him the medium machine gun and its crew, and a platoon as escort. They walked straight into the ambush. The enemy, a rifle company from a regular battalion of the Pakistan Army, the 1st Battalion The 15th Punjab Regiment, had chosen an almost perfect site for the ambush and, dropping the major number of the party with well directed fire, rushed in with the bayonet. Lt. Col. Khanna, whom a bullet had struck through the chest, narrowly missing his heart, was fortunately assumed to be dead and was spared the thrust of a bayonet. Regaining consciousness after some time, he managed to reach a nearby hut, which he and the survivors of the ambush made into a strong point and engaged the enemy. The enemy withdrew after some time, but only one rifleman with a wound in the neck and Lt. Col. Khanna survived the action.

While lying in the hut, with slender hopes of being found and recovered in time, a local villager, Jumma Mohammad, happened to arrive on the scene and looked into the hut. Lt. Col. Khanna offered him all the money in his possession, and a very substantial reward if he would assist him to get back to his battalion. The villager immediately agreed and led a relief party to the seriously wounded officer and rifleman. Having done so, the villager refused to accept any reward, monetary or otherwise, stating that what he had done was a normal assistance to a wounded comrade. His name was, however, brought to the notice of the Emergency Government of Jammu and Kashmir. Jumma Mohammad was awarded the Vir Chakra by the Government of India and Rs 25 a month for life. That Lt. Col. Khanna survived was due to his good fortune and the gallant act of the villager. His incapacitation was, however, a severe blow both to his battalion and 161 Infantry Brigade, as he had proved himself to be a thoroughly competent and skillful leader.

A sixth sense is said to be always an asset. In the battlefield it is invaluable. While not claiming to possess a sixth sense or even a semblance of one, on 24 June, soon after the dawn patrols had returned and reported all clear, I got an extraordinary feeling that something strange was taking place on the left flank of the Brigade. Calling up Lt. Col. Kalaan, whose Rajrif patrols had moved out in that area earlier in the morning and had reported no signs of the enemy, I asked him to debrief them again. I explained that I was particularly anxious to know whether they had noticed anything strange in the area, or had seen anyone, even a local, moving about. Lt. Col. Kalaan reported, in due course, that the patrols had not seen a soul in the area and that everything had been normal.

As the morning progressed, the queer sensation grew stronger and stronger, until unable to tolerate it any longer, I ordered 6 Rajrif to despatch a platoon patrol up the spur running between the Goalta and Nawa Rundan Nullahs, as soon as was possible. The platoon set out at 1000 hours and at 1115 hours it flashed back a message that it had spotted the enemy, estimated at about a battalion in strength, moving down from the crest of the Pir Panjal Range on the spur that it was occupying. I phoned Major General Thimayya immediately, and he was fortunately at his Headquarters. I told him of the recent development, and asked for two battalions from 77 Para Brigade to be placed under command of 161 Infantry Brigade immediately, so that I could move out to combat what would develop into a most dangerous threat.

Major General Thimayya was naturally rather dubious at first, and reminded me that the Brigade's Situation Report, received only two hours earlier, had reported everything clear. He could not understand how the situation could have undergone such a radical change in so short a period, and wondered whether the patrol had assessed the situation correctly. Giving me two battalions of 77 Para Brigade, he stressed, would seriously affect the operational efficiency of that formation, which was undesirable. I informed him that I was completely convinced that the patrol's report was accurate, and knowing how short he was of units, I would never have made the request had I been in a position to deal with the threat with my own resources. I promised him that if what I intended doing turned out to be a wild goose chase, I would send the two battalions back to Uri within forty-eight hours. Major General Thimayya finally agreed, and said that he would issue the necessary orders to the Commander 77 Para Brigade, on the telephone, immediately.

A quick conference followed with the Brigade Staff and the unit commanders in the Urusa area. 7 Sikh, with 2 Dogra under command, was made responsible for holding the Brigade defences in the Urusa area. 6 Rajrif was ordered to move up the spur between the Goalta and Nawa Rundan Nullahs and to take up a position in the area already occupied by its patrol which had remained in observation. One battalion of 77 Para Brigade, I informed the conference, would be sent by me from Uri, and on arrival was to be guided on to the spur which lay between the Goalta and Kaliane de Kas Nullahs. Tactical Headquarters, consisting of the Brigade Intelligence Officer, Captain Harpal Singh Bedi, and a signal detachment, would move with me to Uri and from there, with the second unit of 77 Para Brigade, move onto the Salamabad feature and make for Khilla Dher, which lay about 4,500 yards to the north-east of Ledi Gali. Calls for artillery support were to be made to Main Brigade Headquarters at Urusa by battalions, but they would have to direct the shoot themselves, while Tactical Headquarters would pass to Main Headquarters any demands for air support and Main Headquarters would brief the pilots on the VHF set. When all three columns were ready, I would give the order to advance. With everyone clear about their various roles, I hurried off to Uri.

Brigadier Nair of 77 Para Brigade was not particularly pleased when ordered by Headquarters Sri Div to hand over two battalions to 161 Infantry Brigade. His annoyance can well be appreciated. 77 Para Brigade had been wanting to see some action, and while two of the battalions of the Brigade would now probably be engaged in battle, it was to be under another Brigade Headquarters. He suggested that 2/3 GR should remain in Uri and the unit manning the piquets withdrawn and handed to me together with the Sawai Man Guards. Time, however, was of paramount importance, and the delay that the withdrawal of the piquet battalion would entail was quite unacceptable: 2/3 GR and the Sawai Man Guards were handed over. 2/3 GR was embussed and rushed off to Urusa, and on arrival guided to the spur on the right of 6 Rajrif, and which led to Pir Kanthi, while the Sawai Man Guards were ordered to accompany Tactical Headquarters to the Salamabad feature and on to Khilla Dher.

At 1315 hours all three battalions reported readiness to start, and the three-pronged advance commenced at 1330 hours. While the right and left prongs made unopposed progress, at 1430 hours 6 Rajrif, in the centre, reported contact with leading elements of the enemy who were being forced back. This continued until 1800 hours when, with darkness setting in fast, all three battalions were ordered to halt and to firm in for the night. Tactical Headquarters 161 Infantry Brigade and the Sawai Man Guards, and 2/3 GR had made reasonable progress, but 6 Rajrif, facing increasing opposition as it advanced, was slightly behind in terms of distance advanced.

The climb to the crest of the Pir Panjal range on all three axes of advance was extremely stiff. In places it necessitated dragging oneself up with both hands. To increase the difficulties, a drizzle started soon

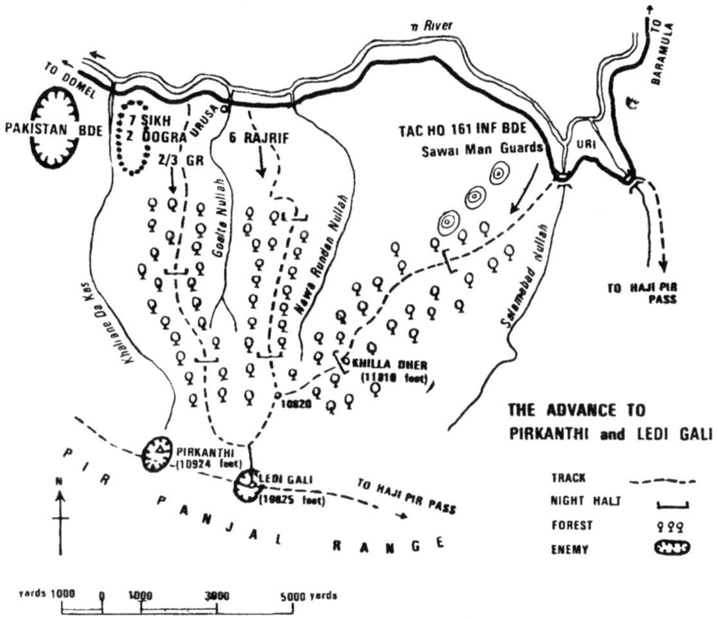

THE ADVANCE TO PIRKANTHI and LEDI GALI

after darkness had set in, and then it poured for the greater part of the night. With no cover, everyone was soaked; and the cold breeze that blew after the rain did not make life any easier. 6 Rajrif and 2/3 GR not only faced steep ascents but had to move through very thick scrub and forests. The advance commenced the next morning, 25 June, at 0600 hours, and followed the pattern of the previous day, the two flank battalions meeting no opposition, and 6 Rajrif, although faced with stiff resistance, steadily forcing its way forward.

At 1100 hours, Tactical Headquarters and the Sawal Man Guards reached Khilla Dher (11,010 feet), which gave an excellent view of Ledi Gali and Pir Kanthi. The enemy could be seen moving about on the crest of the Pir Panjal Range. 2/3 GR continued to report unopposed progress, while 6 Rajrif reports indicated that the enemy resistance was showing definite signs of weakening and he was falling back fast. This was, perhaps, due to the enemy detecting the presence of the Sawai Man Guards on the flank at Khilla Dher. This position was visible from both Ledi Gali and Pir Kanthi, and it was impossible to conceal the fact that troops were present on it in large numbers. The enemy on the 6 Rajrif spur was clearly visible to Tactical Headquarters and the Sawai Man Guards. He was withdrawing as fast as he could towards the crest of the Pir Panjal Range. It was a wonderful target, but unfortunately out of the range of the light automatics of the battalion. The unit had, however, brought with it a section of three-inch mortars, and this section was ordered to get ready for action.

This was not a simple matter, as the ground was extremely rocky and undulating, and it was difficult to find a suitable spot on which to lay the mortar base plates. A couple of possible spots were eventually found, but they were not entirely satisfactory, and there was a live possibility that the base plate would shift when the mortar was fired, and throwing the barrel off alignment, hurl the projectile in the wrong direction. A round of smoke was, therefore, fired, but instead of landing near the enemy, towards whom all eyes were focused, it caused white smoke to spiral from what would have been almost the centre of the Rajrif position on the middle spur, and about sixty degrees to the right of the intended target. 6 Rajrif lost no time in informing the Sawai Man Guards what it thought about it. Fortunately no damage had been done. The mortar section pleaded that it be given another chance but it was refused, as although it would probably have rectified the error and engaged the enemy, it was much too great a risk to take.

An air strike against both Ledi Gali and Pir Kanthi was called for, and aircraft struck both targets, but it was not possible to assess the extent of the damage done. The strike must, however, have had some effect on morale and left the enemy in no doubt that we knew exactly where his positions were and that they would be subjected to an attack in the very near future. However, the air strike was limited to two sorties, and was not heavy enough to cause serious damage to the strongly bunkered positions. Only a much greater air effort would have produced any appreciable result.

At 1600·hours, 6 Rajrif and 2/3 GR reached points on their respective spurs, almost in line with the Sawai Man Guards and about the same distance form the Pir Panjal Range. Lt. Col. Kalaan walked across to Tactical Headquarters, but the Commanding Officer 2/3 GR, who was a little too far off to come over and return to his unit well before last light, was told that he should remain with the unit, and that the orders would be sent to him by hand. It was decided to spend the next day, 26 June, in reorganisation and reconnaissances, and to attack Ledi Gali and Pir Kanthi on 27 June.

The plan of the attack was for the Sawai Man Guards to attack Ledi Gali, and 2/3 GR, Pir Kanthi. 6 Rajrif, the centre battalion, was to be in reserve. The assault was to be mounted at dawn on 27 June, and with only very limited supporting fire available, limited to a few mortars. The targets being out of the range of the field artillery, Headquarters Sri Div was requested to provide as many air strikes as were possible during the morning, afternoon and evening of 26 June. With the extremely difficult terrain facing the attacking battalions, especially 2/3 GR, the final ascent to the defences being almost sheer, it was impressed on both the battalion commanders that they must adhere very strictly to the timings laid down, and press home their attacks, or else the enemy would be afforded the opportunity of taking on one battalion first and then turning on the other.

I was unfortunately not to witness the plan operating. Soon after arriving at Khilla Dher, I developed a splitting headache and began to feel feverish. Ascribing it to a touch of influenza, brought about by the soaking during the hours of darkness and the cold breeze, I obtained two aspirins from the Regimental Medical Officer of the Sawai Man Guards. After discussing the plan for the assault with Lt. Col. Kalaan, who then returned to his battalion, I sent the RMO a request for some more aspirin. He came to me, felt my pulse and immediately took my temperature which turned out to be 104 degrees.

I was provided with a blanket from the Regimental Aid Post, and although it was damp from the rain it was a luxury. Wrapping myself in it I rested against a rock. It was not possible to lie flat because of the sharp rocks, and the result was a restless night. The next morning, 26 June, the RMO took my temperature and said that it was 99 degrees, but a couple of hours later it shot up again to 104 degrees, and proceeded to alternate throughout the day. At 1500 hours, the RMO decided that I must be evacuated, stating that he was not prepared to have the Brigade Commander die on his hands. With the attack due to start the next morning, I insisted on remaining on the feature, but at 1600 hours, when I tried to move forward to have a last look at the preparations made by the Sawai Man Guards, I found that my legs had turned into rubber and would not support me. The RMO, armed with a signal from Headquarters Sri Div, had meanwhile organised a party of porters, who had arrived with ammunition and rations for the battalion, to lift me down to the road on a stretcher. This, however, proved impossible because of the steepness of the terrain, and I was carried down a re-entrant in-between the 6 Rajrif and Sawai Man Guards held spurs, pick-a-back, and delivered to a jeep of 60 Para Field Ambulance which was waiting on the main road.

Detained for the night in the Field Ambulance in Uri, I was evacuated to the Military Hospital in Srinagar the next day. Whatever ailment I was suffering from certainly mystified the doctors. Malaria, influenza and pneumonia were eliminated as they did not fit in with the symptoms, the temperature continuing to rise and fall throughout the day. As tick typhus was suggested as a possibility, intravenous arsenic injections followed. After four days in the Military Hospital in Srinagar, I was evacuated to the Military Hospital in Delhi Cantonment, but not before I received the very heartening news that Ledi Gali and Pir Kanthi had been captured.

It had been a stiff battle, and Lt. Col. S. S. Kalaan, who was entrusted with the command of the operation, conducted it extremely well. The Sawai Man Guards and 2/3 GR had advanced according to schedule, but the extremely steep terrain that they encountered had slowed them down. The enemy had also reacted violently, but the two battalions grimly held their ground and, having weathered the storm throughout the hours of daylight, had scaled the last bit of the climb after darkness and successfully assaulted the enemy defences on the morning of 28 June. With the two battalions firmly established on the feature, the Pir Panjal Range from Pir Kanthi, through Ledi Gali and on to the Haji Pir Pass was now firmly in the hands of 161 Infantry Brigade. Both the right and left flanks of the Brigade were now secure.

At the Military Hospital in Delhi, my illness was diagnosed as relapsing fever and the arsenic injections continued. Lt. Col. Man Mohan Khanna, also a patient in the hospital, and now walking gingerly, used to come in for a daily chat. One morning he arrived in a very agitated state of mind, and announced that Pandu had fallen, and with it the enemy had recovered quite a bit of further territory on the Kazinag Range, only being halted with difficulty. I was speechless. It was unbelievable that such a thing could happen. Then, before I could say a word, he added very quietly: "They did what you resisted so strongly, they took 4 Kumaon away and placed 1 Bihar on the feature."

When it was decided to evacuate me from Srinagar to Delhi, and the doctors stated that I would not be able to return to 161 Infantry Brigade for at least six weeks. Brigadier T. B. Henderson Brooks was sent to the Valley and took over command of the Brigade. A few days after his arrival Major General Thimayya contacted him and offered 1 Bihar as a relief for 4 Kumaon on the Kazinag Range. Henderson Brooks, who was a virtual stranger to the area and apparently had not realised what the holding of the Kazinag Range demanded, unfortunately disregarded the advice given to him by the Brigade Staff who informed him of my views on the subject, and accepted the Divisional Commander's offer. It was a militarily unsound decision, and 161 Infantry Brigade was made to pay dearly for it.

With 1 Bihar in position, 4 Kumaon moved to 163 Infantry Brigade. Its presence in the Tithwal area did little to alter the existing situation, but its absence from Kazinag did. The Pakistanis, learning that an inter-battalion relief had taken place, decided to test the new battalion, and sent forward a strong fighting patrol to Pandu. The 1 Bihar company holding Pandu fought well, and having failed in its object, the enemy patrol decided to withdraw and proceeded to do so. In order to thwart any attempt to harass his withdrawing command, the Pakistan battalion commander left a platoon in position to act as a rearguard. This enemy platoon naturally kept the Pandu garrison under fire.

Whether it was lack of knowledge of the terrain, or garbled reports received from the Pandu garrison, confusion soon overtook the inexperienced battalion. For no cogent reason, the 1 Bihar company which had in fact held the enemy attack was ordered by the Commanding Officer to withdraw, and did so. The enemy platoon, which must have been utterly amazed, walked on to the position and the enemy battalion, informed of the success, hurried back. It then proceeded to advance along the Kazinag Range from west to east. Its progress was arrested only by another battalion being rushed to the Kazinag feature, but not before much valuable territory had been lost.

What 4 Kumaon had gained through careful planning, skill and unbounded courage, had been thrown away in a matter of hours. It was a very expensive mistake. With Pandu in its possession, the Pakistan Artillery established an observation post, from where it was able to bring down fire by observation on Uri. The occupation of a portion of the Kazinag Range by the enemy also changed what had been a secure right flank into one of partial security the enemy now being able to harass a section of the main road with fire, and interfere with the line of communication from the road to Kazinag via the bridge over the Jhelum River at M.S. 68.

The five and a half months between the loss of territory on the Kazinag Range and 31 December 1948, when a Cease Fire Agreement between India and Pakistan came into operation in Jammu and Kashmir, were more or less uneventful so far as military operations affecting 161 Infantry Brigade were concerned. There was normal patrol activity intermingled with the laying of ambushes, but nothing in the shape of a major clash disturbed the atmosphere. It was clearly evident that both 161 Infantry Brigade and the Pakistan Brigade facing it had realised that, with the mountainous terrain favouring defence and the opposing forces equally balanced, a major attack would probably result in minor gains being achieved at a relatively high price in casualties. There was no possibility of a large scale offensive being launched unless strong reinforcements were brought forward, and a stalemate developed along the front.

In the Tithwal area, 163 Infantry Brigade faced a similar situation. The paucity of troops, the difficult terrain, and the logistical problem becoming more acute with every step forward in the face of increasing enemy opposition, any spectacular advance was almost an impossibility. 163 Infantry Brigade therefore engaged itself in consolidating its gains, and strengthening its positions by evicting hostile elements from tactical features which overlooked its defences and were proving to be of nuisance value.

Headquarters Sri Division, realising the futility of pressing either 161 or 163 Infantry Brigade to hammer their heads against a brick wall, and accepting the stalemate on these two fronts, now turned its attention to the mounting of an operation on another front—the relief of Ladakh. In this sector, elements of the enemy force that had been deployed to conduct Operation Sledge were still very active. The small gallant party that had set out from 161 Infantry Brigade, and which had been reinforced by the two companies of 2/4 Gorkha rifles and the Jammu and Kashmir State Force detachment at Kargil, was in dire need of relief. The relief operation, carried out by troops inducted into Kashmir and supported by Stuart tanks of 7 Cavalry, proved successful and a link-up with Leh in Ladakh effected. It is not intended to probe deeper into this operation, as the factual story can best be related, and will doubtless be placed on record, by someone with a first-hand knowledge of the operation. It is mentioned here as it was the finale to that great effort by the small party from 2 Dogra of 161 Infantry Brigade, who underwent immense hardships to reach and hold on to the area until relief eventually arrived.

Jammu Division, formed simultaneously with Sri Div, and responsible for the conduct of operations in Jammu and Poonch, opened its campaign with the relief of Poonch as one of its main tasks. Ever since 161 Infantry Brigade had moved from Uri across the Haji Pir Pass and placed 1 Kumaon in Poonch on 21 November 1947, all land communications with Poonch had remained severed. An airstrip had been constructed by the Poonch garrison and further reinforcements had been flown in, but for all practical purposes Poonch had remained under constant threat and under a partial siege. The enemy tried to neutralise the advantage bestowed by the airstrip by bringing it under fire at every possible opportunity, but Brigadier Pritam Singh thwarted all their designs in this sphere.

Jammu Division's operations to link up with Poonch were watched with keen interest by those who had served and were still serving with 161 Infantry Brigade. Poonch had been spared the fate that befell Baramula by one of the Brigade's original battalions, 1 Kumaon, and this unit had played the main role in saving the town. Although in no position to assist materially, 161 Infantry Brigade had been watching closely the actions and exploits of the Poonch garrison. The eventual link-up was, therefore, greeted with much jubilation when the news filtered through. A patrol from the Ledi Gali–Pir Kanthi area moved out to the north from Poonch.

With the capture of Ledi Gali and Pir Kanthi, the siege of Poonch could, in fact, have been lifted by Sri Div had it been given the troops to do so. With these two features firmly held, the Haji Pir Pass was once again an open route. A small engineer effort at the burnt bridge at milestone 7, which had caused the Brigade so much trouble on its return journey from Poonch to Uri on 22 November 1947, and the cutting of a path into the Batar Nullah near the bridge destroyed by the State Forces about eleven miles from Poonch, would have enabled a motor convoy of 15 cwt Dodge trucks and jeeps with trailers to make its way to Poonch with little difficulty. A column on foot, supported by animal transport, could at any time have made the trip. Had Jammu Division run into serious difficulties or been subjected to abnormal delay, Poonch could have been afforded relief with a move from Kashmir.

An error that had cost us such valuable territory on the Kazinag Range was, however, to be followed by another. This one was to have even greater repercussions. It was a tactical mistake of the highest order, and there is not a single argument that can be advanced to mitigate the seriousness of the lapse. With negotiations pertaining to a Cease Fire well under way, and every possibility that it would come into effect, extreme caution and care was called for to ensure that all territory in our possession was securely held. A usual feature of any Cease Fire Agreement is the all important one that all forward movement will cease from the time that the Cease Fire comes into effect, and the initial Cease Fire Line is normally traced on a map in-between the territory in the physical possession of the two contestants.

Attempts at eleventh-hour nibbling by the enemy into one's territory had therefore to be guarded against with the utmost vigilance.

The withdrawal of 4 Kumaon from the Kazinag Range, and its replacement by the inexperienced 1 Bihar, had resulted in a severe loss of territory, but there was at least one consolation, that it had been lost after offering some resistance. Ledi Gali and Pir Kanthi, and with it the Haji Pir Pass and a deep salient beyond it, were lost without a shot being fired. What 161 Infantry Brigade, reinforced by two battalions of 77 Para Brigade, had sacrificed lives to secure, was unfortunately presented back to Pakistan on a platter.

The Brigade Commander, on the score that the snow on the Pir Panjal Range was too hevy, withdrew the Ledi Gali and Pir Kanthi garrisons a few days before the Cease Fire came into effect. In doing so, he not only threw open to the enemy the firmly held Pir Panjal Range but, worse still, he left 161 Infantry Brigade with its left flank unprotected, permitted the route to Poonch over the Haji Pir Pass to be cut, and presented to the enemy the ability to pose a threat to Uri from the south. Snow, no matter how deep, had never been considered nor proved to be an insurmountable obstacle to the troops of 161 Infantry Brigade during the winter of 1947–48, and at that period they were neither fully outfitted nor fully acclimatised to face the heights and the weather conditions. By the winter of 1948, the experience gained during the previous winter was available, and the necessary administrative and other requirements had been well taken care of.

Had the piquets established by 161 Infantry Brigade, during the winter of 1947–48, ill-equipped as the men were to combat snow conditions, with the snow no less heavy than that experienced on the Pir Panjal Range, been withdrawn on the excuse that the snow was too deep and the piquet positions therefore untenable, it is not improbable that 161 Infantry Brigade would have been thrown back from Uri and Mahura to the Srinagar Valley. The Cease Fire Line would then probably have been drawn somewhere in the area between Baramula and Uri.

While the snow on the Pir Panjal Range was considered to be much too heavy and deep to be faced by the troops of the Indian Army, it proved to be no obstacle to the Pakistanis. The excuse is, therefore, quite unacceptable. Even troops coming from areas devoid of snow such as Rajasthan and Madras had operated extremely well in the snow of the winter of 1947, and had not found it either too heavy or too deep. The officers and men of 2 Dogra had braved snows which were probably six times deeper than anything that the Pir Panjal Range is subjected to, when they crossed the Zoji La Pass.

With the flood gates thrown wide open, the Pakistanis lost no time in occupying the abandoned Ledi Gali and Pir Kanthi piquets, and advanced even further to the east. It was a heaven-sent gift and Pakistan accepted it with grateful hands. With the Haji Pir Pass now once again in their possession, the Pakistanis fanned out rapidly to the north-east, east and south towards Poonch, creating a very deep salient. The extent of this salient is shown on the sketch map. While the whole of it may not have resulted from the abandonment of the two important piquets, the areas closer to Poonch being the responsibility of the Poonch Brigade, there is no doubt that the lapse by the Brigade Commander responsible for the Pir Panjal Range left Poonch Brigade no opportunity to salvage the situation, as the Cease Fire came into operation almost immediately.

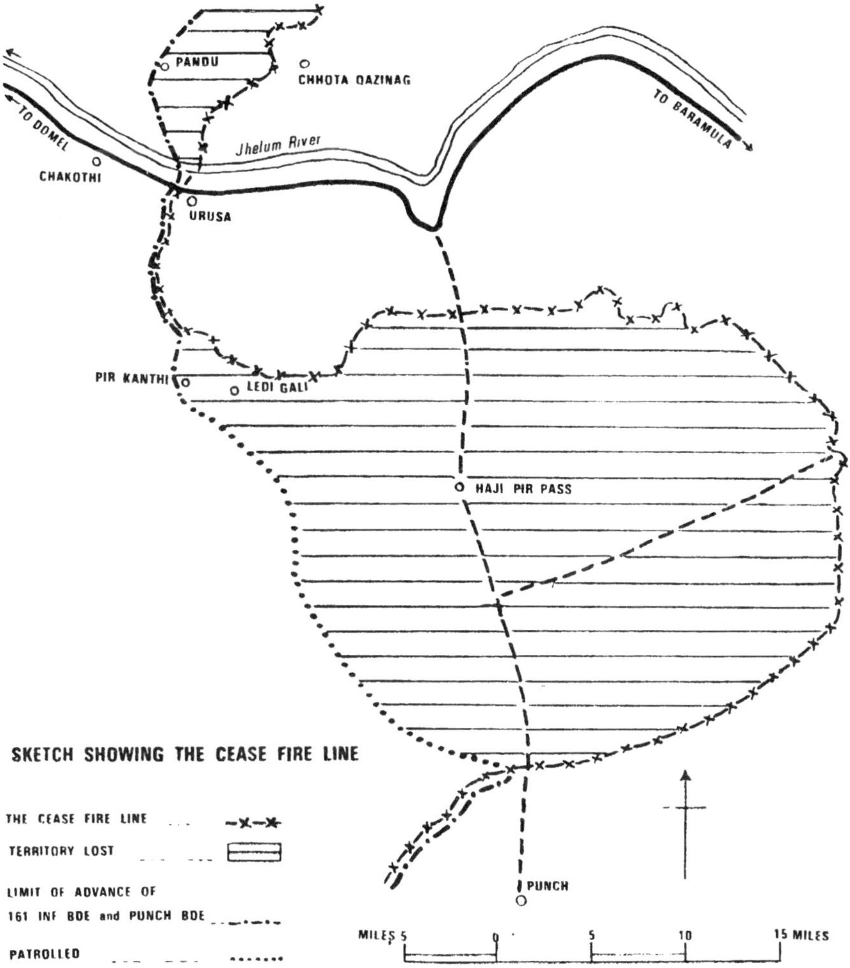
PANDU
CHHOTA QAZINAG
TO DOMEL
Jhelum River
TO BARAMULA
CHAKOTHI
URUSA
PIR KANTHI
LEDI GALI
HAJI PIR PASS
PUNCH
SKETCH SHOWING THE CEASE FIRE LINE
THE CEASE FIRE LINE
TERRITORY LOST
LIMIT OF ADVANCE OF 161 INF BDE and PUNCH BDE
PATROLLED
MILES 5
0
5
10
15 MILES

Chapter 22

A Costly Legacy

THERE are few campaigns in history in which an Infantry Brigade formed of hurriedly assembled bits and pieces, with units and sub-units having their leaders removed and replaced by others who were strangers to the men, and without the full complement of weapons, has been pitchforked into a serious battle while still in the process of being built up. It speaks volumes for the officers and men of 161 Infantry Brigade that it welded itself within a few days into one of the hardest hitting Brigades of the Indian Army.

Had it been otherwise, it is not difficult to visualise what might have happened to the Valley and to Ladakh. Srinagar would probably have met the fate of Muzaffarabad and Baramula, and a pillaged Leh would have become the name of a dead city on another country's map. That they survive and are flourishing is due to a band of warriors of unparalleled bravery who accepted every disadvantage without murmur and who had an uncanny knack of producing the impossible at the right moment.

Could 161 Infantry Brigade have done even better, and cleared Kashmir altogether of the raiders, in which event the unresolved issue would not have remained a legacy of the sub-continent's partition bedeviling the relations between India and Pakistan and enabling foreign Powers to advance their own interests by playing one country off against the other?

The answer to the question will be evident from the foregoing narrative. 161 Infantry Brigade would certainly have made a good attempt, and with every chance of success, had it been permitted to advance beyond Uri, along the axis of its offensive, on to Domel, with the reinforcement of striking power that the situation demanded. The Brigade had fought from Shalateng, through Baramula and on to Uri with two infantry battalions, one troop of armoured cars and later a Mountain Battery. There were six infantry battalions in the Valley when 161 Infantry Brigade set out from Baramula for Uri, and five when ½ Punjab was removed from it on flimsy grounds and sent back over the Banihal Pass to far-off Jammu. The Brigade advanced 62 miles to Uri with two of these five battalions. If it could crush the enemy strength at Shalateng with just two battalions and gain 62 miles of territory thereafter, Domel, which lay 45 miles further, was not beyond its compass had it been given all the five units.

The Government of India was keen that Domel should be recovered, and so were the popular leaders of Kashmir. 161 Infantry Brigade, riding the crest of a wave, was ready and willing to move forward and make a resolute attempt at achieving the object.

Unfortunately, the military hierarchy in New Delhi did not appear to share the objective. It was admittedly Headquarters Jak Force which stayed the advance of the Brigade to Domel and ordered a change of axis towards Poonch. But Headquarters Jak Force had no autocratic powers to change the aim of an operation; it was receiving its orders from Army Headquarters, and only Army Headquarters could effect such a major change. Evidently the latter did not find it difficult to persuade the new and inexperienced Government to accept the change of axis.

The halting of 161 Infantry Brigade's advance from east to west and the switching of the axis from north to south certainly saved Poonch, but at the same time it eliminated all chances of the Brigade making any further gains to the west until the Spring of 1948. When it was ordered to halt and not to make any further advance towards Domel, the enemy was on the run and his morale was very low, and it was unlikely that he would offer any great resistance. Further, the capture of Domel would automatically have relieved the pressure on Poonch. The Azad Kashmir Poonch forces had not been formed and the Pakistan Regular Army had not yet entered Kashmir in strength. The breathing space allowed to the enemy enabled him to arrest the flight of his battered forces, to raise the AKP units and to present 161 Infantry Brigade, starved of extra units, with a serious problem during the period that it was virtually marooned in Kashmir during the winter months.

The only conclusion that one can draw is that the rout of the enemy in the battle of Shalateng shattered not only the tribesmen but other quarters as well. When Baramula fell within twenty-four hours of Shalateng and the Brigade set off for Uri, its advance had to be arrested and so one battalion was withdrawn without relief. When this failed to prevent the capture of Uri, something else had to be thought of. Hence the change of axis towards Poonch. It is little wonder that the Government of India began to sense something wrong and decided that General Sir Rob Lockhart, who had been appointed Commander in Chief of the Indian Army in August 1947 for a four-year tenure, should have had his services terminated after he had been in the chair for just over six months. He was replaced by General Sir Roy Bucher. But the change made no essential difference to the higher direction of the operations in Kashmir from Army Headquarters.

Sri Div, from the date of its inception in May 1948, met with the same frustrating denial of encouragement and support as 161 Infantry Brigade. As long as the proposed attacks were from east to west, the Division was stifled by a refusal of more formations, though even one uninitiated in military strategy and tactics would have seen that the extra formations asked for were not a luxury but a vital necessity. The Spring offensive had to be launched without teeth to it, because of the denial of the reinforcements necessary to provide the punch for effecting a breakthrough. When the two advances from east to west were bogged down and the operation to be mounted took a south-to-north direction, extra Brigades were immediately moved into J&K State.

Army Headquarters's handling of the operations in Kashmir in 1947–48 leaves more than a little room for speculation whether the formations deployed there were really intended to score a decisive success, which they could and would have achieved had reinforcements been moved in, or whether it was the intention that their capacity should be limited to a strength where only a stalemate could result. From the attitude adopted by Army Headquarters, the second would appear to be the correct assessment.

The Cease Fire which came into effect in Jammu and Kashmir at the end of December 1948 proved to be a mockery of the term. Although the Agreement was formulated by the United Nations (UN), and has been supervised by a large team of Observers assembled by the UN from countries acceptable to both India and Pakistan, more bullets have whined across the Cease Fire Line during the last 21 years than in the course of the fighting in 1947–48. Violations of the line by infiltrators from Pakistan, despatched on missions aimed at sabotage or at creating unrest and confusion, are legion. This is no reflection on the personnel of the UN Observer Groups. They have operated with efficiency. But it is virtually impossible for them to seal every route and to control the triggers on weapons. Nor is this expected of them. They are only able to carry out investigations of complaints and to submit the result of their findings to the Chief UN Observer for an award of "Violation" or "No violation".

Britain, which furnished the Commanders in Chief of both India and Pakistan at the birth of the two Dominions, could have prevented the problem of Kashmir from arising in the first place: by preventing the tribal raiders' attack on Kashmir, an operation that was planned in the same building that housed Pakistan Army Headquarters, or failing that, by carrying out the threat of withdrawing all British officers when Pakistan's Regular Army entered Kashmir early in 1948. Instead, Britain's representatives connived at Pakistan's gross violation of the Mountbatten Plan which had given the Rulers of Princely States unfettered discretion to accede to the Domination of their choice. That this was no aberration on the part of some individuals became evident from the UK's role in the ensuing proceedings of the UN on the Kashmir question.

Free India's Army, which had been planned to be in the region of 300,000 all ranks, had to be maintained at a much higher figure in order to provide adequate garrisons not only in Jammu and Kashmir but also in the area of the India–Pakistan boundary in the Punjab. With an extensive border to protect, and a limited budget, many equally sensitive areas had to be denied troop deployment.

The situation was aggravated when the United States of America decided to offer, and Pakistan readily accepted, military aid. The modernisation of the Pakistan Armed Force and the considerable increase in their strength imposed a heavy defence burden on India. It was not the American intention that Pakistan should be strengthened in order to threaten India. Military aid was supplied to enable Pakistan to take her place as a partner in the treaty alliances designed to contain the Soviet Union and Communist China in West Asia and South–East Asia. India reacted promptly to the military aid being poured into Pakistan, and pointed out to America that it would be used against India. The US gave assurances from time to time that she would never permit American equipment to be used against India. When it actually came to dissuading Pakistan from using American military aid against India, first in the Rann of Kutch early in 1965 and again when Pakistan attacked Chhamb in Jammu later in the same year, sparking off the Indo–Pakistan hostilities, America found herself powerless to restrain Pakistan.

Communist China, meanwhile, was not slow to exploit the situation. Having overrun Tibet, she initially adopted a policy of ostensible friendship towards India but soon grabbed Indian territory in Ladakh and constructed the Aksai Chin road. Then she laid claims to other areas, and refused to accept the long established McMahon Line as the border between India and Tibet.

Faced with two hostile neighbours along her land borders, India found herself in a most unenviable position. American military aid to Pakistan enforced the deployment of the major portion of the combat formations of the Indian Army to face that country. There was little left to deploy against a World Power which was threatening the northern border from Ladakh to North–East Frontier Agency (NEFA). It suited China to capitalise on the situation by making overtures to Pakistan and forging a joint front against India. This meant that the bulk of India's armed strength would remain committed and incapable of deployment from one front to the other. The areas chosen by China for rattling the sabre against India were as wide apart as Ladakh in the north-west and NEFA in the east. There were more than 1,000 miles of land border between them, and each of the sectors was garrisoned with a mere pittance of India's 625,000 strong Army.

The NEFA hostilities of 1962 have often been described as a debacle of India's Army. It would be more correct to describe the action as the defeat of a handful of troops of the Indian Army, composed of four Brigades, which attempted to combat four Chinese Divisions over a frontage of 600 miles of most inhospitable terrain. The Indian public and the world were led to believe—unfortunately by the Indian Government itself—that an Indian Corps had moved into NEFA. It was even given a number, IV Corps. Had a Corps been in the area, it would have amounted to between 100,000 and 125,000 troops. That a truncated Corps Headquarters moved in is true. But the troops available to it for operations were at no time more than one fifth of the strength of a Corps. The Chinese, on other hand, had available the equivalent of a strong Corps. The lack of strength for deployment in NEFA arose precisely because the Indian Government was not prepared to weaken the troop deployment in the Punjab and Jammu and Kashmir in view of the live possibility that Pakistan might take advantage of the situation.

The Indo–Pakistan conflict of 1965 followed the NEFA pattern, but now in reverse. Considering herself strong enough to cross swords with India, Pakistan attacked. But in order to arrest any transference of the formations located in eastern India, China delivered a boisterous ultimatum to India. It was a gesture of thanks to Pakistan for what she had done for China in1962 by arresting the movement of troops from Punjab to NEFA.

With the Indian Army's strength substantially increased as a result of the experiences of 1962 and 1965, and sensitive areas formerly devoid of troops now firmly held, Pakistan and China have stepped up their assistance to the hostile Nagas. The situation in Nagaland was rapidly being brought under control when NEFA erupted. The hostile Nagas, who did not embarrass India during the conflict with China, have now been persuaded to look in that direction for assistance. Recent events have shown that they have received both training and arms from China. The pattern is typically Chinese. They have pursued this course of action throughout South–East Asia, and it is directed at all countries which have no use for Mao Tse-tung's ideology and which will not submit to dictates from China.

With Pakistan falling even more deeply into the bosom of China, and China—now also the Soviet Union—filling the void left by the halt of American military aid to Pakistan after 1965, it is difficult to visualise when, if ever, the unsavoury situation faced by India will terminate.

It has been a long road from 1947 to 1969, and India has had to face many crises in safeguarding her rights. There can be no doubt that any further challenges that might arise in the future will be tackled with the same tenacity. In the perspective of history, the pity is that these crises were allowed to develop in the first place. Had their genesis in Kashmir in 1947 been dealt with firmly and in time, India could have avoided what has proved to be a very costly legacy.

Index